The Mysteries of Religion

Philosophical Introductions

Series Editors
Anthony Ellis & Gordon Graham

Philosophy for Education   *John Harris*
The Philosophy of Art   *Peter Lewis*

The Mysteries of Religion

An Introduction to Philosophy through Religion

Stephen R. L. Clark

Basil Blackwell

© Stephen R. L. Clark 1986

First published 1986

Basil Blackwell Ltd
108 Cowley Road, Oxford OX4 1JF, UK

Basil Blackwell Inc.
432 Park Avenue South, Suite 1503,
New York, NY 10016, USA

British Library Cataloguing in Publication Data

Clark, Stephen R. L.
   The mysteries of religion: an introduction to
   the philosophy of religion.
   1. Religion—Philosophy
   I. Title
   200'.1   BL51

ISBN 0–631–13419–0
ISBN 0–631–14295–9 Pbk

Library of Congress Cataloging in Publication Data

Clark, Stephen R. L.
   The mysteries of religion.

   (Philosophical Introductions)
   Bibliography: p.
   Includes index.
   I. Religion—Philosophy.   I. Title.   II. Series.
   BL51.C555   1986   200'.1   85–28698
   ISBN 0–631–13419–0
   ISBN 0–631–14295–9 (pbk.)

Typeset by Cambrian Typesetters Frimley, Surrey.
Printed in Great Britain by Page Bros (Norwich) Ltd

Contents

Series Introduction   _____

This series has its origin in the conviction that the best way of introducing beginners to philosophy is through philosophizing about issues on which the student already has views: politics, morality, religion or art, for instance. It is possible to identify these views and, by asking comprehensible and obviously relevant questions, to show how philosophy arises out of what is simply a sustained attempt to think clearly about such issues. It then takes on its true appearance as a way of thinking with which most people, initially, are familiar. Such an approach is most naturally adopted in the area that has come to be called, unhappily perhaps, practical, or applied, philosophy. So the books in this series will cover such aspects of life as ethics, politics, the law, religion, art and education.

It is important to note that each of the books is conceived to be an introduction to philosophy, not merely an introduction to the philosophy of religion, or political philosophy, or whatever. Consequently, there is no attempt in them to introduce students simply to the range of issues which have traditionally been included in such titles. That is inherent in the approach that the series adopts, since if you remain true to your intention of philosophizing about views that the beginner already has, then it should not be assumed that you will quickly get into the traditional and familiar questions; sometimes you will, and sometimes you won't.

Though the books are introductions to philosophy, each is as seriously concerned with its subject in hand as with its philosophical dimensions. Consequently, they may be expected to be of value to students both of philosophy and of the discipline the philosophy is about.

The books are introductions, not in the sense that they are easy to understand, but in the sense that they presuppose no prior knowledge of philosophy. So they make no attempt to engage deeply in current controversies. On the other hand, it is an inevitable result of the approach of the series that some at least of the books will have a character that is entirely distinctive, and it would be dishonest to pretend that we do not hope that they will make some contribution to creating new perspectives in the subject.

Department of Moral Philosophy,   Anthony Ellis
University of St Andrews   Gordon Graham

There is a supreme God in the ethnological section;
a hollow toad shape, faced with a blank shield.
He needs his belly to include the Parthenon,
which is inserted through a hole behind.
At the navel, at the points formally stressed, at the organs of sense,
lice glue themselves, dolls, local deities,
his smooth wood creeps with all the creeds of the world.

Attending there let us absorb the cultures of nations
and dissolve into our judgement all their codes.
Then, being clogged with a natural hesitation
(People are continually asking one the way out),
let us stand here and admit that we have no road.
Being everything, let us admit that is to be something,
or give ourselves the benefit of the doubt;
let us offer our pinch of dust all to this God,
and grant his reign over the entire building.
(William Empson, 'Homage to the British Museum': (1955) p. 35.)

Preface

When I was first asked to write an introduction to the philosophy of religion, my reaction was to doubt that such a thing was needed, or that I was the right person to write it if it were. It did not take me very long to persuade myself that there was room for a study which took its start from ordinary experience of religion, rather than from scholastic argument for and against the existence of God, or the meaningfulness or otherwise (on some sophisticated theory of language) of religious language. I thought that it might be possible to show how even very technical questions could arise when we began to think about what went on in religious services, or the religious life in general. I also believed that it was time for philosophers to take a rather wider look at the field than has been conventional. It is not enough to rake together a few abstruse arguments about 'the God of the Philosophers' without acknowledging that most 'religious' persons would not recognize any such entity as the object of their devotion. Not every religious person is a member of the Abrahamic tradition, or even a theist, but all might still be coaxed into seeing that there are philosophical puzzles of great intrinsic interest and possible spiritual profit.

These are things that I still believe. Unfortunately, it has also become clear to me that an introduction to the philosophy of religion, as I originally envisaged it, amounts to an introduction to the philosophy of absolutely everything, and that questions were constantly presenting themselves which lay far beyond my competence, or beyond anything that this series could reasonably accommodate. I have, in particular, concluded that I could not do justice to the interface between philosophy of religion and political philosophy, and have postponed my reasoned account of the Kingdoms of God and of this World to another date. I have also excluded discussion of particular issues raised by Christian Incarnational Theology – an area which I do not think beyond the reach of rational enquiry, but which involved me in so much subtlety and Neo-Platonic speculation as to make it inappropriate in anything that purported to be an introductory volume. There are doubtless many other omissions. I hope, however, that what follows will be comprehensible to anyone, religious or otherwise, who is prepared to devote a little time and effort to try and think sympathetically through the thoughts of religious persons in all ages, and that it may serve as a beginning.

Undergraduate students of philosophy (and some of their elders) believe that the task of a philosopher is simply to criticize, and to find fault with arguments even for conclusions that no-one has any serious interest in rejecting. I do not share this view. Analytical criticism, even destructive criticism, is often a good thing, but the real aim of philosophy is not to destroy, but to understand and explore. I do not think it is profitable to imagine that our predecessors, even when they were mistaken, were fools. Nor do I think it profitable to deny ourselves the chance of thinking through some unfamiliar hypothesis merely because there is no conclusive proof – in advance of those explorations – that it will be found to be true. What follows is an investigation of the possibilities, and an attempt to sketch the metaphysical picture which, so it seems to me, makes sense of much of our experience. Even if that metaphysics is false, what I have written may serve as a map with which readers can begin to explore the terrain.

My thanks go to the editors of this series, who insisted that I make myself a little more intelligible, and to friends and colleagues over the years who have doubted that this was possible. My thanks especially to Dr Gillian Clark for saving me from many errors of taste and judgement, and to Mrs Carol Cullinan for dealing on my behalf with a recalcitrant word-processor.

University of Liverpool

Acknowledgements

The following poems or extracts from poems have been reprinted by kind permission of Chatto & Windus: 'Homage to the British Museum' (p. viii), *Collected Poems of William Empson*; The National Trust: 'We and They' (p. 12) and 'Buddha at Kamakura' (p. 63), *The Definitive Edition of Rudyard Kipling's Verse*; Faber & Faber and Farrar Straus Giroux, Inc.: 'Sole Watchman of the Flying Stars' (p. 93), by John Berryman; Faber & Faber and Harcourt Brace Jovanovich, Inc.: 'Little Gidding' (p. 147), *Four Quartets* by T. S. Eliot; Faber & Faber and Oxford University Press: 'The Combat' (p. 149) by Edwin Muir; and Miss D. E. Collins: 'The Last Hero' (p. 158) and 'The Ballad of the White Horse' (p. 160), *The Collected Poems of G. K. Chesterton*.

1

Introduction

On Being Religious

People who are 'religious' make some effort to practise 'a religion'. They go regularly to some 'place of worship' or (at the least) feel some connection with the usual meeting-place of those who do attend a 'place of worship'. They usually mark the major events of their life, and their community's life, by joining in a 'religious ceremony', and are glad that someone professionally employed to conduct such ceremonies leads them through to a satisfactory conclusion. Births, marriages and deaths; midwinter festivals and spring festivals and harvest festivals; coronations and launchings and inaugurations – all such occasions deserve notice, and 'the religious' will want them to be given a sort of 'cosmic setting'. The religious may also impose minor austerities upon themselves (sometimes major austerities): they do not drink alcohol, or do not use a particular range of expletives, or do not eat the flesh of particular animals, or give up some minor indulgence during some season of the year. Sometimes they wear distinctive clothes, and will not send their children to schools that do not enforce the regulations to which they are themselves accustomed.

Some of those who are thought 'religious' will attempt to persuade others to join them at their place of worship. Sometimes they will rely simply on personal influence, sometimes they may try to argue for the truth of certain doctrines usually to be heard in their own religious fellowship. Often they rely, for their own support and in conversation with others, on some body of 'religious' or 'sacred' writings. These writings usually play some part in the ceremonies and regular meetings of their fellowship, and are usually held to date from very long ago. In fact the writings that 'the religious' rely upon are usually translations of still earlier texts. The majority of the religious probably do not much care for scholarly exegesis or reinterpretation of those first texts: if it was good enough for King James it's good enough for them. Even if some more modern translation is preferred it is usually not preferred on 'scholarly' grounds, but because the newer words have a more familiar 'feel' to them, as they come in the same style as the preaching and prayer-life of that particular fellowship.

Opinion polls regularly reveal that those who think of themselves as 'religious' are more likely to be bigoted, racially prejudiced, authoritarian, in favour of corporal and capital punishment than the 'irreligious'. At the same time it may be admitted that (mere hypocrites apart) the 'religious' are more likely to stay sane and well-meaning under severe deprivation than the merely irreligious, those whose life is structured only by personal desire and satisfaction. Notoriously, some of the most destructive and wicked acts of human history have been committed by religious persons. Conversely, some of the noblest, most courageous and most loving acts have been committed by the religious. On the one hand, religious fellowships are often havens of back-biting, malice and all uncharitableness. On the other, such fellowships often contain a high proportion of those who are genuinely trying not to be bad, even perhaps to do some positive good.

In some ages the common style and fashion is to be religious, and those who are not must content themselves with being called atheists and libertines. In other ages the fashion is to be 'irreligious', or even so far gone in impiety as not to care at all. In those latter ages even those who remain 'religious' may not be so by older standards. Even the most bigoted of modern religious rarely plot to have their theological opponents tortured and burnt alive 'for the glory of God'. Not to plot such an end would once have been a notable impiety itself.

Those who are 'now' religious, of course, may be people of quite a different character from those who were 'religious' in the 'ages of faith'. Then, religion was simply the dominant mood of the community, and the irreligious were sceptical individualists, or members of some subculture that could not share the rewards open to those who were fully accepted in society. When the dominant mood of society is itself 'irreligious', it is the religious who appear as sceptics, foolish doubters of the 'way of the world', the received wisdom. To be 'religious' in such an age is probably to be a member of an uneasy minority, unwilling to accept whatever the dominant myth of society may be. Secular commentators may, consciously or unconsciously, so exaggerate this sense of alienation as to suppose that the only people to be 'really religious' are those who refuse to accept contemporary theories of life and the universe, who continue to believe in older moral codes and older myths. 'Real religion' is to disbelieve in evolution, to expect an anthropomorphic god's descent from the sky, to think attendance at a place of worship more important than ordinary duties of citizenship or human feeling.

Two things should be obvious about this sketch of what it is to be 'religious'. The first, that I have tried not to specify what particular religion is involved. In using the phrase 'for the glory of God', I have perhaps been too specific: not all religious would ever have identified the object of their devotion with 'God' or even with 'the gods'. Whether there is anything that could be said to be the one object of religious devotion is a question I shall be trying to answer later on. For the moment it is enough to insist that my main interest lies in studying Religion, not one religion or another. The religious I have described may be Christian, Jewish, Muslim, Buddhist, or animist. It is one of the characteristics of religion that the religious separate themselves not only from the clearly irreligious but from members of other communities and traditions. 'Heathen' and 'unbeliever' are titles freely given not only to those who do not believe at all, but to those who believe something different. What divides the traditions may often be important. The first impression on any outsider must surely be the similarity of the traditions. Some of that similarity rests merely on the common humanity of the people concerned: religions are similar to each other because all human institutions are similar to each other. A football crowd, a political rally, a pop festival, a rioting mob and a religious ceremony will be similar to each other; the 'religious' behaviour of extraterrestrials may be quite unlike any human behaviour – except that it is, somehow, of religious import. But the religious of any tradition are probably more like each other, in outward show and in the meaning of their actions, and more unlike the merely irreligious, than they usually suppose.

The second obvious feature of my sketch is that it is intended to be an outsider's view, and not a very sympathetic outsider's. This is how religion and the religious are all too likely to strike puzzled observers in an age when the dominant mood and myth of the educated and semi-educated public is 'irreligious'. Those who still profess and practise 'a religion' should not ignore this view of their lives and characters. Equally, those who can identify themselves with contemporary myths and ideologies should not be allowed to ignore the other perspective. People who are 'irreligious' may be decent citizens and comfortable neighbours. They may observe codes of professional ethics, and try to live according to their own best ideals. They may have optimistic, or pessimistic, visions of how the world is likely to go, and devote themselves to causes that may involve discomfort or disgrace or death. What is characteristic of 'the irreligious' is a disinclination to believe that anything but human pleasure and pain much matters (with perhaps some sympathy for the feelings of the non-human). To be irreligious is not to feel bound by obligations not of one's own making, to think nothing sacred, to be unmoved (except in sentimental moments) by any overmastering beauty or sense of history. It is also as characteristic of the irreligious as of any religious bigot to suppose that their way of construing things is the way any reasonable being would take, unless they were led astray by guilt or wish-fulfilment or conceit.

In 'ages of faith' critical philosophers have often seemed like irreligious sceptics, questioning what all 'reasonable people' accept. Their questioning has doubtless played a part in the historical processes that have, it seems, unseated true religion. In 'ages of irreligion' (which are not ages of doubt, since 'irreligion' is as complacent as 'religion' was) philosophers may reasonably urge the claims of faith, and point out how insecure the dominant myths may be. Very few people (if any) believe what they do simply because they understand that any other belief would be less reasonable. It follows that any dominant or majority view is usually held for other reasons, from other causes, and may be the more unreasonable simply because almost no-one understands what reasons there might be for it.

The dominant self-perception of the modern intellectual is that she believes only what it is 'reasonable' to believe. If that is to be more than a piece of hypocritical self-deception good intellectuals must be prepared to ask what grounds that duty, and how it may best be fulfilled. That 'religion' is the 'wrong' response to make to life, the universe and everything is not self-evident. Neither is it self-evident that 'religion' must take the shape that 'irreligion' prefers to see.

Religion and Religions

The 'religious' practise 'a religion'. W. Cantwell Smith has argued, plausibly, that our predecessors would be puzzled by our interest in 'religions' as things that could be clearly distinguished from each other. When they spoke of religious practice, feeling and belief they concerned themselves with 'religion'. 'The Christian Religion' originally meant much the same as 'Christian piety', piety as it drew upon and manifested the tradition flowing from the figure, real or imagined, of Jesus of Nazareth. 'Islam' meant (and means) only submission to God, and any religious person would accept the title 'Muslim' (that is to say, One who submits to God). A Buddhist, similarly, is one who has 'entered the stream', and dedicated herself to the path of enlightenment, salvation from the changes and chances of this mortal life.

But although it is right to insist on this, and to declare that 'the mysteries of religion' are the mysteries of piety or the spiritual life, it is also fairly clear that no-one is ever just religious. Attempts to reach towards the essence of religion, and to be 'religious' without practising any particular religion, are tempting especially to intellectuals who would rather not be associated with the sort of people to be found in any worshipping community. It may also be tempting to suppose that we might achieve 'true religion and undefiled' by 'stripping off' the merely human accretions to an original revelation, and so passing behind the disputes and particularities of competing religions. The usual result of such attempts has been to establish yet another sect, in woeful dispute not only with established 'religions' but with rival claimants to the title 'Universal or Original Religion'. Part of what it is to be religious is to join with others in ceremonial and symbolic exercises, to share a perception of things as imbued with a certain sort of meaning. Someone who claimed to be 'religious' in a way that no-one else could or should understand or share, who claimed a literally unique route to the appreciation of a divine reality no-one else could grasp, would not easily be distinguished from an ordinary hobbyist: if 'my' God cannot be anyone else's, how is He God at all?

Insofar as being religious involves sharing in a way of worship, conduct and professed belief that may be expected to last longer, and to be older, than the individual religious, any philosophical study of these mysteries must be concerned with the nature of those ceremonies and customs. A full understanding of them must involve both 'objective' and 'subjective' elements. The 'objective' study of behaviour requires that the behaviour be described without any sense of what it would be to be engaged in such behaviour. It is to be identified solely by statistical regularities and evolutionary function. 'Altruistic behaviour', for example, is identified by students of animal behaviour simply as those patterns of behaviour which might be expected to eliminate the animal and its near relatives from the evolutionary line. Not surprisingly, such behaviour is extremely rare. In saying that such 'altruism' does not exist the ethologist (who studies animal behaviour in the wild) says nothing about an animal's own motives and feelings: ethologists have for many years imagined that true scientific rigour required them not to consider such 'subjective' factors. The arguments for this position are unconvincing. Where human conduct is concerned we cannot escape the necessity to identify it 'subjectively': that is to say, not that it is a matter of our 'subjective' and incorrigible opinion what a person is (in this sense) doing, but that what she is doing, the action she is performing, must be understood in terms of her goals and beliefs. Human conduct cannot be described merely 'objectively' (in terms of what may be observed entirely from the outside: movements, or chemical changes), since 'conduct' is itself a 'subjective' concept. To know what the religious are doing it is necessary to consider what they think they are doing.

The initial assumption must be what Leszek Kolakowski proposes: by and large, people mean by religious ceremonial and creed roughly what they say they mean. They are doing what they sincerely suppose themselves to be doing. It is unwise to insist that they are 'really' doing something different (e.g. working off surplus male energy) merely because we cannot imagine ourselves meaning such a thing (as e.g. summoning the god of battle). Maybe something is happening that they do not appreciate (and we do): it cannot be that *that* is what they are doing, that those are their actions, if it has never occurred to them to imagine any such intent or purpose. Equally, it is unwise to suppose that all religious groups or individuals 'mean' just the same things, even if there is a sense in which they 'do' the same things. Two different tribes may regularly perform rain dances towards the end of the dry season: one tribe may seriously suppose that its dance is a necessary condition (by natural law or by the grace of the rain god) for the subsequent rain; the other tribe may think the anthropologist who takes its dance to have that purpose merely naive or stupid. They are not dancing 'to make it rain', but to make the rain a significant event. It is not that it will not rain if they do not dance, but that they will not receive the rain 'in the right spirit'. There is a certain vulgarity about those conceptions of religion that suppose all religious rituals to be technical or persuasive. There is, on the other hand, a certain fogginess about those conceptions of religion which deny that religious ritual is ever intended to make a 'real difference' to the world. Maybe most of our prayers for healing lead only to acceptance; some prayers for healing are followed, in the most vulgar way imaginable, simply by healing. There are literalists (the rain-makers) and symbolists (the rain-blessers) in every tradition, and no good is done by insisting that only one group is 'really religious'.

The fact that people do interpret their own acts so differently, of course, does create the temptation to revert to merely 'objective' description. There are memorial feasts, and cult-meals in honour of great heroes, and meals shared (in imagination, maybe) with the gods: what remains constant through the historical transformations, and under the different interpretations, is eating and drinking. This 'residue' may be expected to survive all cultural change and conversion. People will always gather in groups and eat and drink together. How they choose to regard their own actions, what face they choose to put upon their motives, may not matter. The 'real explanation' of such festivals lies not at the level of individual intention or social stereotype, but in the 'natural' impulses of a particular species of hominid (other such species preceded Homo sapiens, and may succeed her). People developed early the habit of sharing their food (which even our closest relatives do not do as consistently). By analogy, although sexual and marital practices may change, and although different individuals in different societies may imagine quite different things about the sexual act, we can be sure that people will go on having sex. The changing ceremonial and psychological structure of such acts are merely 'epiphenomenal', byproducts of the 'real explanation', which lies at the 'animal' level (where animals are understood to be moved entirely by positive needs, and not motivated by their understanding of the situation).

But there are at least two reasons to resist such simple-minded analysis. The first, that it deliberately misses the 'religious' (or indeed the human) point of the behaviour it analyses. Husband, lover, ritual priest and Tantric mystic may all be 'having sex', but to understand only that much is to understand very little. If 'religiosity' lies in the emotion and attitude of the agents it can only be detected by our perceiving their actions with their eyes and minds. To identify an act as religious we have to 'participate' in the action – we must, that is to say, sympathise and feel with the agent. Lovers are not only 'having sex', but delighting in each other, seeking mystical experience, confounding their parents, making babies, establishing themselves as members of the with-it generation. To say that they're only 'really' having sex, and that they would be sure to dream up some other excuse if their present one were punctured, may simply not be true, and is at least unhelpful if we wish to understand human experience.

The second reason is that we have in any case no usable theory that can distinguish patterns of animal behaviour, and isolate 'real' causes, that is independent of our ordinary, 'participatory' identification of behaviour. If we were really unable to think ourselves into an agent's skin and could only break up his behaviour into isolable units by statistical analysis we should never get anywhere. That might be the only available technique if we were seeking to understand genuine aliens. It is the technique that a few generations of ethologists have (mistakenly) concluded was the proper way to study non-human animals. But in fact we understand even non-human animals, even non-mammals, far better than that. Who does not appreciate what a male spider does in offering a carefully wrapped fly to the female with whom he wishes to mate? Even identifying a behavioural unit as 'having sex' requires more than statistical analysis: how do we identify interrupted acts, errors and perversions if not by sharing in the 'inner' reality of what is going on?

So religion cannot be distinguished as merely epiphenomenal, because 'it' has an inner structure of its own that deserves comprehension (as does eroticism), and because the notion that there is a describable level of 'merely physical' events is itself an illusion. We have no prospect at all of explaining any human or animal behaviour as the result of the collisions of elementary particles. We cannot even, before the event, explain them as the result of the biochemical processes arising from the strands of DNA which constitute the genetic programme for the creature in question. We have no biochemical theory capable of rendering the move even from acorn to oak more than a brute fact. How much less can we expect to explain human behaviour as a determined result of the biochemical events? We may believe that there is some such history as would show that no natural law was confounded when the acorn, or the foetus, grew up. We may *believe* that nothing happened in those processes which would require any addition to the system from outside to make it 'intelligible'. Whereas simple mechanics can tell us where e.g. the planet Neptune would be if there were no other gravitational influence on it than the ones we know (and thence infer that there is some other influence, since Neptune isn't where it was supposed to be), we have no such complete biochemical theory. Insofar as we do not know what an acorn in its physical environment *would* do if this were a closed system (if nothing else had any influence on the result), we do not know, even of the acorn, whether what it does is truly compatible with the acorn and its physical environment's being a closed system. There may indeed, for all we know, be a 'ghost in the acorn'. More important, it makes no difference to the significance of 'participatory understanding' whether there is such a ghost or not. Maybe, if we only knew, the human being at prayer does all and only what a certain sort of physical organism would do. It remains true that her doing of it must in practice be identified and understood by ordinary human sympathy.

On Being Sacred

But what are the motives and meanings that we may characterize as specifically religious? One way of identifying 'religious' acts and objects – by default – is much used by archaeologists: if some object does not strike the investigator as obviously useful (a comb, a carpet-beater, a knife for getting stones from horses' hooves) it is often labelled 'Cult-object, for religious purposes'. Ritualists may require that priests attend upon the building of a house, but carpenters and bricklayers come as well. No-one supposes that such things are built by prayer alone. The priest's implements are those material objects that seem to serve no practical purpose. But the archaeologist may be deceived: perhaps the object does have an immediately practical use, or maybe at least the builders thought it did. Would it really not be a religious tool if it were also a practical tool? The ancient distinction between the sacred and the profane suggests that this may indeed be so: to profane something is to use it for merely practical purposes or immediate ends. To use what is sacred for one's own immediate purposes is blasphemy, or simony, and brings down a curse. What is sacred is not for use. It hardly follows, of course, that what is useless is sacred.

To acknowledge something as sacred, accordingly, is to understand that it is 'out of bounds', no tool of ours. What can move and motivate a creature like ourselves to let things she might want be put out of reach? One reply, the simplest, would be that God, the gods, had claimed them for their own. But though that may be the 'ratio essendi', the explanation of why they *are* out of bounds, it is not always the 'ratio cognoscendi', the reason that leads us *to suppose* them out of bounds. It may be that our recognition of a God rests on our prior experience that some things are sacred. We do not believe them sacred because we believe that God has fenced them round; we believe that God exists to preserve them, because we are constrained, or inclined, to believe them sacred. Sacred things include stones of a peculiar shape, animals that do not easily fit the usual patterns, language transformed to verbal music, women set aside – by their own will or another's – from the normal processes of child-bearing and child-rearing. What cannot be or will not be employed for our practical ends may sometimes be impressive enough to avoid being classified as merely useless detritus. We cannot use it, but we cannot forget it or dispose of it.

But though the awe-inspiringly unusable constitutes one category of the sacred – the fringe-sacred – there is at least one other class. The tools employed by craftsmen may be sacred, whether these are tools that every adult male or female uses, or ones that only a particular guild may touch. The tools of adult males, of course, (such as spears) may themselves be the tools of a guild to which adolescents must be initiated. Such tools are sacred (taboo) to all outside the guild (of adult males or of smiths), and sacred also to all inside the guild, the badge of their office and the things by which the craftsmen themselves are used. To treat them as sacred, in this sense, is not to allow them to exist in awe-inspiring uselessness, but to acknowledge their authority. To profane the tools of one's trade is to try and use them against their nature, for aims of one's own: to acknowledge them as sacred is to serve one's trade. What is sacred in this sense (sovereign-sacred) may be indistinguishable, to later archaeologists, from the ordinarily useful. The difference lies in the attitude of those who use the objects, an attitude that may be difficult for determinedly secular minds to appreciate.

These two aspects of the sacred are not really in opposition. What is awe-inspiringly useless and unusable by us is the province of diviner spirits. What is used (in fear and trembling) by guild members and initiates is not to be touched or even looked upon by any others. The sacred permits itself to be used, on its own terms, but is not ordinary, not accessible, not defenceless. Those mysterious rocks, and more mysterious crafts, are the lineaments of the sacred cosmos, which exists beyond human contrivance and without our aid. The rites of religion can be understood as ways of linking our ordinary lives to that cosmos, even of establishing and securing its boundaries and pathways. The gods of the cosmos, the figures in which human imagination cloaks its awareness of the sacred, are both our bulwarks against chaos and the loss of meaning, and also themselves a part of chaos, an aspect of that which lies before and behind all merely human endeavour. Just as what is 'holy' is only a step away from what is 'dirty' (since both are useless), so the sacred cosmos is at once that imaginative reality that gives our life its significance and what may at any time overturn our comfortable security.

In saying this, and seeming to offer some account of the 'religious feelings' of our ancestors, I claim no special psycho-historical insight. What our ancestors felt is impossible to tell, unless they have left clear literary or oral records. Cave-paintings and figurines and unblemished axe-heads only speak to us if we ourselves give them their voices: the religion of our ancestors is, all too often, only our 'religious' response to antiquity, beauty and mystery. For all we know most of our ancestors took 'the sacred' a lot more lightly. Craft-secrets were, for some, only the symbols of their own power and authority; oddly marked stones were simply stones, even if stories were made up, and half-believed, about the gods and giants who had thrown them there. People can be very practical, even about sacred objects. If they were 'sacred' at all it may often have been only that they were named in the rituals. We have no good reason to suppose that 'primitive humanity' lived, or lives, in a sort of 'religious haze', with weird significance staring from every crumbled rock. Our own experience is that religious enthusiasts are the exception, that people who acknowledge the boundary between sacred and profane do not always feel that boundary, or take any pains to protect it. Cemeteries and churches are widely felt to be something more than mere buildings, so that the 'desecration' of a church or graveyard is a deliberate offence to popular decency. But there are few who feel any religious awe when they pass the parish church ('how terrible is this place!'), and few who take seriously the efforts of genuine enthusiasts to preserve the 'holiness' of sacred vessels. It is probable that we are not so different from others. In some societies, at some times, a sensitivity to such sacredness is cultivated (whether by all, or by a trained elite). In others, or at other times, people take their own 'holy things' very lightly.

In understanding 'the sacred', therefore, it is unwise to suppose that this is an emotional category and nothing more. There may indeed be 'experts' in sensing the sacred, people who do respond deeply and emotionally to some things (even, sometimes, all things) as being sacred or holy. A sort of humble half-awareness of such things is perhaps more widely spread. But the classification may sometimes be no more than to say 'priest-craft'. Priests may have the terrifying task of guarding the sacred fire from enemies – or guarding their people from the sacred fire – but they may also have the ordinary and humble task of dealing with the Powers that rule the world as it might be with a blocked drain, or a broken fence. Any job can be filled with romance by those who choose to see it that way, but it remains a job, and nothing to be all that excited about.

These shifting emotional responses are familiar even in a secular world. Medical practitioners attract fear and respect because they are recognizably dealing with matters of our life and death. For our comfort's sake we must believe them something out of the ordinary, people who have the skill and courage to tamper with our lives (which are themselves half-sacred to us, as not being in our gift). But we may also know that such medics are, after all, only human, and we may prefer to hand over our bodies to them only as coats to be patched. 'The medical' does not reside in the emotions of awe and terror we may sometimes experience (encouraged by music, romantic fiction and a deliberately oracular manner in the physician). Equally 'the sacred' need not reside in a response of awe. Books, animals, rites and people are sacred because they are set aside from ordinary careless use, but it is not necessarily true that what is sacred is experienced to be profoundly significant, or the centre of our individual or social lives.

Accordingly it is probably unwise to follow William James (in other respects a fine observer) in supposing that the essence of religion is to be found in the religious enthusiast, the one for whom matters of religion are of vital and emotional concern. Not everyone is obsessed with the need to preserve the centres of the sacred cosmos; not everyone is strongly aware of the presence of such sacredness. It is not reasonable to suppose that the rituals and stories that preserve the memory of what is sacred are themselves preserved merely by the efforts of enthusiasts. Causes served *only* by enthusiasts – political, military, literary or religious – do not survive and spread. All causes need a mass of non-enthusiasts, who take the cause more or less for granted and whose emotional involvement is rarely at fever-pitch.

Philosophical Analysis

If enthusiasts are relatively scarce, so also are philosophers. Most people take the traditional scheme of belief and practice so much for granted that no real question arises, at least until they become aware that there are other peoples with quite different traditions who have to be taken seriously. One result of that realization may be an equally unthinking relativism, the casual acceptance of a world in which truths are only truths-for-someone.

> But if you cross over the sea,
> instead of over the way,
> you may end by – think of it –
> thinking of We
> as only a sort of They!
> (Rudyard Kipling, 'We and They')

That casual and unthinking relativism, usually combined with a fair degree of bigotry about particular dogmas, is one of the most pervasive of rhetorical styles in our present age. It is usually confused, particularly by its practitioners, with the philosophical attitude, whose effort it is to try and understand tradition. Those with a philosophical bent are perturbed by traditional utterances even before the existence of alternative traditions is revealed to them. They find to be obscure what 'everyone' takes for granted, or they do not see what reason there is to take it for granted, or they see further implications or plausible corollaries of what is believed. Whether their particular bent is critical or speculative usually determines whether they become resident sceptics or imaginative metaphysicians. In neither case are they content to remain entirely within the tradition: either they undermine that tradition, or they seek to amplify and expand it. Whether their work receives any recognition depends upon the mix of temperaments in their society, and its cultural situation. Sometimes they are doomed to find no sympathetic companion, until a social anthropologist arrives to question their tribe about its beliefs. Victor Turner recounts most movingly the delight and growing enthusiasm of one witch-doctor at last allowed to speculate about the theoretical entities of his tribe's cosmology, to isolate the laws of contagion and similarity. Such people are enthusiasts for understanding, and are happy to talk about 'what their tribe believes' when their fellows are busying themselves about the 'practical' affairs of life. Sensible anthropologists know very well that their accounts of tribal belief and custom, filtered through such a speculative intellect, may bear little enough relation to what 'ordinary folk' would say.

Speculative philosophers expand upon and embroider traditional belief. True outsiders, or more critical philosophers, may think that these expansions lack any theoretical justification, and regard the baroque structures of speculative cosmology (Hesiod's Theogony, or the medieval Kabbalah, or current debate about what preceded the Big Bang) as no more than fantasies, that reveal (no doubt) the psychological structure of the narrator, or even the 'logical' structure of human imaginative discourse, but that cannot reasonably be regarded as well-founded theories. Once the religious abandon the illusory security of what is believed 'always, everywhere, by everyone' (a canon to which churchmen occasionally appeal) it is difficult to establish a coherent and believable principle upon which tradition may reliably be expanded.

Critical philosophers, who are exercised chiefly by the need to find the real evidence for what seems to be said, must themselves confront the problem of how any rule of evidence is to be defended. Carried to extremes, the claim that we ought not to believe anything which cannot be proved must issue in a blind agnosticism. Where nothing is taken for granted, nothing can ever be established. The retreat to acknowledged ignorance (not merely of things divine, but about all our customary convictions) halts this side of open insanity only when customary conviction is powerful enough to prevent any real dissent. Thoroughly critical philosophers may then relapse into ordinary convention: so David Hume, one of the greatest of critical philosophers, took refuge in the convictions born of beef and backgammon, binding himself (as traditional Sceptics wished) to the quadruple compulsion of Nature, custom, desire, and the rules of craft. Lacking any argument to convince him that he was rationally bound to believe even that food would not poison him, or that the sun would rise tomorrow, he was happy to forget argument and rely instead upon irrational conviction, strengthened by good food and company. Those who begin as enthusiasts for understanding may end as lazily conventional. If they do not, they may be regarded with the same tolerant amusement as greets the speculative philosopher.

But though real enthusiasts for understanding are as rare as any other brand of enthusiast, it is probable that the speculations and criticisms they develop sometimes trouble the contented sleep of ordinary 'believers'. Just as any of us may occasionally experience the movement of the spirit that enthusiasts desire (even if we do not take it all that seriously), so any of us may sometimes wonder what is going on in our own lives or in the lives of our neighbours, as these are structured and suffused by 'religion'. There are puzzles, to be sure, that only committed philosophers are likely to notice. Working scientists are not much exercised by problems about the reality of the past: those are problems for some other craft than physics or zoology. But too bland an acceptance of current theory and practice, without any thought of what their words might mean, makes for bad scientists. Similarly, ordinary churchgoers or the still more ordinary 'vaguely Church of England' non-churchgoers, are not greatly troubled by the thought that no-one else is real in quite the way they are, or that everyone else is a member of some vast conspiracy. Thoughts like that are taken seriously only by the mentally disturbed, and by philosophers. But too bland an acceptance of whatever the parson, or the television personality, says (even if this 'acceptance' is combined with total neglect at any practical level) makes for bad believers.

In the following chapters I shall be trying to philosophize about religion, not with the intention of proving it a nullity, nor with the intention of proving it a necessity. Judgement and understanding are related acts, but my aim here is to understand, not to judge. What I seek to understand is the religious tradition, not merely the standard 'arguments for God's existence', and not merely that tradition in which I was reared myself. That the idea of God is central to religion is one of those speculative untruisms that darken counsel. That the standard arguments for God's existence are central to religion is plainly false. For a philosopher to concentrate on those arguments and ignore the living context within which speculative philosophers have elaborated their theories is to run the risk of missing the point entirely. It would be equally unfortunate to ignore the cognitive and intellectual aspects of the religious endeavour: if theology is not central to religion, neither is the ceremonial intoning of religious ritual – as if that could go on unchanged when believers have wholly abandoned the attempt to relate what they do to what they and their neighbours believe about the world.

Any claim I make to 'objectivity', in the sense of impartiality, must not, of course, be taken too seriously. Those who think themselves impartial and dispassionate inquirers are usually recognized by everyone else as the most obviously bigoted of us all. It is, after all, a mark of the bigot that her own thoughts and judgements seem obviously true to her, and therefore not things she needs to be dispassionate about. Those who aim at a careful understanding of themselves and of the world must recognise that they are likely to suffer from the usual astigmatisms, that they are not themselves the best judges of their own impartiality. Those who offer themselves as map-makers must be judged by the results. I would hope that anyone, of whatever persuasion, may find my maps of use, even if some areas are more closely mapped than others, even if I have failed to see some interesting track, or not marked all the swamps. Map-makers should also make their allegiance clear from the start in case partiality should have led them to read the boundary lines incorrectly. In matters of religion, especially, map-makers need to display their credentials: how far may they be believed as trustworthy reporters of the tradition? Is their knowledge mere book-learning? Accordingly: I am myself a philosopher, an 'enthusiast for understanding', reared in the Anglican Communion, and with some experience of 'conversion' and 'baptism in the Spirit'. Book-learning and personal experience have convinced me that there is something to be learnt from all branches of the religious tradition, and that those irreligious who foresee an end of religion have a naive and etiolated concept of the world and human history. I believe, with Gautama, that there is an Unborn and Indestructible, that there is a way to realize the presence of that Unborn in one's own life and the world's, that there is a fellowship of all believers. I take refuge in the Dharma, in the Buddha, in the Sangha, as good Buddhists do. I believe in Father, Son and Holy Spirit, as catholic Christianity has taught us to say. What these declarations really mean can only be made clear by exploring them. What they do not mean is that I would insist on reiterating verbal formulae no matter what the logical and evidential problems posed by doing so. The irreligious have no monopoly of intellectual honesty, any more than the religious do.

Further reading

Clark (1982); Hume (1976); James (1960); Kolakowski (1982); Leeuw (1938); Smith (1978); Smith (1981); Turner (1967).

Helpful introductions to the philosophy of religion include Hick (1973), Nielsen (1982), Davies (1980). Evans-Pritchard (1965) is a fascinating survey of anthropological discussion: see also Banton (1966). Berger & Luckmann (1967) and Berger (1969, 1970) introduce concepts, such as that of a 'life-world' (on which see Schutz (1971)), which are helpful in understanding human action empathetically.

Difficulties faced in interpreting behaviour are the province of philosophers of mind, and of language. Nagel (1979) is a good place to start.

2

The Natural History of Religion

Sacred History and the Great Religions

The sacred texts of any religious tradition define its history as that is conceived within the tradition. The great 'religions of the Book' understand themselves, as it were, as the inheritors of the Creator's promise to Abraham. The world and humankind were made by the Lord; humankind, in the person of Adam and Eve, fell away from the divine purpose by disobedience, and eating of the tree of knowledge; the Lord chose to favour successive patriarchs who served the divine purpose in that generation, and brought Noah out of the flood, Abram from Ur, Moses out of Egypt. The people He had made for His own possession perpetually repeated the error of our first ancestors, but the Lord raised up new prophets for them, and will yet write His laws more firmly in their hearts. The people of the Promise may be Jacob's children, or the spiritual Israel which is the sprawling body of 'the Christian Church', or those other descendants of Abraham, the Ishmaelites and their converted friends. Judaism, Samaritanism, Christianity and Islam share a common self-perception as the heirs of Abraham, in whom the divine purpose for all humankind is preserved. They differ, of course, in many important particulars, and each local variant of their traditions has a little more of sacred history to unfold. Histories of the Caliphate, or the Imams, or the conversion of the English, or the Reformation and Counter-Reformation, or the Dispersion and the Holocaust – these constitute the sacred history of the community, though they are not understood as central to it in the way that the events recorded or imagined in the primary texts may be.

If the 'religions of the Book' report their derivation from Abraham, then the multiple versions of Buddhism, reporting their own derivation from Gautama, might be called 'religions of the Baskets', the Pali Tripitaka, though these fundamental scriptures seem only to have taken final shape in the reign of King Asoka (three centuries after Gautama), in opposition to heretical views (such as the doctrine of the eternal soul). Buddhist sects and, more generally, the civilizations that identify themselves as broadly Buddhist, conceive themselves to have inherited the discovery made by Gautama Sakyamuni under the Bo-tree, that the way to the cessation of suffering lies through the elimination of desire. Those sects that conceive themselves to be travelling in the 'Greater Vehicle', Mahayana, report that Gautama left secret teachings, of a kind that most of his first followers could not bear. Those who hold by the simpler meaning of the Pali scriptures, Theravada, would generally profess to think that the Mahayana is a concession to the human weakness for ceremonial and spiritualistic fantasy, though the figure of the Buddha (as historical figure or as metaphysical reality) may be as honoured in Theravadin as in Mahayana cultures. It is in the stories of Gautama's struggle and self-sacrifice, revealed in the life of Sakyamuni and in the 'lives' that preceded his enlightenment, that the core of Buddhist self-definition is found, surrounded by the local histories of Milarepa (the black magician who repented and achieved a life of naked simplicity in Tibet), of Tripitaka (who journeyed in the company of Monkey from China to India to obtain the scriptures), of Kuan Yin and Nichiren and the Buddhist monks who burnt themselves to death in Vietnam. Just as the religions of the Book take their beginning from Abraham, but require a cosmic pre-Abrahamic, pre-Adamic history within which Abraham (and then Moses) simply returns to the primordial lore, so the religions of the Baskets conceive of uncounted millions of years within which the Buddha-nature was at work, and occasionally manifest. Just as the Abrahamic tradition looks ahead to the Great Day when God shall indicate his faithful servants, so the Buddhist prophesies of the last Buddha, and the Day when all things, every blade of grass, shall be enlightened and the Bodhisattva's vow fulfilled.

Alongside these two vast elaborations of a personal summons and revelation, the taxonomist of religion may place the 'religions of the Vedas', the interlocking cults and philosophies and caste-ceremonials that constitute 'Hinduism'. What history the sacred texts of 'Hinduism' contain is of a magical and fantastic kind, by contrast with the Abrahamic and Buddhistic traditions, but those embedded in the tradition probably see little difference. The world is a moment in the dream of Brahma, and the gods renew their presence in the world, their opposition to the demons who would destroy good order, in every age. The stories of Rama, Arjuna and his brothers, Krishna constitute the base from which the good 'Hindu', secure in her caste and in her obedience to the stages of life, looks out. Saivism and Vaishnavism are as like, and as unlike, each other as the warring Abrahamic sects, though the underlying creed that all phenomenal events are *Maya*, 'illusion', has perhaps diverted 'Hindus' from the worse excesses of the more serious-minded traditions. What matters to a child of Abraham is to be part of salvation history, a member of God's people upon earth, waiting for the promise to be fulfilled. What matters to one who has 'entered the stream' is to realize *Nirvana*, through the power of the Buddha-nature once manifest and now remembered. What matters to a Hindu is to play the part allotted to her in the eternal dance.

Religions with no literal texts, whose sacred lore is stored in memory and ceremonial painting, may still constitute a sacred history. Amerindian religious tradition, for example, provides in mythological form a tale of how the people came up from the earth or from the hand of the Creator to serve His will on earth. Landscape embodies sacred history, even if the land is only settled in the last few hundred years. Great shamans have composed new dances, seen new visions, led their people on long treks and into battle. The long betrayal of a people's hopes by their white brothers is 'written' into the sacred history of the tribes. A similar story can be told of the Australians, who locate themselves in time by reference to the Dream-time and to the complex rules of intermarriage that – so Levi-Strauss supposes– some intellectual genius of the level of Einstein or Newton devised long ago.

Naturalistic Explanation

The sacred histories of our various traditions, now being (willy nilly) forced to come to terms with each other, do not always say just what any dispassionate observer might conclude from a study of the evidence. We may reasonably doubt that the Buddhist Scriptures, or even the central core of them, took canonical shape directly after Sakyamuni's death and were refined and corrected under King Asoka. We may reasonably doubt that the Pentateuch was written by Moses, or that the story of pre-Abrahamic days descends by true tradition and the Holy Spirit from the forefathers of humankind. We may doubt that the Koran is, word for word, what Muhammed was told by Gabriel, just as we doubt that Smith ever had any golden plates from which to translate the story of the pre-Columbian Israel (which is the sacred text of the Mormons, a late Abrahamic sect). Where sacred histories see the action of the gods, 'natural history' sees only the sort of thing that usually, or for the most part, happens, and explains the birth and rise of any particular tradition in 'merely natural' terms. This may disconcert believers.

The Abrahamic religions took shape from the experience of dislocation and dispossession, from exile and defeat and the need to find a cultural identity strong enough to resist the influence of despotic empires and Greek racial prejudice. The Buddhist tradition took its start from the efforts of a semi-Vedic, urban populace to escape the constraints of caste and *karma*. Buddhism, like Protestantism, can be explained by economic causes – or at least its success in subverting decent Hindu morals can be so explained. The visions and ceremonial dances of Sioux shamans are explicable as psychological and cultural reactions to an overwhelming and technologically superior power. Unable to compete in war and business, the Amerindians fell back on magic, fantasy and drug-fostered illusion. Unable to compete upon caste terms, the early Buddhists devised a theory to escape their duties and deny the Brahmins' monopoly of sacred power. Unable to cope with the secular world of a Hellenized Rome, the slaves and lesser bourgeoisie devised reasons to consider themselves the equals of the emperor, and institutions to save themselves from penury.

Explanations of this kind, in terms of political, economic and social realities, may seem inconsistent with the favoured explanations of sacred history. Any particular explanation, of course, might easily be challenged. All of them suffer from the defects that afflict any psycho-historical 'explanation' of anything at all (wars, political institutions, artistic renaissances): all are wholly untestable; none can be understood as instances of any general psycho-historical laws; we have no idea which of the many proposed 'explanations' are incompatible. If we conclude that the rise of Protestant Christianity, or of Buddhism, is to be explained by the needs of an entrepreneurial merchant class, we cannot conclude either that some 'similar' religious movement will occur in any definably 'similar' situation, or that the rise of these great waves of human endeavour is not also to be 'explained' by the agonies of war, the complacency of those hitherto appointed as embodiments of the sacred, plague or the occasional (and unpredictable) religious genius. Why exactly has vegetarianism suddenly moved out of the social twilight, and become a respectable option? Because meat is too expensive, because fertilizer is too expensive, because the oil states formed a cartel? Because more of the populace has been made aware of the significance of evolutionary theory? Because traditional Christianity has come to be seen as standing for an established creed (nationalistic, sexist and authoritarian) that offends modern sensibilities, and so gives way to other and more animistic religious feelings? There is no reason to exclude any of these 'explanations' and no way of assigning any relative weight to them or to the indefinitely many other explanations.

Sensible historians know very well that any supposed explanation is only an exercise of folk psychology, in terms of the usual and foreseeable desires, fears and sensibilities of human beings. We can appreciate why people of a particular kind in a particular era might have found it helpful or even necessary to think of things in a certain way. We can understand why people who have lost economic and social status, who can no longer identify with the motives and values of those whom they conceive as rulers, should bolster their own waning self-esteem by turning on those still lower than themselves. We can, in short, understand some of the games of racism, not because we have any psycho-historical law that is intelligibly connected with a whole system of such laws, but because we can imagine ourselves making that response. We can also understand how just the same situation (as an outsider might perceive it) could lead to religious revival, or cynical despair, or renewed determination to abide by the ancestral code. By the exercise of historical imagination we can think ourselves into other skins, and understand – for example – how what seems to us a trivial insult could really be the 'cause' and 'explanation' of a revolution. The passion of revenge is one of those most subject to cultural relativities: liberal-minded Westerners find it difficult to conceive how far the passion may drive others to avenge not only personal but historical insults. Difficult, but not impossible. In performing that task we may also see that 'the religious impulse', or one of the many impulses that go by that name, may be sufficient cause and explanation of historical events. Abraham's family might have left Ur anyway, as part of a grand tribal migration instigated by the shifting economic situation of the Chaldaean cities. The multiple events, whatever they were, that forged the 'chosen people', the people that conceived itself as chosen by the Lord as His special witness, were ones that we could imagine ourselves participating in, and responding to in just the ways the Hebrews did. It does not follow that part of what made those events what they were was not a religious revelation or discovery. Such explanations as we can give are not in principle incompatible with sacred history, where that is understood as the dialogue and interaction of the ordinarily human and spiritual reality.

Why should it be thought that there is a general incompatibility of 'natural' and 'sacred' history? There are perhaps three reasons. The first, that what is natural would have happened anyway, and that there is accordingly no need to posit an additional determining factor, the divine. The second, that what is natural is itself unmeaning, and carries none of the implications for our life that sacred history does. The third, that natural explanation shows how poor the motives, how irrelevant the reasoning, behind religious movements, and thereby casts doubt upon the rationality of the religions. I shall consider these in order.

Sacred Explanations, and Extraterrestrials

That sacred history is the record of humankind's relationship with the divine, with powers embodied or represented in the sacred, suggests at once that it is an account of how the divine powers have dealt with us and our ancestors. The first model that occurs to us, which may prove defective, is what might be called the 'God as Spaceman' myth. Is a sacred history the record of meetings between humankind and beings (or one being) from outside the range of everyday encounters? If it now turns out that we can find no good contemporary evidence for any such beliefs, and that what was interpreted a such a meeting could as easily be explained in other ways, we have that much less reason to believe in strange encounters. This is not to say that it could not have been true that weird and unearthly beings played a part in the hidden history of our kind. Nor is it to deny that such a story might, even now, be true. There certainly seems nothing unintelligible in the idea that unearthly beings did visit our ancestors, and there can be no conclusive evidence that they did not. It is to say that we have no good reason to believe, of any particular story, that this is a distorted memory of a visitation. One example may serve: it has been suggested that an African tribe, the Dogon, have astronomical information that (conjoined with legends about a fish-god that brought knowledge down to earth) suggests that their ancestors were visited by beings from Sirius. It turns out that the likelier explanation of the Dogon's acquaintance with super-heavy matter, and Sirius' neutron-star companion, is that popular astronomy was more widely diffused (even to the tribes of Africa) than 'ufologists' – those who take stories of such visits, and of flying saucers, seriously – supposed. The story is evidence of the essential unity of humankind, not of extraterrestrial visitations.

We cannot reasonably conclude that unearthly beings have visited the earth, because we can explain stories, relics and religions without recourse to the Galactic Empire. Insofar as we explain events by merely terrestrial instrumentalities we leave no room for the extraterrestrial in any decently economic scheme. There is, on the other hand, a standing puzzle how humankind 'invented language' or discovered the vast range of medical and culinary herbs or learned how to forge metal implements. Language in particular seems impossible for any genius to invent: how could she be understood by anyone, or even by herself? How is it that our ancestors, in struggling bands, could find out so much about the world? Even in the last few centuries, when experimental science has been funded and carried on by millions, we have not equalled the discoveries our neolithic ancestors made. Who found out, who troubled to find out, that cassava could be eaten if the poison was beaten out of it? It is hardly surprising that sacred history so often contains stories of how gods brought down the knowledge of grain and grape. There seem to be so many things that could not have been found out or invented unless we already knew them.

The stories of all sacred histories suggest that long ago the heavens were close to earth, and the gods walked freely among humankind. Since then they have retired up to their homes, shocked by human depravity, or preoccupied with their celestial business, or leaving space for humankind to grow. The stories usually suggest that the gods not only brought us knowledge, but also created us: perhaps they found something that could be made into an image of themselves; perhaps they bred us; perhaps they became us, or let themselves be taken into us (as the infant Zagreus was eaten by Titans, from whose blasted flesh the first of humankind crept out). If we can now understand our coming to be, and even our coming to be knowledgeable, within the framework of a closed, terrestrial, evolutionary system, we no longer need to imagine such creators. The problem, after all, always was to explain the gods' existence. Either there was a God beyond all gods, who simply was from everlasting, or there was an infinite succession of wandering creators. In either case it was not clear that our knowledge and existence were strictly explained by positing such beliefs. If we can explain what happened without bringing gods into the story, we have advanced a little.

If extraterrestrial beings have visited the earth, of course, then many of the stories of our sacred histories may turn out to be literally true. Maybe we shall be revisited, and the new visitors be as surprised by our startled recognition as were the European explorers who were greeted as long-lost godlings or former friends by the Amerindian tribes (who, we may suppose, had encountered stray Norsemen or Celtic saints a thousand years before). But though this might happen, we cannot reasonably count upon it. It may be that those who do count on it, 'ufologists', live more happily and imaginatively than do those who never glance beyond the confines of their local community to wonder about what might be going on amongst the fire-folk dancing in the sky. It may even be that such ufologists will occasionally uncover truths or interesting possibilities that more conventional intellects will never see. But their attempts to persuade the rest of us that we ought to devote intellectual and emotional energy to living out the role of those who wait for the Galactic Empire to make itself known, are unlikely to be successful, except (perhaps) among the bored, half-educated masses.

The powerful analogy, perhaps the identity, between ufologism and religion will continue to exercise me in the following chapters. What concerns me here is the proposed analogy between such unconventional histories as incorporate the visits of extraterrestrials, and sacred histories. Ufologism, of course, may be a religious form, and its texts be a sacred history. But more obviously than most such histories it makes a serious claim to be ordinary history as well. If its believers were convinced that all the texts were fictions and all the reported sightings merely atmospheric disturbances or schizoid delusions, they might retain a vague sensibility about the starry heavens, a wishful dreaming that maybe there is someone up there. They might even continue to keep watch upon the sky, or fund radio-searches of the nearer stars. But they would no longer be believers.

Are all sacred histories of this kind? Do they offer 'unconventional' (or presently unconventional) explanations of events (including those events which are the direct reports of eye-witnesses, as that Pheidippides encountered the God Pan upon his run to Sparta) which compete with alternative explanations (as that people lie, and are deluded, and attribute their own passions and sudden inspirations to some other and 'external' being), and mistake merely 'natural' entities for divine oddities? Consider Elijah's contest with the priests of Baal, when fire leapt from a clear sky to prove the Lord was God. If this is not the sort of thing that, in our experience, happens, no reasonable historian could posit such an explanation for (say) the Great Fire of London or the latest case of suspected arson. If one were convinced that the story was not just a fiction, one would wonder whether the liquid poured over the sacrifice was not naphtha (a tank of which was found in the ruined Temple at Jerusalem by the returning exiles). Suppose that was the explanation. There would then have been no 'miracle', because no evidence of any supernormal, supernatural power. Would it have been a mere fraud instead, the sort of thing that science-fiction writers often describe when they wish to portray a future religious cult? The mass of the population believes that only divine power could explain the events they seem to themselves to see; the elite, the educated priests, know how to bring about these events by the operation of natural causes. Sometimes such imagined priest-magicians are benevolent in purpose; sometimes they are not. In either case they claim to be the servants of a divine power whose effects they themselves bring about, merely by art natural.

Suppose we were convinced that all the events of sacred history were explicable like this, by the operation of natural causes whose behaviour was sufficiently unfamiliar to the mass of the population to make them think that it could only be by supernatural power and divine purpose that the events occurred at all. We need not suppose that there are strange vessels in our sky, visitors from other worlds: it is enough that there are electrical disturbances of a kind that can be replicated, in miniature, in laboratories (if that is so). Equivalently we need not suppose that there are supernatural visitors and powers: it is enough that things sometimes happen unexpectedly, or that some things have unfamiliar powers that can be employed by a knowledgeable elite to impress the laity. Sacred histories, on this view, depend upon a mistake, and realistic history need posit only natural causes, of a kind that we can in principle learn to control. They are *sacred* histories because they involved objects, techniques and persons that were classified as sacred, only to be used on 'their own terms' – or on the terms set by the elite.

Were the priests deceivers? Were they self-deceivers? Anthropologists have recounted how shamans have their tricks to impress their clients, tricks which they guard jealously and which they regard as wholly superior to their rivals' tricks – superior not merely as being more impressive, but as giving a better contact with divine power and with truth. Even a practitioner who first went into the business with the aim of discrediting such tricks may end up believing in the results of his own technique, though he does not (of course) believe the same things about what he does as do his clientele. Is this deception, and self-deception, on a par with a male initiate's attempt to persuade his womenfolk that he no longer defecates? That is certainly possible, but we may perhaps allow the priests a slightly greater sophistication, and thereby allow more credit to the sacred history. The priest or shaman or augur does not suppose – as his clients may – that the gods or spirits have brought into being some new, unprecedented object, or that they have caused the animal's liver to be suddenly corroded as the knife descends, or even (maybe) that fire from heaven had licked up the water. He may think that, in a sense, nothing 'out of the ordinary' occurred. What occurred was, in another sense, 'unordinary'. What happened was significant for the priest (or for any sophisticate) not because it was wholly without ordinary parallel, but because it happened at a particular moment, in a particular context. The event which naive believers count as an 'act of God' because it is in all respects unusual, is significant for the elite because it is part of a communication. In the same way, there is no contradicition in describing a spoken human utterance as a stream of sounds, of which every one (or the whole sequence) is emitted in accordance with natural law. Such an utterance is both a physical, and a semantic, event.

To return to the ufologists' cause: a sophisticated believer might conclude that the supposed events on which she had based her case were not indeed any other than the unbelieving historian reports. There were no extra creatures wandering the earth in the days when the extraterrestrials were active here. They acted only within terrestrial agents. The evidence for their agency is not that something was done which would have required greater power or wisdom than is available to ordinary people. It is rather that human utterances, human activities are seen as communications of a stranger kind. What was uttered, and understood in one sense, is now understood to have hidden meanings, made evident by the agreement – under those rules of interpretation – of human utterances from different places and times.

Sacred historians do not need to include any events that might not also appear in 'natural' histories. What the religious think 'happened' need not be incompatible with what we know of 'ordinary events'. Nor do they need to think that extraordinary power is needed to 'explain' those happenings. It is rather that ordinary events, ordinarily caused, of a kind that serve as instances of general natural laws, are also to be understood within a 'sacred' setting, as communications or contracts with other hidden realities. Maybe when Homer described the goddess Athena's arrival on Ithaca in the shape of the human Mentor, he did not suppose that Athena came in her own body, different from any terrestrial or human body, but that Mentor himself spoke words with an additional layer of meaning and significance. No amount of merely naturalistic enquiry will reveal this meaning, any more than chemical analysis of a human brain will reveal the thoughts that issue in speech.

This is a solution of sort to the problem posed by the contrast between sacred and merely natural histories. The divine realm is not understood as an explanation of material and human events which are otherwise inexplicable, but rather as the giver of meaning to events that are, in their own right, entirely ordinary. Not all religious will agree to this description of the situation; some will prefer to take as 'literal' a view of their sacred texts as any ufologist. But it is likely that the less 'literal' reading has always been available. Witches did not 'literally' fly off to their Sabbats: they might be lying in jail at the time. The Olympians were not 'literally' transmogrified into owl or wolf. The birds of good omen that were, momentarily, Olympian had histories of their own, and the god who was present then did not always make them do things that were not in their natures. When creatures act 'out of character' they may be possessed, by gods or ghosts or devils; it does not follow that those who are inspired, or animated by a god, must act out of character. Sacred histories sometimes do include events that could not ordinarily be expected, but the evidence for their sacredness does not rest upon the extraordinary quality of those events. Rather the reverse: we have more evidence that something odd did happen if we are already justified in seeing the whole sequence of events (including very ordinary ones) as divinely significant. The Bible is the Word of God – if so it is – not because no human being could have written the texts it contains (they manifestly could), but because the writings can be understood as a whole, beyond any human intention of the writers. What the Bible *qua* sacred text means is not merely what its human authors meant. When we read it we are not only acquainted with the thoughts of priestly editors or eighth-century prophets. The Bible is for its believers what the history of Israel itself was to the author of the Books of Kings: a communication floating on the water of natural, historical events.

Natural Fact, Sacred Value and British Israel

The second reason for doubting the compatibility of natural and sacred history is that natural events carry, of themselves, no moral. Suppose it to be the case that some of the Israelites evicted from the Northern Kingdom when that Kingdom was conquered by Assyria did manage to hold together as a community. That sort of thing, after all, does happen. Suppose that after some years they seized the chance provided by political and military turmoil to escape out of Mesopotamia into the lands beyond the valleys, as the Book of Ezra says. Suppose that, although they soon lost all sense of their ancestry they did maintain (father to son, mother to daughter) a legend that their ancestors had once been favoured by the gods but had been cast out of their homeland for their offences to the deities. Suppose that the tribal migrations of the last millenium BC and first millenium AD brought substantial numbers of such half-breed Israelites, still with a few remaining taboos and political habits, to what are now the British Isles. Suppose, finally, that archaeologists and anthropologists and genetic counsellors found sufficient evidence in the present and past artefacts, customs and chromosomes of the British to think that this story was substantially correct. There is clearly a sense in which the sacred history of British Israelites might match the 'natural history' I have outlined. I doubt that any uncommited historian would believe it did, but certainly it might. That sort of thing does happen, and we should not allow a characteristic 'liberal' distaste for wondering about ancestry and tribal origin to make us deny the possibility.

Suppose things turn out like that, and it is generally admitted that the British may trace the main or most interesting line of their ancestry to the ancient Hebrews. Would this validate the sacred history, or even be compatible with it? As it stands, such a natural history would not imply that God had summoned British Israel to witness to His power, nor that we should take any steps to preserve the line against dilution or infiltration. Some of the story, as natural historians might uncover it, might not fit very well with British Israelite history even on a factual level: I can conceive no evidence that would convince an ordinary historian that Elizabeth Mountbatten-Windsor was the lineal descendant of King David, even if her subjects were descendants of the Northern tribes (who were, after all, in revolt from the house of David). That Elizabeth is David's heir can only feature in a sacred history: it is because there must be such a sovereign over Israel that British Israelites conclude that there was a hidden line of descent (known only to God and His angels) through the wilderness years. They deduce what Is from what Ought to be – which is almost a definition of sacred historiography (and a rule of Spinoza's, himself one of the greatest of rationalist philosophers). They also appear to deduce what Ought to be from what (imaginably) Is. Because these things have happened we (that is to say, the native-born British) ought to preserve and reposses our heritage. This requires at least an attempt to keep the dietary laws of Leviticus, to forbid intermarriage, to resist all changes in the sexual mores of society.

That we ought to remember our roots may, of course, be true. We find earthly happiness in part by identifying ourselves, our interests, our being, as members of a long-standing community or line. To lose the sense of what our ancestors were; to re-order town and countryside merely to suit our passing profit; to abandon traditional loyalties and household gods: that is to leave ourselves without fixed footing upon which to stand, and to license the destruction of whatever we achieve. We can only hope to achieve any lasting good in a landscape and society that preserve what came before, for we ourselves and all that we have done will be the antiquities of a later age.

There is good reason, accordingly, to think that our natural history is not quite as meaningless as some suppose. Simply in being 'our' history it is made sacred, something that we disregard at our peril and which fills properly conducted persons with a sense of community and pride in possible achievement. Even the villains of our history books (Henry VIII, Napoleon and Jack the Ripper) are *our* villains, and our heroes are made the inspiration and example of our future age. Historians are the guardians of the tribe's useful myths, but to do their work correctly they must try to see that the stories are not wholly false. We are mostly realists, and prefer to believe the truth, even if there are imaginable stories with some more obvious and heroic moral.

Nonetheless, it is also true that whatever our psychological reaction to what is understood as 'our' history, there is no sacred meaning in the facts of history as such. If the history of the Northern Tribes were as I have described, these migrations would simply be some of the innumerable such migrations. There would be nothing special about them merely because they linked the present British people and the squabbling tribes of eighth-century Israel. To study such matters with an eye to historical plausibility and the 'sort of thing that usually happens', is to make it something other than a sacred history. *Qua* sacred history it is a story, a communication, a divine encounter: *qua* natural history it is only the sort of thing that happens. If it were not the sort of thing that happens, no historian could have any right to assume that it did. If it were essentially a sacred history, it could not consist only of what is usual.

Being 'just what usually happens', such histories are not normative. That the Tyrians came down from Caphtor may be historically true: that God led them is an element of sacred history. If my earlier argument is correct it is not always true that 'God' here stands for some additional *explanans* without whose applied power something else would have happened (of an historically more usual kind). The Tyrians did just what such people might be expected to (though perhaps they might have done otherwise). That God led them is to say that what happened (at one level) for sufficient natural causes, was also (at another level) a declaration of God's purpose. Any natural history must leave divine purpose out of it; any natural historian must strive not to see the hand of God in what she studies.

Does it follow that to consider matters from the standpoint of naturalistic history is to deny the importance of the sacred dimension? It is not clear that it should. The sacredness of an event is not to be identified with its natural properties, any more than the sacredness of a sacred cow resides in her biological properties. To study the cow as a member of a given biological species, or as suffering from bovine tuberculosis, is indeed to put aside her sacredness. But the fact that such a cow is of a particular species, or that she is sick, does not prove that she is not also sacred. The fact, if it is one, that we ought sometimes to try and see things outside sacred history does not show that we ought never to see things within sacred history. The fact that a human being can be contemplated as a merely biological organism, without attention to her thoughts and purposes and her existence as an end-in-itself, does not show that this approach is always adequate, nor that a more respectful attitude is inappropriate.

Furthermore, it is not entirely clear that ordinary historians should always be so ascetic. The idea that we ought to try to understand all human history 'without affect', without forming any judgement of its significance and moral worth, is really nonsensical. To describe human beings as if they were no more than matter in motion, part of the unending transformations of the material world, is a trick beyond us, and if we were capable of such a vision we should have no interest in describing them at all, nor any way of distinguishing action (or even animal behaviour) from material event. It may be true that we can, with an effort, refrain from drawing moral or religious conclusions from what we know of our past. If may be true that, with care, we can describe things in such a way that any moral or religious judgement on them be logically intelligible. It does not follow that we could easily understand someone who made certain moral or religious judgements, nor that there are no objective criteria for such judgements. If all the great bullying empires of the past have gone down hill and all their peoples been dissolved into the general human stream, we have good reason to think that, if there is a God, She is not upon the side of the big battalions, however arrogantly their leaders say She is. As the Greeks (or some Greeks) said, God loves small things, and the overweening God delights to humble. That is not a deduction strictly so called: rather an educated hypothesis, that draws upon the evidence of normal history-making for its support.

Religious Feeling and Intellectual Virtue

It may be true that sacred history need not constitute a rival explanation for what has happened, but rather a different way of identifying what has. It may also be true that the attitude of a normal historian is neither incompatible with the simultaneous cultivation of sacred historiography, nor even all that different from sacred history in its search for what is humanly significant. But it must surely be admitted that the reasons which most religious have for forming or holding on to their sacred histories are so contemptible as to cast doubt on the rationality of such belief. Though it might be true that the British are descended from the Northern Tribes, and though there *might* be evidence that would establish this, it is quite clear that British Israelites do not really believe the story because there is any evidence for it which is independent of their belief that it *ought* to be true. How else could we believe it true that God has fulfilled his reported promises to Abraham, to Joseph and to David? What recognizable body of nations other than the English-speaking Anglo-Saxon stock has grown from small beginnings to cover and dominate the whole earth (supposing that even the Anglo-Saxons have)? Outsiders are likely to suspect that it is racial pride, half-educated ignorance, uneasiness at the speed with which the times are changing that encourages people to hang on to such a story. If these are the sort of motives that lead people to maintain allegiance to a sacred history instead of trying to discover and understand what happened through the normal causes of natural history, can sacred histories be respectable?

If this claim is to be of any general interest, of course, it cannot be merely that some people believe their sacred histories for unworthy or ridiculous reasons, or that some sacred histories cannot be believed upon good reasons. Both those claims may be true, and yet religion as such be rational. After all, some scientific theories cannot now be believed upon good reasons, and some people have no good reason to believe the true scientific theories that they do. The interesting claim is rather that sacred history is essentially unreasonable, and an offence to the historical conscience. The earlier objections to sacred history were that there was no need for supernatural explanations for and no occasion to draw religious morals from the events of our past. The present objection is that we ought not to view things from this point of view, that only the intellectually depraved could prefer a sacred to a natural perspective. Natural history shows that people are very easily deceived, that they are so far self-obsessed as to imagine that the whole world is obsessed with their small purposes. We are in the position of one who imagines that every passerby is talking about her, or laughing at her, or that there is a conspiracy against her. Those who do not share this illusion can understand it: they can conceive what it would be like to feel like that, and may make some progress in uncovering the psychological or physiological causes of her aberrant system of belief. Is not religion similarly self-obsessed? Not all the religious feel themselves the victims of an omnipresent eye (though such guilt feelings are not rare), but all (presumably) suppose that what they do 'matters' to the gods, or even that they are of especial interest to the gods. Religion, in some of its forms, is often praised precisely for giving people the sense that they are loved and valued. Is this not simply the manic opposite of paranoid depression?

Could we go further in uncovering the roots of 'religious feeling'? Maybe our alternation between complacency and despair is a function of our lengthy childhoods? Would creatures who were not slowly maturing mammals have any disposition to conciliate superior force, even to need superiors in order to enjoy conciliating them? Are not all the attitudes and dogmas of religion much like the paranoid delusions we may all endure, but which self-knowledge and maturity put behind us? Natural history understands us as we are, quite ordinary primates with the gift of language and an easily disturbed psycho-social system. To understand that no-one is particularly interested in us, that there is no vast conspiracy, that things are not arranged with us in mind (for good or ill) – these are the discoveries we need to make. Religion, as such, is a retreat to adolescent fantasy, the dream that there is someone who will 'take us out of this', that we are waiting to be transformed into Captain Marvel, that everyone must be a friend or enemy. The universe is neither friend nor foe, and happiness is knowing who we are, and that no-one else much cares.

Those who argue like this cannot reasonably claim that the facts of history 'require' this belief in any logical or scientific sense. Some of the suggestions that have been made about the genesis of religious feeling are indeed quite plausible, in general terms. But in the absence of any genuine control experiments, any evidence either that there are intellectual but irreligious species who have a different way of bringing up the young, or that there are no religious species who have such different customs, we cannot claim to have demonstrated such an account. Nor, if it were true, would such a causal story itself cast the theory of religion into doubt. There is just as much reason to suspect that there are biological determinants of our tendency to distinguish individuals, to believe in the continuous existence of material bodies, to expect genuine causal regularities, to be able to devise elegant theories of the universe: insofar as we are biological organisms our capacities and preferences will be appropriate to the kind of biological organisms we are. Such an hypothesis no more discredits 'religion' than it discredits 'science'. It might equally turn out to be true that we only believe in the existence of an orderly, elegantly mathematical and causally continuous universe because we are slow-maturing mammals whom security has rendered curious and gratuitously optimistic. 'Maturity', on this account, would come with the discovery that the universe cares nothing for our standards, that we cannot make the 'little agitation of our brain that we call thought' (a phrase of David Hume's) into the model of the universe. The assertion that the religious are immature because their attitudes are not unlike the paranoid depressive's could be met by the equally gratuitous assertion that the self-styled sane and irreligious are immature because they imagine that the universe makes sense, or because they have failed to remember the old joke: 'The fact that you're paranoid doesn't mean we're *not* out to get you!'.

Mutual insult and recrimination apart, both sides – if they have any concern for intellectual virtue – will agree that there are intellectual vices, that those who hope to discover the truth must practise humility, and be willing to be proved wrong. Those inquirers in particular who believe that what happens in the world and history is 'the work of God' (or some equivalent) have a very powerful motive for finding out what really did happen, and ought not to be content with their own first guesses, or their wish-fulfilment fantasies. Such believers do not need to be afraid that what they will uncover will destroy their ordered cosmos, and it is precisely because they believe that 'their God' is indeed the Lord of history (both natural and human) that they concern themselves with history. If they do not, if it is enough for them to recite what already occurs within the sacred texts, they give evidence that they conceive of 'their God' and 'their sacred cosmos' as something that exists within a wider and chaotic world which it is death to examine. If God is only 'our God', is He God at all?

The belief that the cosmos is established within chaos can very easily be seen as evidence that people are conscious that it is their own ordering and myth-making capacity which creates the tidy world in which they imagine themselves to live. What goes on outside that tidy history is of no human significance, and too much interest in it would destroy the sense of neat boundaries, belonging, and intelligible sequence that we rely upon for our human happiness. Religion can then be understood as the chief apparatus for keeping people's minds off the chaotic and meaningless outside. True knowledge is then defined, in opposition to religion, as acceptance that the universe is a great, meaningless vacuity. The only honest posture for a 'modern intellect' is to understand that all value, all order is a product of our own emotions, and that what is is supremely indifferent to us.

This result is clearly paradoxical. The assertion that 'what matters' is the product only of the emotional illusions of a creature that arises in and from what does not matter, is itself a sketch for a religion, and those who advocate such a creed and attitude – for which there are no clear demonstrative arguments – are recognizably proselytizers, seeking to amend and recreate our vision of the world into something that supports their own emotional demand, that they be unfettered 'creators of value', without an obligation to submit to rule and authority. This emotional demand is for a cosmos in which nothing matters except what 'we' choose should matter. It is defended by all the usual rhetorical tricks of religious apologists, and its advocates want the rest of us to turn from our own personal and ancestral creeds to accept this new vision. A not unreasonable response must be that if such a picture of the universe were true there could be no standing obligation to believe it. The only coherent pictures of the world in which there is an obligation to believe and hunt the truth (as distinct from our own imaginings) are ones where believing the truth, or trying to believe the truth, transforms one's life into something recognizably and really better, nobler, happier. Such pictures are ones that accept the existence of hidden order, unseen beauty in the world itself, outside our own first imaginings of it.

From this a further moral can be drawn. Religion is indeed, in part, the apparatus that establishes a sacred cosmos. But it can also be understood, in its radical moments, as the apparatus for breaking out of a once-sacred cosmos. Abraham's movement away from the Chaldaeans, Gautama's movement away from caste-nobility and orthodox asceticism, the Sioux visionary's revelation of the breakdown of the ancient dances are all recognitions that the sacred is constantly renewed from 'chaos'. It is because genuinely religious persons believe that the world in which our fantasy pictures are set is itself greater than our imaginings, that they should be able to accept new revelations with some equanimity.

Many of the themes on which I have touched in this chapter will return to plague us. It is enough for the moment to insist that sacred history and natural history need not conflict. The sort of explanatory hypotheses that are involved in sacred history prove their value (if they do) in the coherence and wider helpfulness of the cosmos they establish. Some sacred histories do have the failings that the irreligious comment on. To draw from this fact the conclusion that we ought to abjure sacred history can only result in the construction of an alternative sacred history, establishing another cosmos that we have (some) emotional reason to affect.

On the other hand, the overtly religious should be prepared to let their sacred history submit to the demands of logical rigour and plausible explanation. Not to do so, to insist instead on keeping what is already known or imagined, is implicitly to admit that one's religion is of the kind that maintains a comfortable cosmos. Those who genuinely believe that all things are 'in the hands of God', or that all things 'have the Buddha-nature' ought to accept the leadings of the truth, as that is manifested in our best and most serious imaginings. It is now not uncommon for proselytising atheists and religious 'fundamentalists' to conspire in restricting the name of 'true religion' to those who refuse all alteration and development in what they suppose themselves to understand from the sacred texts. It is assumed that 'liberals' are weak or hypocritical, or conceptually confused. There seems good reason to disagree. Religious traditions do develop, do draw upon the insights and arguments and experience of all humanity. Those who refuse to develop may be, on occasion, right to hold on to some truth that is momentarily out of fashion, but in general, *a priori* refusal to develop is profoundly irreligious.

Further reading

Clark (1984); Hume (1976); Larner (1982); Toynbee (1956).

The philosophy of history falls into two parts: the first deals with problems of historical method; the second deals with 'the meaning' of what has happened in the past. Philosophers in the analytic tradition have been shy of the second set of problems (see Popper 1957)), but 'reading the past' may still be an important aspect of our self-understanding, even for the atheist. Nationalism, which is one of the major religious forms of the present century (see Lutoslawski (1930), Larner (1982)), depends on our memory of the past, as that is enshrined in monuments, landscapes and texts.

A useful compendium of sacred texts is Smart & Hecht (1982).

3

Rituals and Rites of Passage

Beginnings and Endings

Religious traditions are constituted by sacred texts that record sacred history, but also by the rites and ceremonies that mark the community's response to the 'major events of life', and by the regular liturgical programme. I shall consider the regular forms of prayer and public worship in chapters 9 and 13. In this chapter what concerns me are the rites of passage which even a generally irreligious society tends to maintain. Seasonal festivals, inaugurals and ceremonies of birth, maturity, marriage and death are the great occasions of life. They are the peaks which the rising waters of irreligion cover last of all, or the wells that take longest to run dry. Even the irreligious tend to want these rites maintained, and are indignant if the regularly worshipping community and its scholars should change the established rituals. It clearly matters to people that the rites be as they were, or as they are commonly thought to have been. They are a way of reaffirming our relationship with the past even as we step into some new future. Beginnings and endings are the moments when people are reminded of mortality, and of their contact with the abiding reality that contains our more transitory and parochial concerns. The sacred is what comes before and follows after, that sets the framework for our mortal lives.

Beginnings and endings are sacred occasions. When we mark them off by ritual we also (sometimes) provide the participants with reminders of their lost, imagined past. If the ritual is recognisably the self-same ritual that we attended in our childhood we may be reunited, in memory, with our past selves, given a sense of who we are and what our limits are. We may also feel that others will attend such rituals when we are no more, and so momentarily confront our own mortality and understand that life goes on. The wish to maintain such ceremonials unchanged is a recognition that the refusal to preserve the past is tantamount to the reduction of all things to an unreal present. If the past is not to be preserved, why should the future preserve what is now our present? If there is no general tradition that past achievements are allowed to stand, we can ourselves count on achieving nothing, and our goals must shrink to those of immediate satisfaction (unless, just possibly, we find ourselves directed outwards, to eternity – but that is another story).

Larner spoke for sociological orthodoxy with characteristic clarity in pointing out that Russian atheistical scientist and Free Church minister alike might acknowledge the force and importance of a people's heritage, quite independently of any clear theological doctrine. 'A minister who spent some years in a parish in Aberdeenshire told me that he regarded his main function as being a word-merchant. He provided the utterances which gave meaning to some people's everyday lives, and to most people's life crises – by relating them to a cultural pattern of the past' (Larner (1982) p. 84f). It is also interesting to observe that the supposedly 'new' and 'modern' rites to which traditionalists object are usually attempts to 'get back' to an earlier original. The central rite of catholic Christianity, the eucharist, has constantly been refined to fit current scholarship about the first-century ritual. Some participants, accordingly, can think that they are doing what the first disciples did; others can think that they are doing what was done by the founding mothers and fathers of their own particular sect. Both sides in the debate can then describe the others as mere sectarians: those who prefer the ritual revised to suit current scholarship are separating themselves from the community of the folk-religious in their land; those who prefer the rites of 1662 as they were performed in school chapel and parish church some thirty years ago are separating themselves from two millenia of catholic Christianity. Both sides, of course, heatedly insist that they are identifying themselves with the true tradition, and display for their opponents all the charity and understanding which religious people reserve for those who disagree with them about an iota.

Beginnings and endings are disturbing, even dangerous, occasions. It is not surprising that we try to mark them off with ceremonial and festival. Succession of days without a pause or alteration in the pace of time is also disturbing. It is, accordingly, not all that surprising that we arrange to mark the seasons, and to say the year *begins*, and has a middle and an end. We want time to have a proper narrative form, and not be merely one damn moment after another. It is not that we first notice great occasions (the birth of a child, the marriage of a man and a woman, the death of a great chief, the dawn of a new year, the days of harvest and first-fruits), and then decide to mark them with a festival. The great occasions are created by the festivals. Unless there were such ceremonials there would be no beginnings, no middles and no end.

People would still be born without such ceremonial. But 'being born', as medical technicians and moralists now realize, is not a clear line, as though one first were 'not-born-yet' and then, all of an instant, 'born' (though it is true that there is a distinctive difference between being inside and outside the womb). Passage outward from the womb is a laborious and long-drawn process that does not 'begin' nor 'end' in quite the way our ordering intellect requires. It is as true of birthings as of any other process that the first moment at which we realize it is going on is also the moment at which we realize it has already 'started'. It started, indeed, some 'nine months earlier' (to use a largely ritual measure of very doubtful statistical accuracy). If we define birth (or conception), death (or burial) as the first and last of life it is not because we 'observe' it to be so, but because we thereby name and create the individual, that segment of humanity and of the whole world-process that our age and our society considers real.

If rituals do not merely mark occasions, but create occasions, the question we must answer is not 'Why do people feel a need to celebrate such occasions, such passages from one state to another?' but rather 'Why do people feel a need to insist that there are such different states, between which they pass?'. The first question can be answered, roughly, in the psycho-social terms I have suggested: in passing to a new state it is necessary for our mental stability and continuity to remember the old, and to remember that this passage has been made and survived before. The second question is not so easy to handle: granted that such passages are felt as dangerous why do we imagine them into existence? A passage from being to not-being is alarming, even when we know that we lose only an aspect of our former life: we move away from being-child to not-being child, or from being-a-single-person to not-being-so. But what are we to say when we realize that what underlies these notional changes is a continuum, that it is our rituals that create the illusion of a real passage? Why do people want to place a grid across the continuous? Why not realize that there are no limits, no straight and absolute lines, and no need for terror or for ceremonial?

The Logical Impossibility of Change

Time and change have been amongst the greater mysteries since first we 'noticed their existence'. There will be more to say about them and their relation to eternity and the unchanging, in later chapters. The point to be made here is that change, understood as a passage from being to not-being, is quite impossible. The first thing to observe is that such a passage (say, from being a child to not being a child) requires the persistence of some underlying subject (a *'subject'* indeed is the English version of the Latin for 'what underlies' such a change by persisting through it). Consider now the last moment of the subject's being a child: is this the same moment as the first moment of the subject's not being a child, or is it not? If it is, then there is a moment at which the subject both is and is not a child. If it is not, then (since time is continuous, and there are always moments in between any two distinct moments) there are indefinitely many moments at which the subject is neither a child nor not a child. Either option is a violation of the laws of non-contradiction and excluded middle. Such change is therefore logically impossible.

This puzzle is unlikely to keep anyone awake at night. Indeed, no one but a philosopher will feel much interest in exploring the several possible answers. Supposing that we insist on the reality of change, we can avoid the paradox either by considering that time is, after all, discontinuous, that it comes in instantaneous frames such that there is no time at all between successive frames (but what could such an absence of time be like?), or else by denying that talk of 'first moments' and 'last moments' is appropriate. On this last view there is no instant at which the subject is both a child and not a child because nothing is true of any subject simply 'at an instant'. The solutions and their concomitant difficulties do not greatly matter: what concerns me here is to observe that there is an obvious puzzle, which seems to stem from the attempt to divide reality, to separate what-is and what-is-not. Applying the laws of logic to a continuum generates paradox: the acceptance of logic implies the acceptance of illogic (unless we are so bold as to abandon temporal experience entirely). Beginnings and endings, accordingly, are felt as paradoxical affairs, and this is a consequence, not of any 'primitive mentality', but of a sophisticated logical understanding. Beginnings and endings are the moments when the mere subject, which neither is nor is not what it was presumed to be, is half-glimpsed, and clothed (in fantasy) with all the outward signs of myth. The demon is to be killed neither with the wet nor with the dry, neither by night nor by day, neither on water nor on dry land. So Indra slays him on the sea-shore at twilight with the foam of the sea.

Our ancestors' recognition of a paradox implied by all attempts to classify and dichotomize a continuum is also evident in the creatures that they picked to be their holy beasts. The cassowary is not a bird, but neither is it anything other than a bird: its character defines it as a betwixt and between thing that is a suitable symbol for what lies behind the oppositions of being and not being. Pigs, similarly, are boundary animals, that divide the hoof but do not chew the cud. The point is not, of course, that these creatures simply happen to fall foul of the orderly classification of kinds. It would probably be truer to suggest that just *those* classes have been formed as will pick out these creatures as anomalies. As before, it is not so much that rituals are a way of coping with the existential problem of boundary conditions, transactions and obviously opposed states of being. It is the rituals, the anomalies that create the opposition. It is because we have a ceremony called marriage that there is an opposition between being unmarried and being married.

My suggestion is in some ways the reverse of one theory propounded by the theoretical anthropologist Durkheim. He proposed that systems of logic and scientific classification were, in origin, copies or replicas of kinship classification, that social order was the first order known to humanity. There is a certain etymological justice in this thought (for taxonomic terms do generally stem from the language of blood-relationship). But it seems more likely that the impulse to classify is expressed both in social order, and in efforts to divide the world up into north, and south, wet and dry, human and unhuman. It is because we have an idea of the continuum, the abiding subject, what Buddhist tradition has called *Tathata* (the just so), that we emphasize the classification of being and not-being that overlays the first reality. We know that we could, in a sense, put the ritual markers anywhere, and make anything a new beginning. More easily, we could mark any of the regular, expectable events of human life and cosmic history (the first baby tooth to fall, first frost in crocus time, first fog of autumn), and so generate a Before and After, and the paradoxical betwixt and between. The rituals we conveniently make are not just memorials, not just preparations for the time to come: they are the occasions we have set aside, by making them a standing paradox, when *Tathata* 'comes to the surface' of our waking minds.

That rituals, rites of passage, ceremonials are meant to be paradoxical explains why it is so easy to discover paradox in them. 'Rational religion', while a noble cause (and one which I would not wish to renounce), sometimes takes the mysteries of religion a little lightly. It is important to believers, perhaps especially to those believers who normally attend only the greater festivals and have no clearly defined commitment to the central dogmas of their tradition, that the ceremonials embody paradox. The religious imagination is one that desires mysteries, or is so quite often. Casual believers in particular do not want to hear that evidence for the fairy-tale Nativity, with the One God born in a stable and visited by shepherds and wise kings, is doubtfully Christian, that the first believers (and the gospels) imagined no such thing. Nor do they always want to be told that the saying 'This is my body' can be given intelligible sense: it is better that it be a mystery, something that both is and is not merely bread. Nor do those celebrating Passover wish to be reminded that they will not be in Jerusalem next year.

The extent to which the religious relish mystery is variable. Some rituals are almost ordinary, and believers happy enough to say they are memorial feasts, or parties, or maybe meditation exercises. Others thrive on apparent absurdity, on chanted assertions that the speakers will not die, that a small round wafer is the very body that once hung upon the cross (nor that it represents it, nor even that it is a miraculously multiplied and disguised part of it, but that it *is* the whole and unique body), that a wooden lingam is the god Shiva, that a cucumber is an ox. Fashions change amongst anthropologists: once upon a time it was assumed that 'primitives' were alogical, and every possible illogicality discerned in their proclaimed beliefs and liturgies. More recently it has been assumed that we could not understand or translate their words without assuming that they were rational, and the number of reported illogicalities has shrunk. It seems likely that both parties had some reason on their side. Some peoples, some of the time, intend to talk sense, and mostly succeed. Some peoples, sometimes, do not intend that what they say should express any intelligible truth. These are often the same people, just as the same people sometimes think that prayer is an efficacious way of making rain, and sometimes that it is only a way of ensuring that rain, if and when it rains, is 'an answer to prayer'. Even supposed primitives may have different views, and even change their minds.

At all events, the sense of mystery as well as the sense of history is often satisfied in seasonal rituals and rites of passage. People do employ them to remind themselves of who they are, and of what lineage. That is why the hope of any genuinely unified religion is about as likely as the mass conversion of all humankind to speaking only Esperanto. Few people, in any tradition, 'really and whole-heartedly' mean what they say and sing, for the songs and sayings were settled in an earlier age, written (most probably) by enthusiasts, and hardly intelligble in their original sense (or many others) except to scholars. Even in small conventicles it is a delusion (from which members often suffer) to suppose that everyone is agreed, or that they speak their creeds both consciously and without mental reservations. What matters to them is that, by sharing in a ritual which establishes a Before and After they locate themselves not only in a historical tradition but in relation to the extra-human, *Tathata*, the subject that escapes all human thought. If this subject could be understood as one thing and not another it would not be the subject that neither is nor is not. For this variety of believers, or of believers in this mood, it is an advantage to ritual that it be not readily intelligible, even that it seem not to make much sense. This does not prevent other believers, or the same in different mood, from seeking to rationalize the doctrines perhaps implied by the rituals, and religious theories.

Realism and Ritual Truths

But do such rites, or the sayings uttered in them, have any implications? In 'ordinary' discourse what is said is assumed, other things being equal, to be *true* or at least to be meant to be true. And being true is, in part, a matter of fitting in to a complex system of mutual implication and evidence. If it is *true* that Tamar is Zachary's wife then Zachary is Tamar's husband, and a marriage ceremony of some kind was performed, and there would be legal complications if they chose to part, and evidence that Zachary was having sex with Rahab would be evidence of his adultery, and so on. If it turned out that our informant disavowed every one of these usual implications, and was disinclined to mention even one supposition that she would consider inconsistent with her first claim – we should have grave difficulty knowing what, if anything, she meant. After a while we should most probably conclude that she was not trying to say anything strictly true. Is this also the situation with ritual utterance? If all usual implications are denied to be implications, and the utterance has no effect upon the network of 'ordinary' information, was it ever meant to be true? What cannot be understood even by the speaker, cannot be an attempt at communication. On this view ritual utterance is not something to be known or believed, but only a verbal magic that perhaps helps to engender appropriate mood and emotion.

This is a thought to which I shall return, but there is a slightly different way of considering the case. Even my example of Zachary and Tamar, after all, was in some sense a ceremonial truth: in Nature 'there is no marriage nor giving in marriage', and Tamar's being wife to Zachary carries no implications about her health, the state of the weather or how old she is. What follows from the fact of her condition is determined by human law, and not by natural necessity. It might even be possible that Zachary was also married to Rahab, if we make the rules comply. This is to say that the proper implications of a truth may be confined within certain limits, merely by how we use the terms and what rules we apply. By contrast, if Tamar is Zachary's natural daughter it follows by natural necessity that he is her father, even though none call him so. The question raised long ago by moralists was this: does it follow by natural necessity, or by custom, that Tamar owes Zachary respect, and that Zachary owes her paternal care? Is it true that they have such duties because natural necessity requires it, or because sound custom does? Those who choose the second option have grown used to saying that moral judgements are not strictly *true*. In other codes it would be Tamar's mother's brother who owed, and was owed, such duties. The status of moral judgement is yet another topic that I must defer. Its relevance here is that religious utterances too might be conceived as made only within bounds, by virtue of the rules we choose and not by natural necessity.

Thus, when a priest (no other) says, within the rite, that a piece of bread is the bodily presence of the Messiah it follows (by custom) that it ought to be revered, that communicants should feed on it (or Him) by faith, that all left-over pieces should be consumed, or kept as the 'reserved sacrament'. It 'is' the Body of Christ in something like the way spades 'are' Trumps, or Michael Hordern 'is' (occasionally) King Lear. Being the Body of Christ consists in playing a particular part within the ritual drama, and that bread 'is' the Body by clear implication of the canon law. If the words are pronounced by any but a priest, it is not the Body. Custom may dispute whether the moral character of the celebrant bears upon the truth of what he says, and conclude that it does not, or on the gender of the celebrant, and conclude that it does. These rules are rules of custom, sound or unsound, and make what is uttered 'true', just in the sense that what is uttered in a game, or play, or legal ceremonial is 'true'. To insist that no-one is a High Court Judge 'in nature', and thence conclude that nothing such a Judge says can have any further implication than it would have done if anyone else had said it, is to miss the point.

On this account religious ritual, like other human ceremonials, defines the context within which its utterances must be judged. Complaining that the wafer does not bleed when crunched is asinine. Complaining that God does not 'exist' (or claiming that He regularly grants requests) is like imagining that Sherlock Holmes might have met Victoria, that characters in soap operas can correspond with fans, or that the king in chess has really been checkmated since the conclusion of the first game ever. Those who have never seen the theatre before may leap upon the stage to save the heroine. Those with some understanding of what is going on know that the implications of what is said on stage are severely limited. Ritual utterance, likewise, is not intended to reach out to 'ordinary life' in quite the way that literalists (atheistical or religious) imagine. The gods exist just in that they are addressed in ritual. Religious rituals are games or dramas, and the logic of their utterances fits this form. Just as the king is checkmated indefinitely many times, or King Lear bids Cordelia farewell in every new performance, so the 'sacrifice of the Mass' is performed as often as need be, yet is no different sacrifice: many performances, one play.

In these terms it is 'true' that in earlier lives what-was-to-be the Buddha sacrificed himself to satisfy a tigress's need to feed her cubs. It is 'true' that Jesus was virgin-born, Brigham Young in communication with the One God, and that there is an ancient labyrinthine web of power round Glastonbury Tor. These 'truths' are not intended to suggest that anything in particular said outside their dramatic context is true. Unbelieving archaelogists will find no trace of ley-lines (the mark of prehistoric tracks linking hills and sacred sites across Britain, having a magical significance for would-be practitioners of 'the old religion'), nor will non-Mormons ever locate the original Book of Mormon, nor will evidence from genetic research ever be relevant to the Christian (or any other) belief in sacred parthenogenesis. Why do human beings indulge themselves in dramas of this kind?

They indulge themselves, of course, in very different degrees. Some people attend upon a religious ritual as they might go to an occasional play. Others will recognise the characters and sequences of the rite as more devoted theatregoers will relish the latest manifestation of Miss Marple or Macbeth. Others again will be absorbed in their religion, like devotees of *Star Trek*, and the final depths are reached with those who take the 'real existence' of their ritual deities for granted, like those who despatch parcel-bombs to J.R. Ewing (mistaking fantasy for documentary fact). What reasons or motives people have for being theatregoers also vary, but (leaving merely social attendance out of consideration) it seems that no-one would go on going to plays or operas or concerts were not two propositions usually true: on the one hand what they see and hear is recognizable as something in tune with their 'ordinary' lives; on the other, that it is such as to involve a greater emotional intensity, a clearer vision, than their ordinary lives. What goes on in a theatre is at once larger and brighter than 'life', and recognizably 'like' life. Exactly what emotions people like to feel with greater intensity than usual (but detached from ordinary consequences) will also vary. Fear, lust, laughter, horror, admiration, pity – these are clearly clients for any and all of these intensified experiences. Religious rituals embody and intensify a similar range of emotions, and serve similarly varied clienteles: not everybody goes to church to weep at her own sinfulness or sorrow; not everyone goes to indulge her pity for a tortured universe, exalting it to the imagined presence of a compassionate deity that would gather all things as a hen gathers her chicks; not everyone goes to share the triumph of angelic voices. A 'good service' is one that raises up appropriate emotions in all or most of the congregation and sends them out content. Where there are other entertainments church attendance falls.

If religious traditions are to be understood on the analogy of theatrical traditions or long-running series, it is solecism to attempt to 'prove' the extra-religious reality of God or the gods or the Buddha-nature – as it would be to try and prove the historical reality of Gondor, or the War of the Ring. Such proofs should only be the working out of unseen implications of the ritual or dramatic discourse with a view to giving the discourse greater 'solidity' and 'depth'. How many children Lady Macbeth had, or what Dr Watson's second Christian name was, may be of more moment than to idle away a puzzle-solver's evening. Such added details may make the next production, or the next reading, an interesting addition to the repertoire, a more fully realized and evocative performance. Similarly with theological argument: the standard 'proofs of God' are not to be taken seriously out of context – they are simply ways of spelling out connections between different ritual elements. That Christ is Alpha and Omega, the Beginning and the End, may be usefully spelt out (for some temperaments) in terms of efficient and final causation (the One who started things, the One for whom all things were made). He exists 'beyond time' as all good dramatic personages do, perpetually represented to believing souls in their appropriate ritual. To ask more than this, to expect Sherlock to step down off the stage and die in an old people's home, or to expect to turn up Juliet's marriage lines, would be to misunderstand the theatre.

Can any fault be found with this account? That most believers will probably reject it hardly establishes that it is wrong, despite the rule adopted from Kolakowski that people be taken to mean more or less what they say they mean. What they say on this matter does not establish the point for at least two reasons. First, it is clearly possible for people to be so absorbed into soap opera as to forget that there is a real world distinct from the world of Dallas. Second, even those who could easily rouse themselves to deal with 'real life' may object to being forcibly awakened: just as children may prefer not to say 'let's *pretend*', but simply to launch into the game. In order to be an effective drama the play must not remind us too often that it is a play. Nor can we dismiss the possibility on the ground that drama and game lack what religion so markedly has, namely moral implications for 'real life'. Successful drama does embody an attitude to life that its audience can live out in their everyday affairs. Even games require distinctive virtues, and admirable games-players conceive of games so structured as to need such virtues as generosity and good faith as well as courage and temperance and courtesy. Games can structure ordinary life, to the point where people respond as they would to a player, or as they imagine one piece does to another. They can do this, without anyone supposing that the assertions made 'in play' have the sort of implications they would have if made not in play.

Sacred history can be conceived as dramatic history, history within the game. It is what 'believers' take for their context and framework when they join in rituals. They may prefer to behave rather as if it were true even when they are not participating in the rite. What then is the status of the 'real world', 'real life' and 'ordinary living'? What looks from one side (the side I have been taking) like an established reality with enclaves of acknowledged fiction and pretence and play might be turned round: is the chessboard white on black, or black on white? What rituals and games and shared endeavours establish ordinary living as the 'real world', the world that must be taken seriously? 'Realists' may poke fun at those religious who, they say, behave like addicts of soap opera, forgetting that a fantasy world is not the final context and framework within which they live. But is that not a possible description of 'realistis'? If it is folly not to think that one might be pretending, that one is involved in a dramatic show, then 'realism' is unrepentant folly.

Let me be more exact. 'Real life' and 'the real world' do not necessarily denote the same thing. 'Real life', as realists use the term, means the business of making a living, getting on with people, finding money for a mortgage or (just possibly) escaping from state brutality. 'The real world' may mean the same network of relationships and worries (as in 'Academics are cut off from the real world': a palpable falsehood, but not entirely unintelligible). The phrase may also denote the network of physical relationships, capable of description by scientists but never wholly known, that constitutes the universe as it is. Entities in the 'real world' may be entirely unfamiliar to those who are involved in 'real life'. Sociologically, knowledge of 'the real world' is constituted as an enclave within 'real life': even scientists do not consciously inhabit such a world for more than fragments of their life. More exactly still, those scientists who do give evidence that they consciously inhabit what is supposed to be 'the real world' are regularly accused (as other academics are) of being detached from 'real life'. Not to think that mortgages and jobs and civil status and romantic ties are vitally important is regularly classified as 'immature', 'escapist' and the rest. Such scholars, in fact, are as ill-considered as religious believers: they take a drama, or intellectual game, as being more 'real', more vital than 'real life.'

A dilemma confronts 'realists' who wish to place religious ritual in the dramatic slot. Either the 'real world' is the proper context of our lives, if we can find it out, or else 'real life' is the context in which even scientific world views must find their meaning. If the former is assumed, then we have a respectable example of elite, separated knowledge of what is the case. The rituals and dogmas of physical science clearly structure the important emotions and beliefs of practitioners in ways that cannot easily (or at all) cohere with 'real life'. The fact (if it is one) that all physical events, including human actions, have a sufficient cause in the physical state of the universe up to the moment of each event, is not permitted (even by scientists) to suggest that crimes ought not to be punished, or that logical and scientific 'errors' are the best that could rationally be expected at the moment when they occur. The relationship between 'scientific' truth and 'ordinary' truth is, in fact, as complex and as dangerous as the relationship between 'religious' or 'ritual' truths and 'everyday' or 'secular' truths. This does not stop modernists from supposing that reality is made known chiefly in the 'scientific' enclave, so it need not stop the religious from supposing that the primary reality is that made known in religion, that the religious 'ontology' (theory of what there is) is as much a candidate for serious belief as the scientific or common-sense ontologies.

If, on the other hand, it is supposed that 'ordinary life' is the primary reality, within which religious drama and scientific theory take their shape and significance, we must enquire what special status the 'ordinary life' of these moderns has to distinguish it from the 'ordinary life' of more religious ages and peoples. We are fairly unusual in the extent to which 'religion' is a matter of holy days and sacred buildings. Other ages and societies encounter religious realities at every street corner, and can conclude no 'ordinary act' without acknowledging a divine presence. Why is that not the 'ordinary life' within which our relatively 'secular', 'mercenary' and 'materialist' ethos finds its place?

This dilemma can, I think, only be resolved by facing up to the essentially religious drive of 'realism'. Realism, so to call it, has its sacred cosmos and its official priests, and it is like all other religious traditions in that most of those whose imagination and practice are directed by allegiance to the power of that cosmic vision do not really permit the full implications of that vision to have any real strength in their everyday lives. That it is, in a sense, 'religious' is shown by the manner in which such 'realists' seek to denigrate other religious traditions. Because they think that physical realism defines a truth that they *ought* to acknowledge, that such acknowledgement brings with it a renewed spiritual strength, they feel entitled to subvert the myths and rituals of their fellows. 'Realism' has its own sacred history, comprising evolutionary struggle and the lives of great scientific saints oppressed by obscurantists. Realists feel themselves to be, somehow, oppressed and militant opponents of 'religion' even when it is the openly religious, over most of the world, that actually suffer.

Realism, as a 'religious' or 'quasi-religious' movement, has its sects. Realists differ in what exactly they conceive the 'powers-that-be' to be, and what exactly is the proper philosophical stance for 'realistic' humanity. One particular sect, the scientistic, has rituals that help to illuminate more ordinarily religious rites. Laboratory experimentation on living animals is overtly conducted to advance 'knowledge' or to train novices in the appropriate techniques for 'advancing knowledge' or 'saving life'. When attempts are made to suggest that these novices do not need such training, and that animals need not be 'sacrificed' for such reasons (because there are alternative training methods, or because the course is not 'vocational' at all), established scientists resist the moves. They do so partly, no doubt, because it is always uncomfortable to have one's chosen way of living called in question: repentance is a painful act, and repression hardly less so. But they also resist change because they think it important that their students divest themselves of 'sentimental' and 'sympathetic' responses. What matters, as it does in most magical activity, is the effect upon the student, not the experimental object. Even a bungled experiment helps to create in the experimenter a new soul, a new way of viewing 'matter in that state known as "living" '.

Such scientists may well not let their 'new souls' take complete possession of their lives. They return home and are as sentimental and as sympathetic, with their children or the family pet, as any unregenerate 'ordinary lifer' would wish. In this they are very like the openly religious who do not choose always to remember that they are looking at embryonic gods and goddesses, that they cannot finish a sentence without the constant aid of the One God, that no act or thought is without its karmic consequences. Is ordinary life a sort of sleep, the ideal of scientific detachment our one route to reality? Is the world of the laboratory a fantasy, a construction, an enclave within 'ordinary living'? Each seems a dream to the other.

Whether the universe as scientistically conceived can be an adequate explanatory hypothesis (compared, for example, with a spiritual universe, or with the idealist claim that ordinary life itself must be the primary universe of discourse) is a matter I shall discuss later. At the close of this chapter it is enough to say that there is as much reason to think laboratory scientism is a complex of dramatic rituals, unbelievable stories and theories judged 'true' only within their own context, as to think that 'religion' or 'religious ritual' is a game or play. The games perhaps have different effects, different successes. Both 'realism' and religion are usually careful not to let every strict implication of their favourite dogmas be drawn or believed. Both depend upon the social education of novices to preserve the way of life that sustains their respective 'realities'. The novice's first incision into living flesh, or her first attempt to see how irritable starved, shocked, blinded rats can be, are events as traumatic in their psychological effect as subincision or clitoridectomy. What went before was childishness: the new soul is born in pain.

Further reading

Clastres (1977); Cupitt (1971); Douglas (1966); Durkheim & Mauss (1963); Larner (1982); Turner (1967); Mackie (1982).
Turner (1967); Mackie (1982).
Robin Horton's classic article, 'African Traditional Thought and Western Science' (*Africa* 37, 1967, pp. 50–71 and 155–87), has been anthologized several times, most accessibly in Wilson (1970). See also Skorupski (1975).
Puzzles associated with the impossibility of change go back at least to Zeno (on whom see Hussey 1972); on the philosophy of time see Gale (1978) and Fraser (1968). Rees & Rees (1961) discuss the love of paradox demonstrated in Celtic (and other) mythologies.

4

Words and the Word

Sentences and How They Mean

The central fact of human existence is language. Creatures that can never speak are not human, or human only by courtesy. Creatures that cannot speak as we do, but only gabble, are barbarians. Everything we human beings do and are and experience is suffused with language. We live amongst named individuals, classes and defined activities. 'I am writing with a fibre-tip pen': this is, as it were, a map or recipe for imagining my situation. There are at least two respects in which such verbal communication or soliloquy is notoriously misleading. The first, that anyone who hears it with understanding is reminded of realities that are not directly mentioned. It takes a definite effort of will for most people to remember that the statement includes no reference to my posture, the colour of the pen, the paper, and no hint of what I am writing. The first lesson of exact scholarship is to attend to what is actually and strictly implied by an utterance, not what is evoked by historical and personal accident. The images and reminiscences evoked by an utterance are not what the utterance strictly 'means'. On the other hand, the second error of our race is to suppose that these words capture a reality. Things and events are always more than any words could say, and anyone who supposed that all that was happening here-now was *my writing with a fibre-tip pen* would not comprehend even that trivial aspect of reality.

Words convey more than they say, and never say all that there is. We have an imaginative grasp of solid reality, but cannot think about reality except by mapping it out in our verbal language, which cannot accommodate more than a particular cut through the manifold of experienced being. In saying of the carpet where I am sitting that it is dark red with black lines in fairly regular patterns I suggest some image to each reader that is quite unlike my carpet here. Even if I add that that it is a vegetable-dye Afghan, that its crimson is now dark, now light, I convey inaccurate images even while I utter selected truths.

> A sentence uttered makes a world appear
> where all things happen as it says they do.
> (W.H. Auden, 'Words')

But the worlds that appear, in the imaginations of my audience, are only, at best, the wildly various clothes of my skeletal utterance. We do not imagine that diagrams and formulae and maps convey all and only the reality they schematize: we are so suffused with words and verbalized imaginings that we are easily misled into thinking that true statements say things as they are, and can be correctly understood to convey the images they evoke.

Auden's comment was justified, though most sentences do not purport to say things as they *are* (but only as they might be mapped), and few convey just one imagined world. Great poetry has this gift, so to order the sounds and meanings of our sentences as to evoke in most attentive hearers and readers a recognizably similar world, so that all may 'see', 'hear', 'feel' more than the verbal meanings of the sentences require, and all see, hear and feel alike. Poetic utterance therefore stands at the opposite extreme to legal or scientific utterance, which we do not wish to mean or to convey more than the rules of syntax and of logic allow. A great poet creates, summons or evokes a rich reality. A great lawyer or scientist will insist that she means nothing more, that no-one should imagine more, than she has strictly said. Ideally, scientific utterance is a confession of ignorance, a refusal to say more than abstract reasoning allows. In practice, of course, scientific utterance, if understood, does evoke extra meanings, does rely on what is not directly said. Bohr's model of the atom, that atoms were in certain respects *like* solar systems, evoked images and additional hypotheses that were not strictly contained in the original verbalized hypothesis. It would probably be a damaging project to try and eliminate these overtones, even though we ought often to be aware of them as overtones. Poetic utterance, conversely, is trivialized when it ceases to have any lucid or systematic meaning, even if it continues to convey broadly similar images and nuances to its audience.

Religious utterance is usually thought to be more like 'poetic' than 'scientific' discourse, as I have just described them. What matters about it are chiefly the images and feelings evoked by the words, sounds, rhythms, not the strict and literal meanings of the terms employed, abstracted from their ritual context. Whereas it does not matter what any particular scientist *imagines* when she conceives that 'pH level in sample 15 is 6.8' so long as she can corroborate or explain this claim, the poems which I cite in the present study are not properly understood if they do not evoke images and feelings of the 'appropriate' kind. A 'literal' and pedantic reading of Empson's poem, for example, would be nonsensical, although a true reading does depend upon an ironical awareness of truths that might have been 'scientifically' expressed. 'People are continually asking one the way': it would be ridiculous to ask for a head-count or to suggest that there must have been a busload of foreign tourists in the museum, or to infer that the author was serving a term as museum attendant. It would also be wrong to read this simply as a metaphorical, uneasy comment on the author's unwilling status as guru or adviser on the Way. Similarly, although religious utterance may incorporate statements that mean just the same as an indefinitely large number of statements in other languages and dialects, and may take a clear place in a network of logical implications, these utterances are not properly and religiously understood unless they evoke images and emotions of the appropriate kind. That is why it is always difficult to rewrite or retranslate the scriptures or liturgies, and why believers do not readily abandon their formulae even if those formulae, 'literally' understood, are not what they *believe*. The words are retained, like the rituals, because, through their familiarity and poetic splendour, they produce the right emotions. Even great doctrinal statements, about God's omnipotence or omnipresence, are valued not so much for the precise truths they convey (few of us have any clear or consistent conception of which such properties involve) as for their moral influence. Whatever we do, wherever we go, we neither escape nor lose the Lord.

If religious utterance is more like 'poetic' than 'scientific' speech, and appreciated only by those who admit to an imaginative and moral sympathy with it (for the moment), this is partly because most speech is unlike the merely 'scientific'. Even this latter is not as strict and literal in its import as some suppose. It is easy to suppose that we have a clear grasp of what it is for a narrow, precisely formulated statement to be true: crudely, 'pH level in sample 15 is 6.8' is true just if pH level in sample 15 *is* 6.8. The truth of a statement consists in its 'structural identity' with the facts: the statement has the 'same' form as reality. More careful inquiry makes this doubtful. The sentence I have used as an example could certainly be used to make a true statement (or a false). We may persuade ourselves that, in that situation, there is an entity identifiable as 'sample 15': are we so sure that there is an entity identifiable as 'pH level in sample 15'? If the pH level were 4.5 would it be the *same* pH level that had a different property (as a chair that *is* white might be *red*)? Would the sample (or the stuff that has been sampled) still have that pH level (6.8) even if there were no chemists, or if a different numbering system had been devised? Doubtless the soil would still be what it is whatever we said about it, but it is difficult to believe that it *is* (independently of our verbalizing efforts) something that it could only be relative to particular modes of analysis and identification. Once *pH level* and *being 6.8* are recognized as not quite language-independent entities we can have doubts about *sample 15*. The worry is not merely the banal one that it would only be labelled 'sample 15' if we were there to label it. The point is that it is up to us what counts as *still being sample 15*: is it still the 'same' sample in two hours' time? Would it be the 'same' if we had collected it with a different instrument?

Worries of this kind have cast serious doubt on the naive belief that statements are *true* just if 'the facts' are as the statement proposes. There is a reality, no doubt, which chemists of many different languages, persuasions and even species might report upon and use. But we have no clear reason to expect that all 'true' statements about that reality have anything like the same structure, or that that reality already 'contains' all the different structures before they are enunciated. Some theorists have concluded to outright relativism, to a neglect of that unknown, indescribable 'thing-in-itself'. We live amongst words, and our statements do not report, but create their own realities. The soil had no pH level, there was not even any soil (as such), until people began to speak of soil, and acid-alkali balances. There being such things now rests simply on the general usefulness of statements about them. Reversing the naive formula: the pH level in sample 15 is 6.8 just if 'pH level in sample 15 is 6.8' is the right thing to say.

What is odd about this powerful 'anti-realist' argument is that it is often used by people who express no doubts at all about the existence of the world before we arrived to grace it. I find it peculiar to insist that things are 'real' only as they take their place within the linguistic universe, and to assume that these 'same' things existed evolutionary ages before the emergence of human consciousness. If that in virtue of which things exist did not then exist, how could anything else really have existed, and how can we possibly *explain* the emergence of human consciousness by reference to imagined entities whose 'existence' is as much a function of human consciousness as Zodiacal signs? For this and for other reasons my own metaphysical preference is for what might be called an absolute idealism. The real world within which human minds took shape was already a mind-suffused world; things really and truly did exist as what our best endeavours now suppose, but did so in virtue of an ever-present, ordering intellect. The truth to which we approximate is not wholly extra-linguistic (there are, it seems, insuperable difficulties in thinking of such a correspondence), but it is extra-human.

This debate has persuaded many that there are indeed sound reasons for adopting some form of theism. It has entirely failed to persuade others. In the context of this present study, there is no need for me to expand or criticize the theistic position. It is enough to insist that the difficulties we experience in saying what it is for religious utterances to be true are matched by more general difficulties, and that we cannot take it for granted that we have any clear cases where the truth of a statement rests simply on its 'correspondence' with an extra-linguistic reality. In practice all statements that are labelled 'true' are so labelled simply as being, in the context, the right thing to say, the usable formula, the helpful and inspiring rule.

Anti-Realists and Magicians

Our failure to find any way of understanding how a statement might 'correspond' to an extra-linguistic reality, as a mirror-image 'corresponds' to its original, has led some thinkers down the anti-realist road. But even the most sanguine anti-realist will concede that words are not the world, that changing the way we speak of things does not change the way things *are*. The trouble for anti-realists is that 'the way things are' consists only in how we speak of them, so that changing that way ought to change the things. This is one way of understanding magic. Magical rituals are founded on the implicit assumption that if we all speak differently about something, the real world changes, not because any power moves (as it might or might not) in response to our pleas, but because the words themselves, our words, are the real constitutive powers of our universe. If we *say* that a cucumber is an ox, or a wafer is the Christ, or a feather is a knife at our enemy's throat, it is, since its being so just consists in what we say of it, and do with it. What is clearly true of many things (as that this piece of paper is worth a sovereign if enough people say it is) the magician reckons true of everything. Accordingly, where early modern anthropologists saw an ignorant and childish confusion between words and the world, late modern reasoners must see a sophisticated anti-realism on a level with their own. Their disagreement must simply be a preference for different rituals.

To this the anti-realist magician may have several answers. The first, that we can indeed make magic and remake the world. The ceremonies that make husband and wife, transfer property and legitimize what would otherwise be crime are obviously magical, in the sense described. There are further ceremonies of naming that distinguish health and sickness, champion and also-ran, savage and civilized, human and subhuman. What things 'are' in our human universe is very often quite obviously dependent on social ceremonial form. There are magics familiar in other societies that 'we' do not employ, but it would be naive to conclude that we are in any metaphysical sense more 'realistic' than others. What we usually mean by 'realism' is that we have failed to notice how many 'realities' are dependent on our ceremonially controlled conviction. When we (or our rationalizing predecessors) sneer a little at (say) Polynesian *tabu* we neglect the identical features of our own society: our readiness to agree that the Government 'owns' as much of our property as it cares to take, or that some things 'just aren't done'. Once we start 'thinking of We as only a sort of They' we can recognize the magical roots of what had seemed 'merely facts'.

Secondly, the anti-realists may emphasize the distinction within our linguistic system between what is amenable to verbal magic and what is not. That some things are true, whatever we say, is itself a dictum that it is right and proper to affirm. The sun rises and the day begins because we say it does (and might have said that the sun sets and the day begins, or the land comes out of shadow, or the earth is turning), but the sun still shines even if we call it black. There are facts that we cannot alter, though we can rename them, and they constitute the ineliminable skeleton of the human universe. We need not suppose that there is an absolute and easy line between 'soft' and 'hard' facts, between the things that would be otherwise if enough of us said so, and the things that must be endured, or affected only by 'technical' means. A good many supposedly 'hard' facts (about the ill-effects of sexual deviance on health and sanity, for example) have turned out to be largely magical devices. A good many supposedly 'soft' ones (as that courage is a virtue) are not affected by any number of people who pretend that we can manage without it. Nor should we suppose that all really hard facts are 'scientific laws' of the sort investigated by physicists: it is the Gods of the Copybook Headings that are most secure. Many facts are hard facts. Metaphysical idealists may suspect that these too rest upon intentions and orderings (even if not ours). Metaphysical materialists may found them upon the cosmic reality of matter in motion. Anti-realists of the kind I am here discussing entertain no view upon their metaphysical status, contenting themselves with finding that some facts are more intractable than others.

The third and last response of the anti-realist, abandoning this last attachment to firm ground, is to agree that 'science' and 'scholarship' are magical in effect. What 'we' (or our elite classes) say does determine what is the case, and how things 'are' independently of our ceremonial and firm conviction is a nonentity. This doctrine is not, perhaps, as fashionable as it once was. In the 1960s and 1970s many a guru, disenchanted with the military-industrial complex and 'the mere touch of cold philosophy', urged us all to believe that a verbal alteration, a 'reprogramming', would bring in the millenium. Paper and base metal have 'worth' only if people think they have. The magicians concluded that the results of technocratic science were similarly unreal, that we could transform not just 'the emotional affect' but 'the reality' of oligarchic control, ecological catastrophe and nuclear overkill by ceasing to speak of them, in the old way. Some of those gurus have perhaps learned that things are sometimes as they are no matter what we say, that actions have their consequences, and that ecological catastrophe is not avoided by calling it 'evolution in action', nor sin destroyed by labelling it 'self-fulfilment'.

Such gurus of the would-be 'alternative society' often had some justice on their side. One of the tricks of tyranny is indeed to make its rule seem obvious and natural, 'the way of the world', and tame intellectuals are regularly hired to help. Current practice in the training of 'scientists' and 'engineers', with its emphasis on supposedly 'practical' and 'technical' skill, has served our masters well, by denigrating the great political and theoretical debates which ought to lie behind immediate decisions. 'Practical' people, all too often, are those who never think about the principles of what they are doing, or the long-term consequences. Dissidents may do well to insist that things do not have to be seen like that, that what seem the obvious fact and the simple way rest upon unspoken and ill-argued assumptions. Dissidents, in objecting to the tyranny of 'consensus reality' (what 'we' all agree is so), may often seem deranged, and may sometimes actually (by better standards) be so. Just occasionally a later generation recognizes that they were right all along.

Particular 'facts' may be revealed as cultural artefacts, and magicians praised for demonstrating that there are other possibilities. But total relativism, in the mouths of anti-establishment gurus or a few 'hermeneutical philosophers' (a continental fashion that has attracted more attention among theologians and literary critics than among professional Anglo-American philosophers), is both naive and ill-defended. If there is no extra-linguistic reality, and 'we' can change what is 'real' merely by changing the way we speak, there is no guarantee that it will be those of vaguely liberal sympathies who fix the future. The major literary evocation of the thesis that language controls reality, after all, is in Orwell's O'Brien: the ruling class determines what is said, and so what *is*. Even if the present-day establishment were to fail, we have no good reason (unless mere hopefulness counts as a good reason) to expect that the 'nice people' will win. Those who seek the overthrow of established law and order are merely naive if they forget the existence of yet bloodier and more violent sects. Past rebels have been able to trust in God, or the Nature of Things, to bring things round their way. Cultural relativists, with only the magic of the spoken or written word to help them rewrite history, have no rationally founded hope of defeating either the establishment or rival gangs.

This would be merely sad if cultural relativism of this magical kind were forced on us. If that is how things are, whether we like it or not, then why should we wish to be deceived? Maybe there is indeed no secure reality, and 'we' must fight against other worlds and languages without any certainty of success. But the notion that *anything* is as it is whether we like it or not, is itself in direct confict with magical relativism (which claims that how things 'are' depends entirely on our chosen way of speaking). Such relativism simply cannot be stated as an over-mastering truth: if it is true, there is at least one truth that does not depend on us, and so it is false. Cultural relativism, by its own standards, has to be judged false, and the magical conclusion is indeed a product of unreason and naive hopefulness. Those religious believers who have made momentary alliances with the magicians, in the face of a common enemy, should break off all negotiations forthwith. Magic, which is the brash and foredoomed assertion of the will to control all things by the way we speak of them, is the very opposite of religious piety, which recognizes an established Order as the root of Truth.

The Three Ways

So what is that established Order, and how may we speak of it?

It is by the word of His mouth that the Creator establishes our world. That word and *fiat* is itself the Pattern to which all things are to move. The Egyptian texts record the creative act of Atum in producing Shu (which is Life) and Tefnut (who is also Mayet, Order). Things are as God has called them, not as our merely human languages decree. Our languages do not 'cut things at the joints': the Divine Language, the First-born, decrees what joints there are. Archaic or unfamiliar tongues (when they do not sound like barbarism) evoke the feelings of awe that properly belong to the First Language, the tongue whose mortal replica was lost at Babel. Artificial and logically exact languages pretend to a universality and accuracy that only the Divine could have. The yearning for a Really Appropriate Language is one explanation for the reverence often felt for 'Science'. Such a language, some science-fiction writers have imagined, would endow its servant with real under-standing of causes, and power to control. Heinlein's *Stranger in a Strange Land*, for example – whose saga belongs in part amongst the magicians of the earlier section, and whose name and example were one inspiration for Charles Manson – thinks in Martian, and can therefore exercise telekinetic and clairvoyant power. The doctrine that lurks behind this case is not quite cultural relativism (though Heinlein sometimes speaks as if it is), but rather the ancient hope of 'Real Language', whose words are things.

When we speak, we know (if we think about it) that 'a cabbage' (i.e. the phrase) is not a cabbage, and that no amount of punning will transform the world. The sort of joke that the Greek playwright Aristophanes used to construct Cloud-Cuckoo land, and that appears in children's stories ('he coughed till he was *hoarse*, then got on the *horse* and rode away') works in our dreams but not in this waking world. But God's Speech has just this effect: God's speech *is* the welter of rocks and trees, butterflies and setting suns, people and electric shocks. He might have used (may use) another medium or tone of voice, and still have said the same.

Have we any hope of finding out God's speech? Three pathways beckon, science, ritual and prophecy: which may be the same three ways defined in the Vedic tradition (knowledge, works and devotion). Those who walk the first way reckon that the words or formulae on which the world is founded, which are the true description and cause of all that is, are accessible to rational endeavour. We may identify certain axioms, uncover worthwhile hypotheses, and hope at last to describe the world as God does, without contradiction or confusion. This confidence is one of the historical roots of Western science, whose renaissance occurred when Galileo and others turned away from merely instrumentalist views of scientific theory to the realist conviction that, by reason, we could reach behind phenomena and 'remember' God's plan. Later transformations of the scientific project have somehow retained the idea that 'science' uncovers truth, that truth is rationally demonstrable, that our minds are adequate to the task, while tacitly abandoning the metaphysical doctrine that makes all this seem possible. In the world described by naturalistic science there is no good reason to expect that our favourite axioms, our carefully 'scientific' hypotheses should have any 'resemblance' to the way things are. If we are not god-born, how should we know the language of the gods?

The second way, of ritual or works, offers the traditional discourse of sacred text and liturgy as the gods' speech. To understand the world 'as it is' we must describe it in the traditional way, and see things charged with sacred significance. Each tradition, of course, has its own favoured language: all reach back to the 'original' language. Even the periodic rewritings of sacred text and liturgy are not directed simply to the utterance of contemporary sentences: the rewriters almost always gloss their efforts by referring back to some yet older model. If the Anglican Communion Service is rewritten it is not a way of disguising theological vacuity by would-be 'modern' phraseology that is outdated before it is in print. Any decently scholarly examination of the rewritten liturgies and their writers' motives reveals that the chief influence is from early Christian texts, before some of the schisms. The 'modern' liturgies are preferred by clergy not because they have been brainwashed into ignoring 'the glories of Cranmer's English' but because they are professionally aware that Cranmer's liturgy is a late and in some ways deviant affair. The true 'original speech' lies further back than Cranmer and King James. Actually, of course, it lies further back even than Hellenistic Greek and Aramaic, even than Hebrew or Sanskrit. The first tongue of men and angels has long been transformed, and all our best efforts to recover it from some few less sullied wells of tradition are flawed. Short of some direct, divine revelation we cannot quite recover Adam's speech. But traditionalists may, with some justice, suspect that much of our traditional speech does embody the same forms. Once again, we are in danger of retaining a prejudice in favour of tradition while forgetting the doctrines that alone give us reason to rely on tradition (or some tradition). If God is not the Lord of history, we have no reason to reject the possibility that our language has changed wildly, and randomly, from the true original (whether that 'original' is the speech of Eden, or Palestine, or Arabia, or Nepal). If on the other hand God has preserved traces of the original in us, we cannot be debarred from a careful inquiry that may uncover them.

The third way, of prophecy or devotion, relies neither on scientific reason nor on liturgical tradition: instead, it is supposed that God pours out His Spirit on believers, and they begin to speak 'in tongues'. This odd phenomenon, frequently decried both by rationalists and by ritualists, is widespread and well-attested. It does not involve 'hysterical loss of self-control' (though it is sometimes associated with a startled loss of social inhibitions), nor is it always wholly incomprehensible (though 'interpretation of tongues' probably has to be regarded as another divine grace). The one feature of *glossolalia* that concerns me here is that the speaker is understood (by her community) to be speaking a language given to her by God. Anecdotes are told within such a community of such-and-such a one who turned out to be talking Hebrew or some minor New Guinea dialect. There is certainly no way of showing that these 'tongues' are not 'real languages', but it does not seem relevant to the actual occasions that they should be. What they are in practice is, precisely, unknown tongues, with a faint resemblance (sometimes) to known languages. For all we know, they are one language, though the speakers seem to regard them as personal, idiosyncratic languages that perfectly (though incomprehensibly) catch the speaker's own character and world. They may feel as if they are speaking and half-understanding their 'original' tongue. They may do so (though there is sometimes a faint unease about this) even in apparently 'non-sacred' contexts. A person newly 'baptized-in-the-Spirit' may find 'her' tongue is the very 'nonsense language' she has spoken with her children, may feel able to talk of things in 'her' tongue without knowing quite what any particular string of sounds 'means'. It may prove impossible to be bad-tempered in that tongue, and easy to slip into it while singing songs not usually thought 'religious'. Of particular relevance to my present concern is the way the use of such a tongue transforms the object-world. Instead of thinking 'the cats have torn this chair' one may (still considering reality so far as it concerns what we call chairs and cats) invoke the presence of the always-present, offer Him one's tongue and voice and find oneself saying 'ondrovum hesh garindrovee'. How exactly such a sequence of sounds (only arbitrarily divided into 'words') is to be mapped against the first (English) thought is entirely obscure. Most probably (even if we concede that, somehow, it means *something*) it says nothing about chairs or cats. What it seems (subjectively) to catch is something about the battered majesty of this particular (as we say and see) apricot-coloured, grubby arm-chair. What the tongue uncovers is a universe refracted through this simple point, and so an image of the Lord. This thing here-now, this universe here-now is only superficially described in English, Welsh or Dutch: what it is, is to be grasped without intellectual analysis (though I have made some effort here to sketch a part of what the tongue *may* say). 'Nonsense-language', insofar as that is spoken in the honest intention of worship, may be more accurate than we usually think.

Pentecost, in Christian tradition, was a foretaste of that Day when the curse of Babel is undone. Even without *glossolalia*, the language of devoted worship may be more appropriate than efforts to state the forms of things. When a lover's language dissolves into incoherent admiration and delight what he says may be more appropriate than a series of statements analyzing the beloved's shape and character. It is at least not unintelligible nor unreasonable to say that he knows her better *then*, than when he is in a position to try and identify particular facts about her. The way of devotion, in which the worshipper speaks and acts out of that sort of appreciation of the Real, similarly prefers the more or less 'unintelligible' utterances of the God-struck to the precise discriminations of scientist or theologian, or the liturgical dance of ritualists. What is paradoxical about this suggestion is that it has been made, in philosophical cricles, chiefly by the sort of liberals that are least at home in pentecostalist gatherings. On the one hand, liberal theologians have often fallen back on the suggestion that religious utterance is frequently 'expressive' (like the lover's 'Yum' and 'Ah') rather than 'assertoric' (like the commentator's 'She has served seven aces so far in this match'). On the other hand, they are less than enthusiastic about those congregations who take to *glossolalia*, although conventional hymns (on liberal terms) are as nonsensical when thought of as a string of statements as 'ondrovum hesh garindrovee'. If what matters in religious utterance is simply the awakening in us of a love and awe directed at the rationally incomprehensible Beginning, the proper speech may well be deliberately nonsensical.

The Way of Negation

The negative way, which takes seriously the difficulty faced by finite intelligence, requires that we abandon any thoughts we have of knowing what God is. We can use words to describe the Deity, but we cannot know what it is for God to be omnipotent, omniscient, eternal and the like. Even when we say that God is not bodily, not contingent, not malicious, we cannot infer that He is therefore anything we might ordinarily call non-bodily (and the like). Nor can we have any clear idea even of what it is for God to 'have' properties at all. A finite and contingent being (say, this chair) 'has' properties (being apricot-coloured, grubby, used as a scratching-post for cats, in the sitting-room, more than fifty years old). It 'has' these because they are distinguishable properties that it might lose, or never have had, and that other things might have. But a great many of the things we say of God require that God cannot lose (and cannot not have had) certain 'properties', and that nothing else than God could have them. In which case His being omnipotent is not something that He might have been without being omniscient or just or loving. Such description, couched in language suitable to finite creatures, is deeply misleading. God is not omnipotent by virtue of 'sharing' in a general property (omnipotence) that others might have, that He might not have. Nor is there any other Love than He. If finite creatures 'love' it is by the 'presence' in them of the Undying.

Considerations such as these have led even Abrahamic theists, peoples of the Book, to a seemingly abstract and philosophized Divinity: the One, which *has* no properties other than itself, of which we cannot say anything that is not misleading. Students of other traditions, such as the Buddhist or Vedic, have placed still more emphasis on the essentially incomprehensible nature of Reality, the failure of all our petty descriptions. Such students, all too often, have imagined that

Abrahamists – familiar to them only in the shape of missionaries struggling with a foreign tongue and the misapprehension that they must preach a particularly crude version of the gospel for supposedly simple-minded natives – must be idol-worshippers. The tragi-comedy that even decent and pious people have made of cross-cultural relations is a warning to all 'comparative religionists'. The Christian missionary who thought that 'the heathen in his blindness bows down to wood and clay' impressed those 'heathens' as one enslaved by outward forms and ceremonies. Modern Western converts to non-European traditions, with no more than a superficial understanding of Biblical religion, often repeat the error. The mask of rituals and stories that all religions wear is not to be taken too seriously. It is God, the Divine, that the religious serve, and what we say of Him can only be the best we can when we realize that, considered literally, it is always false.

But though it is common doctrine that our ordinary language and finite intelligence do not permit us to construct statements which adequately match the Divine reality, it is unusual to draw the conclusion that we should keep quiet about it. Nor is such a conclusion binding. After all, there are grave difficulties even in speaking of finite existences. Our statements, even if 'true', do not really 'correspond' to reality. Some philosophers have entertained the thought that when I say truly that the cat is on the mat, there is a cat, a mat and a relation of 'being on' out there in the world. Only the monolingual could ever really have taken this seriously: other languages do not employ six words to utter the 'same' truth. What is on the mat is called 'a cat' by taxonomic convention (might it be a lion?); what the cat is on, is called 'a mat' (i.e. a member of a certain vaguely delimited class of floor or table coverings) by mere habit (could it be for a serving-dish?). 'The cat is on the mat' may be true when the tabby is on the Welcome mat, the lion is on the table, the notorious burglar is being heavily criticized by her superior. It counts as true, if it is an appropriate guide, in context, to experience and action, not because it fully and explicitly 'says things as they are', nor because its structure 'corresponds' to real distinctions and associations in Reality.

Nor should we be confident that we can given an adequate account of the principles we use even in such simple cases. In using a referring expression like 'the cat' I presumably employ (and hope my audience will too) some criterion of what is to count as the same cat. But many studies of the identity of things have made it clear that we have no general account of what it is to be the *same* something. What we call one and the same cat, and distinguish from other cats and other non-overlapping substances, may on occasion be recognized (more accurately?) as only a segment of some larger Real, or else an arbitrary collection of lesser Reals. Suppose that one or other of these more 'holistic' or 'atomistic' doctrines turns out to be the final word on the subject: we may still agree that there was nonetheless some sense in saying that the cat was indeed on the mat, in denying that she was not. The higher truth may be that there was no clearly identifiable substance having any appreciable subset of the characteristics we impute to 'the cat'. It might still be sensible to report that the cat was there.

If we have no clear and generally accepted demonstration that our usual language even about finite things embodies a realistic metaphysic, but can still use such language by way of warning and reproof and idle comment, it does not seem absurd to say that our talk about God, while inevitably misleading and inaccurate, should not be absolutely abandoned. Although it is metaphysically objectionable to say that God is Love or that God is not Love or that God is Hate, we had nonetheless better say that God is Love.

This response has been dignified at least since the great Islamic philosopher Averroes as the Doctrine of Two Truths. A thousand years earlier the Greek philosopher Parmenides, perhaps more exactly, spoke of the Way of Truth (that only the One is, and the One is only One) and the Way of Illusion (that there are things other than the One). Only God knows things 'as they are': we must deal with them according to the best rules we have. Some have confusedly supposed that this is a recipe for social division: the knowledgeable few can follow the Way of Truth, while the rest must be content with the strictly inaccurate level of ordinary religious discourse. This is a confusion, simply because the thesis is that we are all in the same boat. The doctrine of Divine Incomprehensibility is not that we have an appropriate but very difficult language with which the theologically expert can speak of God, but that all human, all finitely conceived language is necessarily misleading when used of God, and does not strictly 'correspond' to Reality even when we speak 'truly' of finite creatures.

'No-one has seen God at any time': in attributing these words to John, and adding that 'the only-begotten Son has declared him' (John 1.18), the gospel-writer spoke from within the same intellectual milieu as the Jewish thinker, Philo of Alexandria (whose life's work was to retell Hebrew lore in terms drawn from neo-Platonic philosophy, and who set the scene for the next fifteen hundred years of Christian, Jewish and Islamic philosophizing: he was active in the year 40 AD.) The Father is not an object of anyone's experience, but there is something that both John and Philo called the Logos, the only-Begotten, or the Man. Philo, as well as the Samaritans (those other descendants of Israel whom the people of Judah despised), seems to have entertained the thought that this Logos was visible as Moses, though it is likely that Philo meant only that what was said of Moses could be understood, allegorically, of the Logos. Piety seems to require both that the One cannot be adequately described in any creaturely language, and that there is an intelligible manifestation of the One. Only those in whom the Logos takes its dwelling can attain to a non-discursive intuition of the One; the rest of us must be content (and may gladly be content) with an apprehension of the divine pattern of our own being, of the ideal form of the humanly intelligible universe. This is the Son of God, begotten before all worlds, by reflection of which we are *logikoi*, rational beings.

This approach amounts to a re-evaluation of the way of Illusion (so-called). Whatever God may be, He is at least that which ordains us and our capacities. The way of negation may come round at last to the way of affirmation: our best thought of the Divine (not to be surpassed by the pretence that we can think without using human concepts, or take God as the object of our fleeting attention) is as the life well-lived. As William James observed, our best service is to follow the command-ments, not to indulge the fantasy that we might take intellectual hold of Him. In understanding what we are to do and be, we understand God in the only way we can. Similarly, in the Buddhistic traditions the older (?) distinction between *samsara* (the phenomenal world of individuals ruled by desire) and *nirvana* (the blowing-out of desire's candle) is transcended in the discovery that *nirvana* is *samsara*, and so that our would-be enlightenment is achieved in the Bodhisattva's vow to forswear 'our own' rest.

Kipling, incensed by the obdurate stupidity of those who spoke of 'a Japanese idol at Kamakura' (being a statue of Gautama), wrote as follows:

O ye who tread the Narrow Way
by Tophet-flare to Judgement Day,
be gentle when 'the heathen' pray
    to Buddha at Kamakura . . .
A tourist-show, a legend told,
a rusting bulk of bronze and gold,
so much, and scarce so much, ye hold
    the meaning of Kamakura?
But when the morning prayer is prayed,
think, ere ye pass to strife and trade,
is God in human image made
    no nearer than Kamakura?
(Rudyard Kipling, 'Buddha at Kamakura')

The *Dharmakaya*, the Reality transcending all Categories, inaccessible to discursive intellect, is manifest as *Sambhogakaya* (the whole company, one might say, of redeemed creatures) and as *Nirmanakaya* (the historical Gautama). No one of these 'Three Bodies of the Buddha' is inferior to any other, and piety may in principle be directed at any – save that the *dharmakaya* is made known only by its own activity, in awakening in us an appreciation of *sambhogakaya* and historical person. Whether this model might also serve the ends of Chalcedonian Christianity is not my present concern: enough that both Christians and Buddhists (as well as the religious of other traditions) are prepared to accept a manifestation of the One as something that deserves the same absolute devotion as the One itself.

By this account we come as close as we may to an appreciation of the One by participating in the religious tradition, by using the words and following the commands laid down for us. We are always in danger on two sides: on the one hand, we may slip away from the proper traditional speech and come to speak of things not as God would have us speak but as our desires and prejudices prompt us; on the other, we may forget that the speech ordained for us is not itself the One, but only our best pointer. The Word of God must be perpetually renewed in our hearts, or else it becomes only one changing speech amongst many.

The Angel of the Book

Some traditions find God's Word (or its equivalent) straightforwardly in scripture. Protestant Christianity indeed has tended to reserve the title for the Old and New Testaments, forgetting that these scriptures claim rather that Jesus is the Word. Gobind, the tenth Guru of the Sikhs, appointed the Sikh Scriptures as his successor, the Guru Granth Sahib. The *dharmakaya* of the Buddha (for which I gave a metaphysical account in the last section) is sometimes identified as the Buddhist scriptures. The Pentateuch and the Koran have both been identified as God's everlasting word, ordained before all worlds. Insofar as all these scriptures (as well as myriad unwritten hymns and meditations) are clearly composed of words, there seems no difficulty in principle in supposing that they are God's words, and that (by speaking as they speak) we may be speaking the language God requires of us, even if not the unimaginable discourse He holds with Himself. The evidence that this is so is harder to come by: the anecdote retailed in Christian circles, of the old Russian woman, twitted for her possession only of a Bible, who replied that she could read other books but this Book alone 'read her', is probably an apt reflection of how any traditionalist approaches her own scriptures. In reading them she finds herself interrogated, encouraged, shown how to see things differently, reminded of past follies that had sunk out of sight.

The idea that we might in any realistic sense be interrogated by a book is hard to unravel. It was Plato's complaint, after all, that books can never answer one's particular questions. Their author may have managed to include a response to all the queries she has thought of, but all the written responses imaginable must still be interpreted by the reader. Any author is perpetually baffled by the weird expansions and misreadings that her reviewers commit. Books are vulnerable to readers, and cannot reach out to say 'Look, you're misreading me: that wasn't the right tone of voice to hear me in; that wasn't *my* position, but an imagined critic's; that wasn't what my author used those words to mean'. Because they are vulnerable, and cannot answer back, careless and conceited readers (that is, all of us) frequently imagine that we have 'refuted' some great thinker, merely because we have made some simple response to a crude reading of the text. Who dares to claim that, in virtue of her easy successes in dissecting Plato's text, she would stand up to Plato?

What I have described, of course, is in a sense inept reading. Dedicated and careful readers allow themselves to be changed and challenged by the books they read, even if they also reserve the right to step aside, to close the book, to pack it away as the diversion of an hour or two. To read anything with decent openness is to be changed a little, even if it is only to see that some possible world is not for us, that we will close that door and walk on along the Way. Great poetry in particular arouses in us the enjoyment of our capacity (wholly unrealized as it may be) for some experience, or the enjoyment of our awareness that there is such a capacity. Words, whether they are written down or made a part of oral tradition, may contain more than we ourselves bring to them. They present standards and possibilities against which we are measured, by which (for good or ill) we may be changed. Maybe they are not quite as vulnerable as we suppose: one reader's misreading does not necessarily poison the source. And maybe we are faced by something more than merely the general similarity of educated readers' responses to a particular sequence of words: maybe there is 'an angel' in a book or oral epic.

We speak of copies and editions of books. A copy may, originally, be a literal copy of the author's original script, but, unless something has gone very wrong, to read any one copy is just as much 'reading the book' as reading the original script would be. It may be indeed that there is not, and never was, a true original: what appears in the multiple copies (by the author's design) never appeared in any single script, but has been edited and altered on the basis of telephone conversations, scribbled notes and editorial *fiat*. 'The Book' appears in multiple copies. It is the *same* book whether we read it in paperback or illegal xerox. It behaves, that is, like one of Plato's Forms: Plato believed that when we were confronted, as it might be, by several examples of Justice or Beauty or Humanity, the examples only shared in, or reminded us of, the one thing that was Justice, or Beauty, or Humanity. These forms were not strictly identical with any of the things that we habitually described as just, beautiful or human (if they were, those things would be identical with each other). The situation is still more Platonic in that all copies are, predictably, defective. We cannot tell what The Book itself is merely by comparing copies, even by comparing editions: all available versions may contain a particular phrase, but that may *not* be what was meant. There are, of course, literary critics who imagine that all misprints and textual errors must be incorporated in their reading, but most of us (particularly if we have any experience of ancient texts) are ready to agree that some widely accepted readings are founded on mere error. So there is a Book, reflected or represented in a medium which unavoidably distorts the celestial text. Even the author's script, incidentally, is not immune to error: authors make slips, and do not always notice them. Just occasionally the 'slip' (even the printer's error) makes better sense than what the author would have said she meant.

If there is such a Book as our ordinary way of speaking suggests (not to be identified with its copies, and indestructible in its essence by any human act) could it be understood (as Plato understood his Forms) as causally active? From a non-Platonic position 'the book' is simply an idealized universal, formed from our experience of many texts saying 'the same thing'. The multiple copies are not living creatures, each with its own causal powers and inclinations. Might there be a causal effect of the Book Itself? Some authors, certainly, do speak as if their enterprise were a slow uncovering or reception of a preexistent Reality: things fit together as they seem to 'compose' their work in ways that they did not expect. Some authors distinguish between what they themselves construct, and what they seem to themselves rather to report, though the actual processes of rewriting, striking out and amending may be impossible for any finite observer to discriminate. The usual assumption (for which no argument is offered) is that the author 'really' constructs her own work, perhaps out of subconscious memories and associations, even though her own mental attitude is rather of one listening carefully to try and catch the thing. One variation is to say that 'the subconscious' or 'the right hemisphere' does the creative work, and the conscious mind housed in the left hemisphere merely reports and analyses it. The Book, that is, is somehow made and housed in the author's brain before the author herself has access to it.

Something like this may be correct: the author's daimon, her Other Self (the Latin term is 'genius') may have creative powers unknown to intellect. Certainly one can sometimes detect in a book the moment when that daimon takes over – the fumbling, artificial plots and sentences are suddenly swept aside, and what was a two-dimensional character explodes into Shylock himself, or a sterile argument becomes a world-shaker. Most authors delete their own first efforts to make up the book, once they have (as it were) tuned in. But if the Book Itself is to be a real Platonic Form it cannot simply be a configuration of the author's right hemisphere. If it exists (or subsists) independently of the author, might it not also affect those who read its multiple copies? Great critics sometimes seem to understand a text better than the words before them quite explain, better even than the author: they are, as we say, 'on the same wavelength'. If this were so, might not 'the Angel of the Book' or 'The Book Itself' respond to suitable inquirers? Once the author was 'tuned in' it has, we may suppose, influenced whatever neurological changes are associated with the author's thinking and acting: might It not also influence other material events, the flipping of pages or the toss of coins?

This possibility has been supposed to be actual. The works of Virgil, for example, were regularly approached via the *Sortes Virgilianae*: passages randomly selected as answers to the Inquirer's questions. In a sense this was a profoundly unliterary undertaking, associated with a view of Virgil as a great magician, not a poet, and dependent on taking passages 'out of context', without regard to their setting or the author's conscious intention. It also betokened the respect in which Virgil's works were held, as earthly representatives of a compendium of Wisdom inaccessible to ordinary intellectual means. The works of Aristotle do not seem to have been treated like this, although they were often regarded as an Enquire Within Upon Everything. To understand them it was necessary to think discursively: to understand the Virgilian lottery one need only respond in Faith.

The principal example of such oracular usage of a Book, and a religious phenomenon of some significance, is the Book of Changes, a Chinese work popularized in the West in Richard Wilhelm's translation, with the imprimatur of Carl Jung. Its popularity in the sixties and seventies among initiates of 'the Alternative Society' probably counts as one of the more paradoxical episodes in the history of religion. So far from preaching the laissez-faire, laissez-aller ideology of hippiedom, or offering any comfort to secular liberalism, the Book of Changes is a profoundly religious, and conservative work. Its basic moral message is submission to the Tao, the way things are to be, and it assumes in its readers a readiness to participate in traditional religious ritual, and traditional society. On the shibboleth of romanticism (did Bogart do the right thing at the end of *Casablanca* or *The Maltese Falcon*?) the Book of Changes is clearly unromantic: on both occasions, yes. Anyone who agreed to be guided by the Book's responses (as selected from the range of texts by the random fall of coins or yarrow sticks) would live equably, honestly and piously, not expecting any earthly condition to endure, but conscious that the Well is always accessible.

Jung's philosophy was always somewhat ambiguous. On one interpretation, he was moved to postulate just such real, non-empirical Beings as neo-Platonism proposes, in order to explain the presence in human dreams and imagination of certain 'archetypical' forms. They (he sometimes seems to have supposed) were the real explanations not only of our thought but of the phenomenal world itself. On the other, less radical view, he meant only that people (being conspecifics) tended to respond in similar ways to regular experiences, and that the only reality of his archetypes was as elements in the human imagination. On this latter view, 'asking the Book of Changes' could only be a way (at best) of isolating our own half-formulated suspicions (which might, or might not, be wiser than our conscious intellect). On the former view, it might really be a way of consulting an Angel, the same Angel which had imprinted on its authors the thoughts that led to the multiple copies of the Book. Which view we take will depend hardly at all upon our immediate experience: the decision requires metaphysical backing. When Jung enquired what the Book thought of itself and of his association with it, he received hexagram 50 in answer: the Cauldron, which stands for ancestral tradition, now shockingly neglected.

What about the Book that has been 'the Book' for Christian tradition, the Holy Bible? This too has been used as an oracle. Indeed, so far from reading it in proper 'literary' fashion most believers have taken it for granted that passages selected by liturgical custom, or random opening, will prove relevant to their everyday concerns, over and above any conscious intention of the human authors. Jewish Kabbalists have operated on the principle that even the separate letters of the text may be decoded, and convey further truths to the inquirer. If this is to divert attention from the more obvious messages of the semantic level we may be justly suspicious, but a divine work of art presumably could carry such a weight of meaning.

It may be true that any randomly selected catena of texts, if read with suitable attention and imagination, will come to seem meaningful, whether or not there is any neo-Platonic Angel which is the origin and continuing Spirit of the book in question. That there is such an angel does provide a possible explanation for the phenomena of literary creation, criticism and oracular consultation. If things are like that it is not clear to me how else we should discover or confirm that they are than by the process of pious reading and consultation. If things are not like that, the techniques of pious interpretation do at least allow us an occasional insight.

Science and Piety

The search for God's words, the words by which He founds all things and which he would have us speak, has been conducted through pentecostalist enthusiasm and through scriptural and liturgical traditionalism. There is also the way of intellect, the attempt to apprehend the fundamental structure of the created universe by thinking through the consequences of what we ordinarily think and experience. The ancient Pythagoreans, awe-struck by the mathematically describable order of music, guessed that all things were founded on number. This also seems to have been one of Plato's thoughts: no-one is to rise to be ruler, no-one could be a sound philosopher who had not progressed through simple arithmetic to the study of ratios, and bodies in mathematically describable motion. The world of Plato's *Timaeus* is built up to reflect the ideal world of Forms by means of simple geometrically defined solids, 'the Platonic solids'. The formulae we find approximately accurate in the study of material event (and no formula is ever more than *approximately* accurate) are ones we can uncover in our own minds. Renaissance science began in the conviction that we could reason our way to a realistic understanding of the universe, by relying on our grasp of mathematical relationship.

Scientists from Claude Bernard (the great nineteenth-century founder of experimental physiology, and an unrepentant vivisector) to Einstein have testified that what is needed in scientific investigation is a feeling for the forms behind phenomena. Einstein himself has commented on 'the one unintelligible fact about the universe – that it is intelligible'. Studies of the art of thought are unanimous in reporting that discoveries begin, very often, in sudden insights, metaphorical connections, images and dreams. If we put these facts together it suggests that we discover new truths about the reality 'behind' phenomena by 'remembering' or 'getting in touch' with it. The model of inspiration that has seemed convincing to so many creative artists also serves to explain how creatures like us could be so accurate so often when we reach out to the unknown. We are also often wrong: our dreams are not those of the Cosmic Imagining which bodies forth the phenomenal world (see Fawcett (1921)). But as we move toward a clearer imagining of the structures that 'explain' superificial behaviour we may have a sense of drawing closer to an intelligible order that is already present to us, 'at the back or root of our minds'. As modern physicists work towards an ideal scheme of quarks and leptons, each variety defined exactly by its character and with no room for individual variation and deviation (one Up quark is absolutely indistinguishable from any 'other'), they are constructing (with greater success than the Pythagoreans) a theoretical image of a purely mathematical reality. Or rather, the reality they seek to contemplate is understood, by them, in merely mathematical terms. But if those mathematicals can be found in the human intellect as well as in phenomenal reality then they are not quite the sort of things that the naive suppose.

The 'correspondence' between human theory and reality may be merely a fiction: after all, we have no access to reality save through the eyes of theory, and are in no position to confirm by empirical means that our best theorizing does indeed grasp the real truth. We can, if we wish, abandon that belief, and retreat to the instrumentalism from which Copernicus and Galileo saved us. On that account, all our theories are to be valued only as practical aids, and can never conflict with religious theories. We may, if need be, adopt apparently contradictory theories without a qualm, and rest content with ignorance. If we prefer to believe that there is a reality of which we can form an intelligible estimate, we must reject the anti-scientific views of David Hume and deny that thought is only 'a little agitation of the brain'. If we cannot trust our thought, what reason could we have even to believe that there are brains? What sort of world must it be if our best thoughts do reach out to be truth? What else but a world founded on presences in whom we participate by thought: the living forms and mathematicals that Plato glimpsed? On this account scientific theory does approximate to reality, insofar as the scientist has been entered by the very objective daimon which represents itself at the level of phenomenal reality as the array of facts she seeks to explain. It follows that when we speak, metaphorically as we suppose, of the cosmos as a society, we are quite right. The reality is a complex of intercommunicating spirits.

The idea that scholarly and scientific inquiry is essentially a work of piety may seem strange. Popular culture in the West regularly opposes 'science' and 'religion', though with no very clear idea of what either of these things may be. Popular history is convinced that 'the Church' persecuted original scientists, and believed 'scientific truth' an obstacle to 'faith'. It is considered odd that some 'scientists' should also be believers, and if an apology must be made for this fact it is suggested that science and religion appeal to different aspects of the personality: science to the 'masculine' impulse to schematize and control; religion to the 'feminine' impulse to receive and conserve. There may be some truth or other in this, but it is worth insisting also that science, as the intellectual effort to make sense of things, is as old as humanity and is not essentially linked with egomaniacal schemes of 'conquest' and 'control'. The master of them that know, namely Aristotle of Stageira, was well aware that scientific demonstration rested on strictly inde-monstrable principles (preferred because the alternative seems worse) that we follow in faith. Religion, on the other hand, is not revealed only in a supposedly feminine submission to fate, but in the desire to join the dance, to participate in the cosmic game. So far from contradicting religion, the scientific enterprise requires it, since it rests upon the assumption that the world is humanly intelligible, that we have some hope of bringing our inquiry to completion. Outside the doctrines of a decent piety it makes no sense at all.

Further reading

Bowes (1977); Jaki (1974); Wolfson (1947).

Egyptian religion may be studied in Morenz (1973), Te Velde (1967) and Frankfort (1949). *The Book of Changes* (Wilhelm & Baynes 1951), is discussed further by Wilhelm (1960).

Philosophy of language is an obscure, even wilfully obscure, area of philosophy, to which Blackburn (1984) may serve as an introduction. The use of analogy in religion is discussed by MacCormac (1976) and Palmer (1973). On the effects of literacy see Ong (1982). Cupitt's later writings, especially (1980) and (1982), have followed the anti-realist track to its bitter end.

Studies of scientific invention include Schon (1967), and Wallas (1926); see also Yates (1966).

The charismatic movement is described sympathetically by Kelsey (1973, 1974), and by Gunstone (1982).

Before man parted for this earthly strand,
   while yet upon the verge of heaven he stood,
God put a heap of letters in his hand,
   and bade him make with them what word he could

and man has turn'd them many times; made Greece,
Rome, England, France; yes, nor in vain essay'd
way after way, changes that never cease!
The letters have combined, something was made.

But ah! an inextinguishable sense
haunts him that he has not made what he should;
that he has still, though old, to recommence,
since he has not yet found the word God would.

And empire after empire, at their height
of sway, have felt this boding sense come on;
have felt their huge frames not constructed right,
and droop'd, and slowly died upon their throne.

One day, thou say'st, there will at last appear
the word, the order, which God meant should be.
 – Ah! we shall know that well when it comes near;
the band will quit man's heart, he will breathe free.
(Matthew Arnold, 'Revolutions')

5

New Souls and the Olympians

One Self and Many Selves

William James, seeing no reason to expect that there was a single known system of ideas with which we could handle the world was content that 'science gives to all of us telegraphy, electric lighting, and diagnosis, and succeeds in preventing and curing a certain amount of disease. Religion in the shape of mind-cure gives to some of us serenity, moral poise, and happiness, and prevents certain forms of disease as well as science does, or even better in a certain class of persons. Evidently then the science and the religion are both genuine keys for unlocking the world's treasure house to him who can use either of them practically' (1960, p. 132). Scientific reality is confirmed for us by technical success; 'religious reality' by the success of its techniques for preserving spiritual and physical health.

The mind-cure of which James spoke was the robust 'religion of healthy-mindedness' that, in the last resort, he reckoned less profound than the experience and creed of the twice-born. Some 'mind-curers' are more conscious than others that their goal is an increased enthusiasm and appetite for life and society, freed from the hobgoblins of shame-faced pride, anger, greed and boredom. To awaken that enthusiasm it is often necessary to be persuaded that one is born again, renewed, has a new self. Healthy-mindedness, in fact, is often only the opposite side of twice-born melancholia, and James, for once, does not play entirely fair in depicting his 'once born' as vulgar revivalists, his 'twice-born' as helpless depressives. They may be the very same persons.

The first question that may occur to us is this: how is it that a 'new self' can come to be? What changes are they, psychological or sociological, that change a person's character, make her a 'new creature'? The second question is rather the reverse: how is it that we are not always changing, always trading in an old identity and never acquiring any stable character at all? 'Our ordinary alterations of character, as we pass from one of our aims to another, are not commonly called transformations, because each of them is so rapidly succeeded by another in the reverse direction; but wherever one aim grows so stable as to expel definitely its previous rivals from the individual's life, we tend to speak of the phenomenon, and perhaps to wonder at it, as a "transformation" ' (James (1960), p. 199). The new creature is the more stable realization of a possibility that had perhaps surfaced many times before, and been submerged again in the shifting seas of human personality. Rites of passage, and conversion experiences (which constitute a sort of unofficial rite, with their own expected rituals) are ways of strengthening some particular mode or mood; cutting the victim off from other, past possibilities, or (equivalently) cutting off those other moods from the central pillar of the victim's life. Those other possibilities are now perceived as temptations, or personal demons, against which the rite (maybe repeated, maybe merely remembered) protects the 'new born' person. If we stamp out the boundaries of our parish, or deck ourselves in tribal costume, it may (partly) be to re-establish that chosen identity in which we feed upon our consciousness of being a proper tribesman. When we perform some individually chosen rite (as it might be, the daily or hourly utterance of the words 'Thanks be to God on high') we steer ourselves through life, avoiding the possible identities, demon-possessions that we sense on either hand.

These techniques, verbal reminder and dramatic performance (individual or social), are, in a sense, value-neutral. Any identity may be stabilized like this, and any identity (it seems) may someday crack. We are more likely to fear this breakdown, and so defend ourselves against it more fiercely and rigidly (and so hasten its coming?), if we think that our chosen identity is indeed an attempt to freeze a wave of the sea, to make solid sculptures out of butter on a warm day. We shall be less fearful of collapse if we conceive that the sea itself is the real shaper of our standing wave, that it was the former identities that were the momentarily aggregated flotsam that the waves have swept away. A stable identity, in short, is likely to be one which is believed to be the manifestation of an underlying reality, 'the one original face we had before our births', or at least in touch with 'something far more deeply interfused'. Those who believe that their identities are maintained by their own endeavours, by their own disciplined insistence on being as they were, are very likely not to last the course. Those who believe that there is a spring which will continue to create the fountain of their own identity, according to its own purposes, and without any insistent effort on their part, may more easily live on in their chosen form. It is, accordingly, unsurprising that those who cannot or do not believe in

God, or in the working of the Buddha-nature, may yet suppose that what comes 'naturally' is best, that it is by the forces of nature that their chosen humanism is maintained, that the demons of inhumanity are bound to fail. If we did not believe that, but believed that it was by our conscious efforts only that evil is averted, what leisure would we ever have? And what enormous evils would we perform, with the plea that we must prevent yet worse evils?

Part of the usual ritual for maintaining a stable identity, accordingly, is likely to be a more or less explicit affirmation that this identity is of a piece with the cosmos, that it is just what the underlying 'powers' (the occult causes of what happens) require. Such confidence rests upon our confiding ourselves to the care of an unknown power which we insist on reckoning of one kind with our chosen identity. Only one who seriously thinks himself the Son of the One God, with whom He is well pleased, can entirely afford to abandon the alternative identities that might have served their turn. Such total conviction, of course, has its price. Most of us withhold our absolute consent to be *merely and utterly* a child of the Most High not because we are persuaded by rational argument that the story is false but because we are afraid.

We live between these two extremes. On the one hand, it is imaginable that someone should entirely lack a stable character, a plan of life, a sense of being thus and so. Such an individual would react from moment to moment, with no intention even of keeping faith or carrying out a plan for longer than it was amusing. On the other hand, there are the supremely confident, who have identified that in themselves which they can take to be what comes 'naturally', what is supported and sustained by powers that lie outside the boundaries of their former, merely human personality. Genghis Khan, for example, believed himself possessed of the Mandate of Heaven.

In a pluralistic and relatively mobile society most people will have many roles to play during their lives, and at any period of their lives. The character, behaviour, forms of reasoning and speech that are appropriate in one role are not in another, and we must be able to move between them. In doing so we approximate to the first extreme, and mark these periods of our lives by changing our style of dress, and redirecting our attention. In moving between home and work, and church, and recreation we select different goals, experience different emotions. We are all a little like werewolves. It is the dominant assumption of secular moralists that it would be wrong to think of some one goal as dominant. Many things are valuable, we are told, and there may be no single plain in terms of which those different values could be assessed. The 'good life' is the suitably varied life, without a single dominant pursuit. Such sane and respectable moralizing is a confession that no one thing is worth all our other goods, that there is no single, stable identity to which and for which we can secure happiness. Those who propose that there is, after all, a single goal, that God is to be served and contemplated as the dominant end of any happy life, are not refuted, but ignored. Rather than a longed for purity of intention the modern moralist prefers a *smorgasbord* of values, a wardrobe of differing costumes.

From such a perspective those who are 'reborn' as simple identities yoked to the powers seem to have sacrificed too much. Better that people should share their time out between different possibilities defined by outward shows that help to sustain a particular mood. Those for whom the mask slips momentarily, who start behaving with a childishness suitable to families in their working lives, or who try to organize their recreations in economically profitable ways, are guilty of an error of taste, the more notceable where boundaries are rigid. It should not be assumed, of course, that casual wear and first names in the workplace really lower any barriers between the family and working styles. Such customs merely alter the codes. But perhaps the popular myth of the orgiastic office-party is a wistful product of the wish that barriers might go down, and a more 'natural' identity emerge. Such barriers go down more easily if the participants can persuade themselves that they are possessed, that there is something 'bigger than both of us' that is flexing itself for action. An anthropologist's aphorism: 'people do not behave unconventionally because they are possessed – they are possessed so as to behave unconventionally'. And that is itself a convention.

Office-parties, conferences, summer schools are rarely as orgiastic as wistful rumour imagines. Nor do *we* think of them 'religiously'. But it is not impossible that we should. What the boundaries of our lives, and the wistful imagining of their overthrow, suggest is the double role which religious ritual plays in the operation of stabilizing identities. On the one hand outward performance of an expected kind serves as the code to others and ourselves to summon up one identity, one demon, rather than another. Insofar as all these identities are equal claimants, the person who sustains them does not think herself possessed as she drops one expression, one style for another. If there were a single identity that was felt to be her 'real self', most or all of her overt identities would be experienced as constraints (or believed to be constraints). When she finds herself automatically going into 'parent gear', and quite unable to 'snap out of it' and 'remember' that the one who is her child is not only that, what is that but 'possession', a demon – speaking phenomenologically (i.e. without any implications about the causes of this experience, and merely examining its experienced form) –

that needs exorcism by determined prayer? On the other hand, the sudden emergence of a forgotten self – an emergence made easier by social ritual and the consumption of a mild drug (most usually, alcohol) – may be experienced as a joyful rediscovery or an humiliating possession by something quite at odds with waking values. These changes and orderings can, with a little imagination, be experienced as the manoeuvres of a spirit world. Spirits, gods and demons are the compelling moods and behaviour patterns that are evoked, controlled and manifested by the rituals that establish boundaries between identities and sometimes break the boundaries down again. Religion is the collective noun for all such practices, whereby our changing selves may move in time to some unknown tidal motions, without driving us insane.

I emphasize that I am speaking 'phenomenologically'. These passing moods and different styles of action express different identities that may even be hostile to each other, may seek to exclude or re-absorb each other. What it 'feels like' to someone grown conscious of what is happening is a contest between alien powers, with her soul as the prize. Polytheism, and moral pluralism, is the thesis that all these powers must be given due respect, given their own time in the sun. If this is to be a stable solution, the powers themselves must accept the rules, and not be always fighting. If they were, their human victim's condition would be terrible, and they themselves would never be able to complete a project. Consider an SF fable by Wyman Guin, entitled 'Beyond Bedlam'. In this fable every individual body houses two distinct personalities that take orderly turns. What we now regard as a case of multiple personality, and our ancestors would consider obvious 'spirit possession', is recognized as an alternation of distinct ego-conscious-nesses, who must 'play the game' (or else throw all the social order into disarray). This fable takes the experience of 'multiple personality' as the norm, whereas our own postulate of practical reason requires the 'unity of the ego'. On the one hand, many spirits, moods and personalities; on the other, the single ego that moves beneath the domination of these spirits, and needs to obey the rules.

It is easy to imagine that the 'real situation' is what 'we' suppose, that individual persons are indubitably individuals, and these different moods and styles and roles are indubitably passive, properties of those unitary subjects. It is our custom to insist that there is one person only who endures from birth (or conception) to death, that the same person speaks with this mouth now as spoke thirty years ago – although we recognize that much may have changed since then. That is indeed, as of now, the 'commonsensical' attitude. But if that ordinary affirmation of my identity as a continuing physical presence, as one and the same object through multiple transformations of mood and style and professional standing, is probed, it becomes clear that my 'unity' is rather a demand, a postulate, than a plain discovery, and is also very difficult to analyze. My being that one individual does not reside in my having any particular property of physical shape or psychological condition. Clearly, I could lose any property I have and still be 'me', indeed, I can conceive of 'my' existence in indefinitely many possible worlds, ones where 'I' was born with brain damage, or as one of twins (and which twin would I be?). It may be right to insist that there are such bare identities, that there is a pure ego. But insofar as this is a highly theoretical and abstract notion, we are entitled to try out the alternatives, to see what can still be said if we abandon the search for such a simple subject.

It was indeed fashionable in classical circles some years ago to argue that 'archaic Greeks' had (poor things) no clear conception of the unity of the human subject. Archaic potters break up the body into discrete segments. Homeric heroes apostrophize their heart, their '*phrenes*' (the region of the diaphragm that is the centre of vital strength also in Oriental tradition), and expect death to disintegrate even their seeming unity (ghost, flesh and immortal flame going separate ways). It was, rather oddly, taken for granted that the thought of post-Mycenaean Greece could be illuminated by stories of the North American Trickster, who is sometimes said to have found it difficult to identify his limbs precisely as himself, not letting his right hand know what his left is doing. The idea that archaic Greece was somehow 'closer' to the imagined first condition of humanity, that there is no difference between what happened 3,000 and 40,000 years ago, is not one worth reviving. The degree to which archaic humans should be treated as what we would call dissociated personalities, acting without compunction in any one of several different styles that they made no attempt to co-ordinate, is also very unclear. Homer's heroes do not strike most naive readers as altogether unlike the humans that we know. Nor do they find it difficult to speak in the first person.

But if we reject the claim that our notion of a unitary personality has evolved from a more 'primitive' notion (according to which a human body was a collection of parts and a human self an empty arena for disputing spirits), the way is open to treat the archaic view as a commonsensical view biased toward the opposite metaphysical position. Our common sense assures us that, despite appearances, we are each an individual self. Archaic common sense assured people that, despite appearances, each individual was a medley of competing parts and loyalties. The ego may experience itself as being at the mercy of those struggling powers, or may suppose itself favoured and strengthened by some one of them through all its tribulations – as Odysseus knows himself as Athena's man.

The ego is recognizably mortal, because it cannot sustain itself in whatever condition it chooses. The moods and styles it encounters and lives through are recognizably not-mortal, because they are encountered again and again in the ego's life, and in the experience of the ego's 'significant others', its family and allies and superiors. These moods are also not to be commanded, though they may be coaxed and conciliated. Nor can their onset be entirely predicted, although some may have special domains in which they are to be expected: the panic fear of wilderness, or the despairing rage of the battlefield, or the enchantment of twilight when each bush may be a bear or a benevolent magician, or the clear light of Delos. In brief, such moods and styles are experienced as gods, whom it is death to defy, and death (equivalently) to serve too singlemindedly. Those who try to proclaim their own immunity to Aphrodite find that she is raised up against them, that their wives betray them or their stepmothers pursue them. Blasphemy is the service of one god to the detriment of another, or (equivalently) the hope of rising above the shifting seas of mood and role. Odysseus achieves selfhood under the aegis of Athena: the price is the hostility of Poseidon (the Lord of Horses and the Sea, in their magical and uncontrollable aspect: see Vernant in Gordon (1981)) until Zeus (who embodies that order which must be preserved if all human life is not to revert to fratricidal chaos) lays down the law – and even then Odysseus must conciliate his enemy so that death may come from the sea 'in gentle fashion'

Most of these archaic Greeks who thought and spoke of gods and 'kers' (the spirits of spite and reprisal), and who understood that their lives depended on respectful remembrance of the other phases of life, had no very systematic theory about the world. The presence of the gods was commonsensical, and it was merely common sense to remember that one's humanity consisted in this, that we are not the masters. Odysseus can endure, and contrive, and (with Athena's blessing) prosper, but he cannot order all things to his desire, nor secure himself against mortal sadness and homesickness. Only gods are singleminded. More systematic intelligences organized the major divinities into a pantheon, leaving kers and furies and fits of temper and the onset of insanity as terrors on the fringe of every day. The major divinities are each a world. Only if we go far astray shall we encounter Furies, but the Olympians together make up the universe that any human being must inhabit. Other religious traditions – as the Roman – made of each momentary crisis, each feature of the world, a separate god, with a name but without a character. Archaic Greek thought achieved a more synthetic vision. If the lucky moment was a god (coming of itself, encountered more than once, and shedding its own lustre), that god was likely to be Hermes. The pangs of childbirth and the knot's release were Artemis, untouched mistress of wild things. Over all these deities stood Zeus, who required that gods and mortals alike knew their place, and mounted no rebellion against Themis, what was proper. The possibility of war in heaven, of an alliance between some gods against others, who would thereby be assigned the role of demons, was always there. Moods and styles arose at first from Earth and Heaven, themselves the children of the yawning void. Those first patternings of human life, remembered as the Titans, were cruder, less differentiated passions than the Olympians who followed them. Aphrodite herself – though one story named her daughter of Zeus – was by the older tale a Titan, born from the foam that gathered round Heaven's severed testicles. Athena too was a Titan tamed: Metis (crafty wisdom) whom Zeus swallowed was reborn in his daughter. This 'discovery', so to call it, of the possibility of an orderly world-system in which each god had a part to play, and which the demands of different roles were not settled simply by resort to force, issued in the grant of Shame and the sense of Justice to humankind. Technical ability had been granted already, by Prometheus the Titan. This 'knowledge of good and evil' was what, in Greek thought, prevented human beings from becoming gods: precisely because they could look before and after, and discriminate, they could not be unselfconsciously absorbed in any single role or mood. Prometheus himself lies chained, like Loki of the Northern myth: and knows the name of one who would overturn the order that Zeus defends. The price even of the pluralistic order, the disunities organized beneath the hand of Zeus, is the eternal death of an excluded possibility.

Once again: it would be very difficult to demonstrate that this was really how even a sophisticated Greek actually felt and thought about the Gods. In a sense, that does not matter. If it is not how the Greeks thought, it will still serve as a model for one sort of religious consciousness, and assist our understanding. The greatest triumph of Olympianism, on this view, was the inclusion of Dionysus. Here most clearly is a god known in the experience of possession, the anarchic dissolution of established order, in the grant of Titanic energy that yet serves as a reminder that we ourselves are mortals. If Zeus is the guardian of Law, at the peak of the Olympian pyramid, then Zagreus-Dionysus is the reminder that Law is at last the child of Chaos. He is the man dressed as a woman, the priest and sacrifice, the spirit of make-believe and dramatic action, all that is liquid and alive. In the most perfect of Greek tragic plays, Euripides' *Bacchae*, he reveals himself as the necessary opposite of Shame and Justice, who must be remembered and conciliated lest the bulwarks of our ordered lives collapse. By acting out our guarded dreams of transvestism, eating our food raw, destroying those we love, we may be spared – by the god's casual compassion – the tragedy of our complete overthrow. As generations of rationalistic critics have rather boringly observed, the god's behaviour is unjust, the punishment he exacts far in excess of any fancied crime. The god is not subject to the laws of Justice, and hardly subject even to the hand of Zeus and the defiant competition of other duties. He is not an individual mortal person, but the god he is. If he were subject to change, and many-mindedness, he would not be the god of the whole world.

One final comment: the religious genius of the Greeks did not conclude that 'Dionysus' was 'the natural man', the man as he would be if all restraints gave way. Such a creature is a mere blasphemer, one who tries to step beyond the bounds of his own nature. Dionysus is not the natural man, but a natural possibility that is at once the origin of all this talk of gods, and the temporary destruction of the order founded on this talk. The origin, because Dionysus is the god of make-believe, the power of being what one isn't (as the tragic actor dons his mask to do). The temporary destruction of Olympian order is magnificently accepted into that very order as a moment of human life, because it is when possessed by Dionysus that we see through the shadows. That the organized worship of Dionysus came into Greece from Thrace or Asia Minor in the seventh century may be true, but it is unwise to assume that this *must* be so merely because Dionysus is labelled as a 'foreigner', an immigrant, as unwise as to suppose that 'chthonic' religion (worship of the spirits of the earth, as opposed to those of the sky, the Olympians) must somehow be left over from an earlier civilization: it is part of the essence of such cults that they lay claim to having got there first, as it is of the essence of the Dionysiac that it comes in 'from outside'. Mythology and ritual cannot so easily be transformed into history. Such myths are better understood in their present meaning than as history. Dionysus is remembered, or supposed, to be a foreigner because his nature is precisely to be foreign, alien, the excluded possibility that will always return in power.

In Egypt the god Seth, instigator of confusion, deserter, drunkard, foreigner, homosexual, had a lower religious status (Te Veldè (1967) p. 7). In Norse mythology, it is the sumpreme God, Odin, who looks most like this, 'a chaotic, amoral figure' (Turville-Petre (1964) p. 86), while Thor upholds the world. Perhaps the Greeks had the best idea.

Hebrews and Hellenes

My exposition of the Olympian way draws heavily on the work of W.F. Otto, its last true believer. I believe it to be more accurate than are the sneering descriptions of the Olympians as a band of brigands, the projection into heaven of all the worst features of their worshippers. The gods are emphatically not simply human beings immortalized and given magic powers, beings who are likely to lose their distinctive characters or change their professions or suffer qualms of conscience over eternity. Nor are the stories told of them merely coded histories of political alliances between different states (though it is true that this is part of the process whereby gods acquire their names and natures). The network of divinities that the poets found in human life as it was organized in their historical communities was a way of describing, codifying and ordering the moods and roles of life in those communities. That this was done successfully is proved by the power of the Olympian dream: despite all the complaints of religious reformers, rationalists and 'practical politicians', paganism endured, and its faint echoes are still part of our religious consciousness. We are still aware that blood-thirsty rage can take command of armies and nations, that sex is only denied at fearful cost, that the lucky moment is a joy to which we should give thanks, that 'the god gone mad' had better be conciliated (if US politicians had ever read *The Bacchae* they might have been spared the agonies of the Prohibition Era, and its destruction of civil community and respect for law). The message of all the gods, not only Apollo, is to know ourselves, to know that we are merely mortal. Even if a god possesses us, so that we see with its eyes, and it speaks with our mouths, yet the triumphant god will let us drop. Sometimes a mortal does become a god, his old mortality burned up and the pure being incorporated in the Olympian system: Heracles became, or was revealed as being, the splendid labourer whose presence might be invoked (complete with lion skin and club) upon a lonely road or on the lintel of a house. But his immortality was won through suffering even greater than the common man's, through slavery and madness and an agonizing death. In him a robust endurance in the service of civil order made itself known: a bridge between humans and the Olympians precisely because he was entirely human.

There is another well-known intrusion into pagan lands of a cult whose enemies considered it subversive of all good order, whose celebrants conceived that they had become new creatures by taking their god into them, whose god was born a mortal and endured hard labour and death in agony. Their god was a son of God, like Heracles and Dionysus, and their rites (it was supposed) an excuse for getting drunk in the early morning, and for continuous debauchery.

I refer, of course, to Christianity. If Olympianism is the attempt to provide, through deathless poetry and yearly festival, a structure for the moods and roles of social humanity, what shall we say of Christian dedication to the One God and Father of our Lord Jesus Christ, fed by the sacramental consumption of bread and wine, fuelled by doses of the Holy Spirit in age after age? What is the 'new creature' of Christian conversion, and how is it to be related to the shifting moods of ordinary humankind, stabilized by rites of passage, rituals of social observance? Paganism, according to Miskotte (1967), is the natural religion of humanity, a celebration of 'cosmic awareness', of our knowledge that we are vulnerable parts of a world system with its own laws and beauties. For the pagan, we are mortal, and our only joys must be in momentary glimpses of the pure being of gods: of Aphrodite as she shows herself in sexual partners, of owl-eyed Athena in the prudent anatomizing and judgement of the wise, of Apollo in mathematical order and elegance, even (horrifically) of Ares in the berserk fury we have not learned to live without. Those powers will endure, and though we may call upon the spirit of Heracles in our troubles it is not with any hope that we shall dwell with him. Christianity, on the other hand, is one form of a great protest-movement, the rejection of our mundane, mortal selves, and the circling seasons.

That there is a distinct similarity between Christian enthusiasm and the Dionysiac revivalism that (perhaps) swept seventh-century Greece is a familiar enough thought. Both involve a rejection of standard social barriers between Greek and barbarian, slave and free, male and female. In both cases the worshipper supposes that the god is living in her, and she responds to His presence by ecstatic utterance and dance and an uncommon energy and endurance. Christian revivalists may not tear living animals to pieces (though some sectarians play with snakes as happily as Maenads did), or drink the literal blood of any sacrifice. If Maenads ate the god by eating raw flesh, Christians eat Him by eating bread (that their enemies assumed must be human flesh). The dance-steps of ecstatic enthusiasm (head flung back) are recognizable in many cults and nations. Such enthusiasm often strikes the guardians of official religion as distasteful, dangerous, over-emotional and beside the true 'religious' point – which is understood to involve sound morals and a social conscience and a willingness to be instructed by one's human betters. Those who suppose that the god has spoken to them, that He has anointed them with His spirit, that they are new creatures and have cast off the works of darkness and the older gods, are unlikely to be popular with established sectarians.

Miskotte's counter-paganism is not only that of charismatic revivalism, the sudden creation of a new self that dances to another tune than
the established order. It is also that of Hebrew prophecy, the denial that
God's demands are met by orderly enactment of the season's rituals or
the complacent stages of human life. The prophet stands aside from her
ordinary status, the duties of her station, and feels the weight of another
Lord than Baal (which only means, 'the Lord'). The Baalim of the land,
the little lords who are embodied in good harvests and the serviceable
rites of an agriculture imbued with feeling for the sacred, are to be
supplanted by an invader, the one Lord who is not just another Lord,
but the mastering presence that gives the lion his food, and the young
ravens their meat, who brings the stars up from the east and will not be
identified with the interests of the worldly rich. For paganism (in its
many guises) it is the established priests, the rich, the powerful who
embody or represent the divine power. It is in bowing before the
Monarch that we make obeisance to the powers, and in our rush of
terrified devotion that we experience what mortals must feel before the
immortal gods. At the same time the god is bound to its worshippers:
each worshipping community sustains its gods, experiences itself as
chosen, favoured by the immortal ones who inhabit eternity. They are
'our' gods, whose being lies in being acknowledged and reverenced by
us, in being the atmosphere of our communal living. Let the customs
change, the worship perish, the accepted stages and the moods we
notice alter, and the gods will die, or fade into old bogeys.

The one Lord of Hebrew prophecy is not dependent on His people,
and tolerates their betrayals and continual adulteries. He is not
experienced as a world defined by moods or ritual stages of a human
life, nor yet (as Zeus is) as the abiding guardian of the established way.
His messengers and representatives are not the wealthy, not the
established priests, but whomever He wills to pluck out from the fields
and load down with the intolerable burden of prophetic truth. The great
prophets of Hebrew literary tradition spoke in rounded sentences and,
though they acted strangely, did not dance out upon the mountains. But
there are traces even amongst the Hebrews of colleges of prophets,
speaking with tongues and challenging established order (by convictions
of their own). Christianity seems to have begun as charismatic
revivalism, denying that the one Lord was to be seen where others
looked for Him, among the well-groomed scholars and the rich. God
speaks in the provincial, in the poor and oppressed, and does not need
the careful worship of Israel. This was the message always of the
prophets. 'If I were hungry I would not tell thee: for the world is mine,
and the fulness thereof' (Psalm 50.12). The One Lord is Lord of
Sabaoth, Lord of the powers, and displays His power and purposes in

overthrowing the mighty from their seats, and exalting the humble and meek.

Such a god is not known only in the patterning of human life and the world we inhabit. It is not a mood, or style, that is conceived to arise within the framework of 'Earth and Heaven'. It claims to be the maker and shaker of the earth and the heavens. So the new name that is given to the believer is one that renders her a spectator of the cosmic play, not merely giving her another role within that play. The experience of being 'called out' from all usual patterns is paralleled in other traditions by the thought of an escape from the wheel of fortune, within which (by luck or by the operation of causal law) each mood and stage must be repeated on and on forever.

So in Christian prophecy we find the thought that the One Lord will have neither slave nor free, Jew nor Gentile, male nor female, and demands obedience to laws unlike the world's, finding His chosen among the oppressed and not the oppressors. In Buddhist thought we find the way out from caste-division, age, status, all the shifting duties of a pluralistic life, and the goal is set of a condition quite unlike all others, when desire is Blown Out, and the Unnameable, the end that cannot be pictured, the enlightenment that is not this, not that, is known without words. That there are enormous differences between these traditions I do not deny: where they are in harness is in this, that the one religious truth worth knowing is not to be equated with a service of the powers that be. These gods may merit courtesy, but not worshipful devotion. The One Thing to be worshipped is . . . the Buddha nature, the One that names Itself in Its refusal to be named, the Power beyond all Powers. It was not entirely a mistake that Hellenists in Alexandria, trying to find a place in their city for the God of the Hebrews, equated the One God of Sabaoth (which means 'the Powers') with Sabazios, Dionysus by another name. It now takes some imaginative effort to connect the moralizing piety of Christians or Rabbinic Jews with maenadism, but the parallel is there. The worshippers of the One Lord declined to be assimilated into paganism, as the maenads had been. For them the old ways were entirely disenchanted, the gods who were the moods of worldliness downgraded into demons, whereas the Dionysiac revivalists had acknowledged that the other gods had just as good a claim. Dionysus accepted his filial relationship with Zeus, whose business was to keep the world in order. Yahweh, the Spirit, did not bow to order. Dionysus might work his revenge on kings that would not honour him, but their kingship was of Zeus, who granted 'the god gone mad' his rights. Yahweh insisted, through his worshippers, that the kings of the earth held office only at His will, that there were no norms nor orderly arrangements that could claim rights of their own against the One. Being worshippers of such a One, the revivalists were, by definition, uncivilized, uncouth, unreasonable. Pagans had to experience them as threats, and their god (quite real by virtue of their worship) as the expression of that threat. Loyal Hindus found the Buddha's teaching quite as horrid, and concluded at the last that Vishnu had taken shape as a false teacher to delude and weaken those who might otherwise take arms against the order of the Heavens.

Were the pagans right? Were the spokesmen of the Unnameable entirely wrong? Those who lay claim to special knowledge, and who dance out a life that (so they say) arises from outside the ordinary realm, seem bound to be mistaken. Is it not clear that such revivalism is one of the things that happen, that it is a permanent possibility in the human world, and hence one element, one god, within an ordered world? If it were not brought within the Zeus-protected patterning of mundane life it would, if unconfined, destroy the human universe. Why else is the Wolf bound fast, lest He should eat the world? How can there be an identity that transcends all identities, a life that is not one life among many nor yet the life that lives in ordering the other lives? If Yahweh could be identified easily with Zeus (as philosophical Hebrews and Greek proselytes alike would wish), He would be the God of this world, the support and stay of princes, owed obedience as the guardian of proper order. There is no doubt that many of 'the peoples of the Book' have held this thought, that religion lies in service of that order, in knowing one's place or places, in maintaining due respect for all the powers that be. It cannot plausibly be claimed that they are entirely wrong.

But the other tradition surfaces regularly. By this account Yahweh is not the God of Natural Order, under whom each lesser god and value holds sway. Yahweh is an Absolute Demand, a thing unlike all other things, a Voice that says 'Come out of her, my people', and creates Its people as ones with 'no continuing city' in the circles of this world. All other gods and values are without a value; all are to be traded in for this one pearl, this seed of a new Heaven and Earth. Satan is the god of this world, and what he offers us is fairy gold. Yahweh is not to be obeyed because that way lies riches, nor a quiet mind. Nor is He the object of the world's desire, the ever-receding goal of divine perfection that all things yearn toward. Only those He calls desire to follow Him, and they must follow through the absolute destruction of all worldly tastes. The bourgeois (and well-meaning) congregations that now sing 'Take up your Cross, the Saviour said, if you would my disciples be' do not usually recall to mind just what such crucifixion is: not merely the Herculean endurance of the troubles of this mortal life, enlivened by our worship of the eternal gods, but a stumbling climb up Golgotha to be stretched out and nailed upright to a pole, to be cursed and jeered at: 'I am a worm and no man; a reproach of men, and despised of all the people' (Psalm 22.6). Only in such final dereliction, in having tied one's fortunes wholly to a fallen star, is the One Lord to be known, and the Way Out open. It cannot plausibly be claimed that such visionaries are entirely wrong.

On the one hand, Zeus and obedience to the gods of human ceremonial and meaning. On the other, Yahweh and forsaking of all other goals and meaning save only that we do His will. Each side, to the other, is the worshipper of demons. It may be, indeed, that the dispute goes back further than our records do. It is of interest that both Hindu India and Persia classify divinity as *devas* or *asuras*: but in India, *asuras* are the demons that the orderly gods resist; in Persia, it is Ahura, God of light, that is at war with the Devil (not that 'devil' is etymologically connected with '*deva*': it derives from '*diabolos*', the accuser). On the one hand, order; on the other, the unorderable. On the one hand, laws of non-contradiction and excluded middle; on the other, paradox and the laws only of unfettered Will. The dialectic is complicated by the obvious fact that if the worshippers of 'the god gone mad' should persuade enough people, a new social order will emerge, with its own styles and grades and blessings. Charismatic revivalists, reacting against the established order of their day in the name of the One God, succeed only in establishing new patterns of worship and hymnody, so that bourgeois congregations sing words that take their meaning from the last revival. 'Come Holy Ghost our souls inspire, and lighten with celestial fire'; how many in the congregation really intend to speak in tongues, to prophesy, to dismiss established orders and abandon all their worldly gains? How many Buddhists, for that matter, really rest themselves upon the non-existence of the self, and seek to realize the Unborn? Most Buddhists live within an order of merit and demerit, and hope only for a better birth next time. Like Christians, they rely upon the merit won by others, the 'good outpourings' of the Buddhas gone before, and certainly do not expect themselves to make the supreme sacrifice of all their worldly selves. Like the Olympians, Christians and Buddhists have (to some extent) achieved a synthesis: their ceremonial order does contain a reference to That beyond all orders, and a vocabulary that stands ready for the next revivalist.

What human beings have developed in 'religion' is a magnificent system that sustains their chosen roles, channels their inevitable emotions, and reminds them on occasion that the system is contained within the wholly unsystematized, that human ceremonial and meaning and the orderly progression of our identities may be overthrown, remade, revitalized. On the one hand, Zeus Father of Gods and men.

On the other, He that makes all things new. Zeus-worshippers consider that the other side are atheists and 'enemies of all the human race'. Yahweh-worshippers think that the other side are idolaters, 'the rich who have had their reward'. Both sides have often been correct.

Stable and continuing religious traditions neither wholly abjure nor wholly endorse 'the world'. Even those who are pillars of their respective churches half-remember that their creed and ceremonial is founded on an incursion, an invasion into some more ancient world. Even those who are ridden most fiercely by the Unbounded Spirit sense that what they are about is a 'revival', a re-injection of vitality into the forms that have been made ready for it. Zeus, Father of Gods and Men, was identified by neo-Platonic theorists – almost the last philosophers to take ordinary religious forms seriously as matter for philosophical inquiry – with *Nous*, the ordering intellect and the order it discloses. This was not the ultimately real, the One, which could not be known in ceremonial usage and sacred learning, but only by immediate presence, by ceasing to be (for a moment only) what one was. But the One and *Nous*, though distinct, were not diverse: *Nous* itself had its being only from the One, as ceremonial usage and sacred history stem, in their beginnings, from the Unnamed that lies beyond all ceremonial.

Are There Really Gods?

Nothing that I have said so far need conflict with the metaphysical beliefs of honest atheists. The patterns of ritual that define our changing identities, and make it possible to experience an energy that transcends the usual moulds, are all matters of empirical inquiry. The gods, as I have described them, are indubitably real, and the ritual rejection of the gods, as I have described it, is also religious. As human beings we live within a complex of ceremonial and regular encounter with immortal realities, Birth, War, Lust, Intelligence and that most paradoxical of gods, the voice of Chaos. 'Being an atheist , at the level of religious ceremonial, can only be the rejection of such ceremonial forms in favour of a step outside the usual – whether that step is the Buddha's, or the Devil's. The sort of adolescent cynicism that passes for atheistical intelligence in some circles – the insistence that lust and war and marriage and awe-struck admiration of mountains and the stars do not really engage our energies, that we are all driven only by momentary whims, without plan or passion – is the real enemy of religion. When such attitudes survive into adulthood they constitute the sort of sensualism that gives atheism a bad name. To abandon Zeus and the Olympians in favour of whatever momentary and unmeaning whim may move our souls is to turn onself into barbarian and slave. Such barbarians conceive of the land, the seas, their nation's history as so much stuff, have no respect left for the marriage bed and bond, feel no compunction about 'bits of paper' (that others will call solemn treaties) and sneer at what 'an old man in a wig' (that others recognize as an honourable judge) may say. Irreligion is the denial of human meaning, the claim that nothing matters but the sensual thrills that irreligious people feel, and those only for a moment. Fortunately, most of us grow up, and find our places in the social, ceremonial universe that allows each temporary identity a part to play.

But just as there is an irreligious barbarism that falls far short of civilised community, so there is an 'atheism' that transcends religion. It was a flaw in eighteenth-century apologists for religion that they saw only uncivil irreligion in their atheistical contemporaries. Sometimes they might instead have recognized that the 'atheists' were only denouncing what they took to be a blasphemy against the One, the true reality it was our duty to desire. What it is about the Truth, if that Truth is conceived as scienticists now do, that makes it worthy of our undivided zeal is something that such atheists rarely consider. But their hearts, maybe, were more religious than their heads: they held it right to 'follow Nature humbly' and not be misled, to try and mould the ceremonial forms of human life more closely to the Way Things Really Were (as these were slowly being manifested to the inquiring mind). They were, in short, revivalists, convinced that what was made known to them in scientific mode was the Real Truth, that what was said in customary ceremonial was a hindrance to such 'real understanding'. Whether the religious ceremonials that are now forming in a society entranced by scientific claims to have the one and only Truth are a genuine improvement on older forms is uncertain.

What I have been discussing here is the phenomenon of religion, and the 'reality' of gods as they are constituted by the usual forms of human sociality, including that paradoxical form, the invading critic. Such gods are real, and to be reckoned with, and worship, prayer and sacrifice are ways of keeping order in our lives, preventing our collapse into helpless despair and sensual debauch. That the gods are also real in a more metaphysical sense, that they would still exist even if we ceased to believe in them, even if we ceased to order our lives in anything like a human fashion, is a doctrine that I have not yet considered – its time will come. What I am emphasizing is the primary reality of our human universe, the social community within which we learn to speak and think and do. Our apparatus for distinguishing between what is 'real' and what is 'merely imaginary' is one that works within the field of our experience. The *truth* of a proposition lies, for us, in its having to be affirmed if we are to carry on with the life that we are born to. The Olympians are real in that we recognize certain patterns in our lives, and identify ourselves with certain possible identities, not others. By the same token, of course there are also witches, for as long as competent English-speakers are constrained to speak of them. An old woman accused of witchcraft may be falsely accused (although the mere accusation was usually enough for torture and condemnation), but we cannot seriously say that there 'really are not witches' until we can speak from within a different tradition, a different human ceremonial, and no longer see misfortune and disease as an expression of a neighbour's malice, but as just punishment, or the spleen of gods. Some of those philosophers who have followed this line have given the impression that no single tradition, no human universe, can ever 'really' be more accurate than another, since what counts as 'really being accurate' must be assessed within a tradition. Some of these 'anti-realists' have confused the case still further by claiming that they were really 'realists', since 'reality' can only be what is affirmed as such within a given social universe. As such, they have declared that they are 'moral realists', believing that there are moral statements which must be accounted *true*, within our tradition (as that it would be wrong to operate upon an unanaesthetized dog and leave her tied up in a deserted laboratory with her sides still open). The account I have so far offered of religious discourse could with equal justice be christened 'religious realism', in that it simply avoids the metaphysical issue by concentrating on the ceremonial system that structures our identities, discriminating between 'true' and 'false' divinities only in terms of those systems.

A genuine realism, however, supposes that, for example, it is *true* that the first ten prime numbers add up to 111 because they do. They do not do so because it is correct to *say* that they do, even though 'adding up' is a thing that human intelligence can do. That there are problems about such realism is clear, but it should not be defined into non-existence. The phenomenological account of religious identity that I have given can easily be transformed into anti-realist metaphysics, into the thesis that the gods are 'real' only in that human life is structured as it is. But it is also compatible with a genuine theological realism, that life is structured so because there are indeed such presences, such powers as gods. On an anti-realist perspective the Olympians cannot really be identified with the divinities of any other creed, unless the whole ceremonial and poetic system is brought into a one-to-one identity. When the Greeks detected Zeus in Ammon-Ra they could only have been misled by a superficial similarity of function: insofar as Egyptian life was structured differently, their gods were not the Greek gods, even though certain universals must perhaps be met by all. On the anti-realist view all that is 'true' of gods is what is there to be affirmed within the system that gives them life. The Greeks could not find out more about Zeus, although they might (as religious traditions merged) find that their new Zeus was not quite the old. A realist, on the other hand, may concede that there is some real thing on which Greeks and Egyptians have a different perspective, that they may find that one and the same being fulfils different roles in different ceremonial systems, that both sides may have things to tell the other. Such a mutual exchange will, inevitably, change the traditions, but it need not entirely merge them. The difficulty for a realistic Olympianism is that its gods, as I have emphasized, are 'pure': they do not have unrealized possibilities. In that sense, one who does not recognize Aphrodite in 'the huge tug of procreation', does not recognize Aphrodite at all, whereas a mortal individual need not be known under any particular description in order to be known. Similarly, one who does not recognize the God and Father of our Lord Jesus Christ as the presence of an indignant love, does not know that God. Gods are not the sorts of thing that can be known except in their own proper mode: to know a god is to know as a god. But it does not follow that these gods may not be real and independent presences, made known in subtly different ways in different ceremonials.

Religious structures function as explanatory hypotheses. What happens in the world, that is, is something to be explained as the effect of those powers that are mentioned in ceremonial and sacred texts. Birds court each other in the spring 'because' Aphrodite makes it so. Tribes go to war 'because' Ares falls on them and rides them to disaster. The sea rises to storm 'because' Poseidon Earth-shaker is angry. It is always possible to read these assertions not as offering a causal theory, but simply as expounding what occurs. The storm *is* Poseidon's anger; the obsessional desire of animals to mate *is* Aphrodite. They are not 'caused' by gods; they are gods, or the gods' outward clothing. Some ages, some nations, some individuals doubtless think no more. To complain of them that they are offering unfounded hypotheses, like one who explains large footprints in the snow by speaking of an unseen Wild Man of the Mountains, when there are other, easier hypotheses, is to mistake their point. That Poseidon moves in the sea-waves is a truth of the same kind as that Drake is sleeping down below: a fiction that is still significant, a way of laying claim upon the seas, of making them not just a useless or disastrous waste of waters, of awakening in ourselves a certain patriotic and historic sentiment which it is barbarism wholly to reject. 'That man is little to be envied, whose patriotism would not gain force upon the plain of Marathon, or whose piety would not grow warmer among the ruins of Iona' (Johnson (1924), p. 135). Being a decently cultivated human being requires that we fill our imagination with just such images, that we recognize what happens to us and around us as the sort of thing that does, as the play of a divinity.

This 'expressive' theory of religion stands opposed to the 'realist' theory, that gods and their like are theoretical entities that serve to explain phenomena (as elementary particles 'explain' phenomena in a modern physical theory). Even expressionists will agree that gods are manifested as it were from outside our own past selves. That is why they are *gods*, because they are not to be resisted by any strength of ours (though they can be coaxed, and can come to agreements beneath the hand of Zeus). Whether any given age is more expressionist than realist is a question that we cannot answer, for much of what either party says will be the same. Indeed, it is not clear that there is any clear distinction. Only if we have a clear conception of the difference between fact and fiction, how things are and how we imagine them to be, can we seriously ask ourselves whether the Olympians are to be considered 'fact' or 'fiction'. What is a fact, if it is not simply something to be relied upon? If we can rely upon the gods, and on Drake's drum, they are as much 'facts' as are the current price of oil, the harmlessness of flouridated water, or the benevolence of kings. Those who are convinced that the gods are a poetic fiction must found their case on a vision of things as we *should* believe them to be. They reject the beliefs and make-believe that constitute the humane universe of our historial communities in the name of that universe which is made manifest to those who will to see things 'objectively', without emotional involvement. They advocate, in fact, a new religion, a new cult, a god gone mad in a new way: the doom of the 'objective' eye that strips all human ceremonial, and wills to be only an abstraction, without loyalties or favourite views or even understanding of the gods. Those of us who still insist that there are other values than the scientistic, that science itself is only of value in the context of a humane civility, may reasonably retort that Apollo is become Apollyon, the Destroyer, if he steps outside the frame of Zeus. Greek legend was (here influenced by the unresolved antagonism between father and son in Greek society) that Apollo would one day attempt his father's overthrow. Insofar as the scientific eye is Apollo's, the detached, far-seeing, archer whose delight is mathematical elegance (and whose more compassionate son is Asklepios, god of medicine) that prophecy seems likely to be fulfilled. If it is, it is not obvious that Apollo could maintain due order among his opposites. If humane order and the sense of justice goes, is it so obvious that Ares and Aphrodite, Athena and Artemis and Dionysos, will allow Apollo his crown?

Further reading

Gordon (1981); James (1960); Miskotte (1967); Otto (1954); Te Velde (1967); Turville-Petre (1964).
Archaic Greek thought is discussed by Snell (1953), Dodds (1951), Bolton (1973). Recent work by psychologists and philosophers on the supposed unity of consciousness includes Jaynes (1976), King-Farlow (1978), Lifton (1970), Ogilvy (1977) and Parfit (1984).

Deren (1975) is a study of Haitian Voodoo which sheds light on the actual multiplicity of human consciousness: we are not such simple creatures as we think. Kelsey (1973, 1974) shows the extent to which the imagination can still be a good tool for the exploration of the divine realms.

Sole watchman of the flying stars, guard me
against my flicker of impulse lust: teach me
to see them as sisters & daughters. Sustain
my grand endeavour: husbandship & crafting.
Forsake me not when my wild hours come;
grant me sleep nightly, grace soften my dreams;
achieve in me patience till the thing be done,
a careful view of my achievement come.
Make me from time to time the gift of the shoulder.
When all hurt nerves whine shut away the whiskey.
Empty my heart toward Thee.
Let me pace without fear the common path of death.
Cross am I sometimes with my little daughter:
fill her eyes with tears. Forgive me, Lord.
   Unite my various soul,
     sole watchman of the wide and single stars.
(John Berryman, 'Sole watchman of the flying stars')

6

Sins, Wickedness and Psychosis

Morality and God's Command

The religious are usually understood to have an extra motive for doing those things which, morally or legally, they ought: namely, that they wish to please their gods, or avoid long-term consequences of a kind that non-religious persons have no particular reason to expect. It is sometimes supposed that there could be no other reasonable motive for 'moral' action: if God did not exist, everything would be permitted, and anyone who supposes that God does not exist must be a libertine. Secular moralists, on the other hand, are confident that decent people do not act from fear of the Lord (considered as a capricious despot), but from sympathy and rationally conceived duty. Religious persons, it is held, are dedicated to the service of their god, no matter what, but decently moral or law-abiding persons reserve the right to criticize and disobey even the Almighty. Whereas one view is that morality depends on religion, the other is that religion and morality are actually incompatible.

Philosophers usually discuss the relationship between 'morality' and 'religion' in the context of the question, 'Is God's prohibition (or command) what makes it wrong (or right) to perform a given act, or is the act wrong (right) independently of God's opinion?' It has usually been argued that God (or the gods) cannot be the ultimate source of morality. Either He has a good reason for prohibiting x (a reason which anyone, in principle, might recognize) or He has not. If He has, then *that* is why the act is wrong, not because He said it was wrong. If He has not, then there can be no morally good reason not to perform that act (it may, of course, be inadvisable to defy the Omnipotent).

Another argument: if 'being right' simply means 'being required by God' then it ceases to be possible significantly to claim that God requires or does what is right, and hence it follows that we cannot significantly call God 'good'.

Again: if believers dedicate themselves to following God's commands, no matter what, they are committing themselves, in principle, to do even the most immoral act if God requires it of them – to kill their only son, or commit genocide.

These arguments are actually extremely weak, and rest upon a very strange and even childish notion of what sort of being 'God' or 'the gods' may be supposed to be. Discussion usually begins from the assumption that religious belief posits an entity of peculiar powers and largely unknown purposes and that this entity inhabits the same universe as ourselves. Such a being might be admirable or not, and what it said could only be one more contribution to the debate between rational beings about what was the case, or what was best to do. If such a being could condemn us to Hell for not believing in it, or for disregarding its instructions when they ran counter to our best conclusions about what to do, we might decide that we had best obey, or that we would refuse to live upon such terms. Most of us would find the latter conduct more admirable, even if we did not date engage in it ourselves. From this point of view anyone who commits herself to a policy to blind obedience to such an entity has failed to understand what it is to be morally good, or has at least adopted a programme that most of us would think unreasonable. On the other hand, believing that something is *God* is just to take that thing as one's ultimate authority and object of worshipful devotion.

The argument is complicated further by lack of clarity about what it is to be morally good. There are, crudely, three main views. The first, a strict moral realism, insists that there is such a property as 'being morally good, or morally required', and that some acts, states of affairs or creatures have that property – not, of course, by logical necessity. There is no other property that logically requires the compresence of 'moral goodness' – not even 'being to the felt advantage of all those affected'. We may coherently deny that any particular act or state of affairs is good, even if we do so falsely. There are, that is, substantive moral truths which are independent of anyone's recognition of them. On this account even the divine Creator can only recognize such truths, and is not responsible, by saying that they are so, for their real truth. The trouble is that exactly the same problem can be posed for the non-theistic moral realist as for the theist: granted that moral truths are ones that *might* intelligibly be otherwise (they are not simply tautologies), a moral realist is committed to doing what really is morally right even if it is something she detests. If God *might* have required the sacrifice of one's first-born so might the Moral Law.

On the second view, being 'morally good' is simply being approved within the working system in which we live and choose. Or rather, it is being what would be approved if we were well-informed, prepared to argue rationally and not to make *ad hoc* exceptions in our own favour. For moral theorists of this stamp, the right thing is constituted as right by its being what we would, if rational, be prepared to require of everyone, including ourselves. Moral realists, on the other hand, would probably regard this merely as good evidence of what was right, but not as constituting its rightness.

The puzzling thing about the arguments against a 'divine command' theory of morality is that they are only rarely deployed by genuine moral realists. If 'moral goodness' is a genuinely distinct essence, then there is at least some room for the thesis that even God can only recognize it and not create it (though that needs to be argued). If it is not a real essence, but only the title that we give to what would be approved by genuinely unprejudiced, well-informed and rational judges, it is less easy to see how this should differ from being approved by the one being who certainly is these things: actually, the moralists' demand that we do what we can conceive to be done by just any moral agent in like circumstances is, historically, the descendant of the older view that we should seek to elevate our petty, everyday selves to the universal self, that we should be an agent or incarnation of the Lord. What is even odder is that some philosophers have argued against 'divine command' theory who are not themselves believers in any sort of objective morality, whether 'real' or 'constructivist': theirs is the *third* view – that to say that something is right or good is only to express approval of it, or to demand obedience to some implied principle. Why those who think this should object to others' giving their approval to the One God, and urging obedience to His law, I do not understand.

If moral judgement is nothing but the expression of personal preference, religious believers may quite reasonably express their devotion to their gods by saying that they are good, and such as to be obeyed. If those gods are real, any other preference would be very odd. How, believing that there are presences which cannot be avoided, could I mean anything by the bland declaration that I would defy them? If moral judgements are to be understood as the apparatus of rational preference, then to judge correctly is to judge as the One God, being omniscient, unprejudiced and rational, would judge. Whereas we can make a distinction between what we now judge correct and what we would judge correct if we were better judges, it is clearly impossible to make such a distinction in the case of the One God. What ignorance, what partiality, what self-deception could we coherently attribute to God? If there is such a God, then it would be wholly unreasonable to hang on to 'our' system of moral judgement rather than let it be corrected by divine judgement.

If moral realism is correct, and judgements of what is right are true (or false) in virtue of what is the case independently of our judgement, it seems possible to say that God Himself can only report on what is right, and not create it. But once again, it seems difficult to see why this should be so. If moral truths are facts, why should they not be facts ordained by God, such that if He had chosen He could have made things otherwise? This seems to run into the counter-intuitive conclusion that if God had decreed that all first-born males should be sacrificed it would have been right to do so – but what exactly is meant by that? For God to 'forbid' an action or 'require' it, it is necessary that the prohibition, or requirement, be made known to His creatures. The point is not that it would be 'unfair' of God not to tell us what He had prohibited, and (perhaps) intended to punish us for, but that a mere 'private intention' cannot constitute a prohibition. That God has prohibited some kinds of action requires that He has set some repugnance to the action in our hearts, or so directed natural events as to ensure that, more often than not, obvious disaster follows upon a breach of His law, or caused it to be written into sacred texts that He forbids the deed. The first two routes to knowledge of right and wrong are, essentially, the same as those employed by secular moralists. The third begins from the prior judgement that these are indeed sacred texts, to be read as if they had a single, transcendent author, but this third technique – for that very reason – does not operate independently of the first two. Texts that were wholly repugnant to us, and were not confirmed by general experience, would not be counted as sacred.

So how would God require that first-born males be sacrificed? Not simply by causing writers to set the requirement down in writing, even on stone tablets. Nor yet by setting in our hearts a profound unease when such a sacrifice was not made, though this unease might contribute to our sense of what He wanted. He would cause it to be the case that disaster followed often enough upon a failure, that the first-born died in any case, and the second-born also if the first had not been sacrificed. Evidence would accrue that the sacrificed 'stand upon God's right hand' in everlasting glory, as honoured links between the world of God and humankind. If all this were so, what could any moralist find to say against the act? That it required a desperate struggle with inborn desire to keep one's child safe, and that only the hard-hearted could perform the act? But many recognizably moral acts require us to struggle with ourselves, and many such can only *easily* be done by those whose characters we do not altogether approve. That is not enough to make such acts immoral. Or would the claim be that such acts contradicted the principle of equal respect for humanity in oneself and others? But why? By hypothesis, such sacrifice is the first-born male's route to glory, the particular task for which he is born. The Kantian principle surely does not require that everyone have exactly the same, destiny and duty, or that there always be some reason why just this individual is born to this position. Or is the thought that, although in the world I have described, there would indeed be reason – by God's providence – to think it right to sacrifice all first-born males, there could be no imaginably good reason for God to ordain such a world? This too seems both uncertain and doubtfully relevant. Uncertain, because God (let us suppose) issues all and only those commands obedience to which will create that character and way of looking at things which is necessary if His creatures are ever to be comfortable in His obvious presence. What is required for that (amongst other things) is a degree of humility and ready obedience that *might* be engendered by such deliberate and practical recognition that all one's children are God's gift, not property of ours. That there are other routes to that condition is shown by the fact that God does *not* require such sacrifice, though He may have insisted that we mark the birth of first-born in some ceremonial way.

But suppose that there were indeed no reason, apart from God's arbitrary will, for God to command this or that. Suppose God could, consistently with His nature, command just anything, and decree just any world. There would then be no reason to suppose that any commandments were promulgated to all God's creatures, nor could we hope to find out what His commandments were by asking what commandments could without contradiction be given to and obeyed by all creatures or all rational beings. To suppose this would be to suppose a God whose nature was not to be the highest rational ideal we can envisage, but something quite beyond all categories, quite unknown in Its own essence, and our only duty to submit to the historically promulgated requirements of that unfettered Will.

The effect of the Arian heresy was just this: the One *created* the Second Person of the Trinity, the Logos, the pattern to which our world and souls were to be attracted. The One might without incoherence have created some quite different pattern, according to which it would have been right not only to sacrifice one's first-born son, but to perform whatever 'ordinarily' depraved act It pleased, with whatever motive of contempt or hatred. As it happened, the Logos was the law of love, that we recognize our Maker's hand in all things, and love them as we do ourselves. But it might have been, or yet might be, that the One put out another Word, equally inescapable, as the one pattern to which we must approximate or else die eternally. The alternative view, dominant in mainstream Christianity until a failure of philosophical education in the last half-century, was that the Logos was not created, but 'begotten' and 'of one substance with the Father'. What was meant by this was that the

One could not ever have produced any other word but Love, that there could not ever have been another pattern to be our lode-star. That pattern, Christians believed, was embodied in the very human life and character of a Galilean holy man, but it was accessible to all, the very light that lights everyone.

A 'divine command moralist' holds that the central demand of morality is to obey the Lord: not simply to obey *God*, for that would be merely tautologous. Being God, after all, is simply being worshipful in the highest degree. Any moral axiom could be expressed in terms of taking something or other as one's god: the classical utilitarian, for example, could be described as one who takes the general happiness as god, as something that is to receive her absolute allegiance. By custom, however, we only describe that which demands such worship (or to which we give such worship) as God if it is, in some sense, itself a living entity or person. The claim then is not that we ought to obey whatever being has the requisite properties of wisdom and benevolence. If that were the claim (however plausible it is), it would constitute an impersonal rule, drawing its force not from the dictate of that divine being but from some rational truth not dependent on the divine. The dedicated believer for whom the Lord is God does not think that there is some reason independent of the Lord's will which makes it morally obligatory to obey such a one. Nor does the believer first identify the Lord and then conclude that the Lord requires us to do justice, and love mercy, and walk humbly with her God. The Lord is revealed, for the believer, precisely in those requirements. It is true of any supposed god, as I argued in my last chapter, that it is made known as a compelling presence – in the case of Judaism and Christianity, the presence of an indignant love. That such love is a guide to the character of the Creator is a thesis requiring careful exploration. What it implies first of all is that the divine command moralist's thesis, that the Lord's command is Law, has a misleading grammatical form. In just such a way, when Hindu visionaries identify Atman and Brahman, the Self and the Absolute, they do not mean that the ordinarily known self, the ego, is to be revered as that which lies behind all appearance. The intention is rather to identify as the real self, the heart of one's own continued being, that which is the heart of all things. The unknown self is identified through the known Absolute. Similarly, the Unknown God is identified through the known experience of indignant love.

So far, it could be argued that religious believer and secular moralist might be agreed about what is to be done, but that the believer also supposes that conscience, love, righteous indignation is the voice of the Creator. On this account believer and unbeliever might think it right to do just the same things, and the belief that these things are required by the Lord might be a belief that does no real work. If the believer lost her faith would she not still think it right to keep her promises, refrain from theft, murder and perjury, clothe the naked and feed the hungry? What is added by the belief that it is the Lord who requires these things? It adds to our knowledge of the Lord, no doubt, if we can believe that the deliverances of a properly educated conscience are His words, but does it add to our knowledge of what should be done?

The first reply is that there are some things that believers will think it right and proper to do that unbelievers will not: part of the life-project will be to prepare themselves for eternity, for 'a closer walk with God', by prayer and corporate worship and self-discipline. Ceasing to 'believe' they would, presumably, cease to pray, worship, fast. What 'believing' amounts to, of course, is itself a difficult matter: not all those who practice a religion are realists about their beliefs. Their religion is a matter of spiritual exercise and corporate ceremonial, their reason for engaging in it that it constitutes their particular cultural identity. Losing faith is a personal collapse of meaning, not a change of abstract opinion, even if religious belief does include a strictly cognitive element.

Because religion is a matter of personal and cultural life it cannot be restricted to a small 'religious' sector. Even if there is a cultural division between the 'religious' and 'secular' areas of life, that very fact constitutes a feature of the particular religious tradition that allows the split. Accordingly, the second reply is that believers and unbelievers must always mean different things by what they do. The point is not that believers go to church and unbelievers usually do not, and that a loss of faith would reduce the amount of churchgoing but leave the rest of life unchanged. It may be that the one who has lost her faith will still keep her promises or tithe her income or refrain from murderous rage: in that sense the 'same things' get done. But it does not follow that she is doing just the same things, because actions are individuated by the agent's intention. If an old woman is pushed to the floor on two occasions it does not follow that the same act is performed: on the first occasion, she is pushed down by a mugger, and the act is an assault; on the second, by a concerned friend to get her out of the line of fire, and the act is a life-saver. Murder is not done unless the agent intended to kill or seriously injure her victim. Correspondingly, one who tithes her income solely because she believes it right to share wealth out more equitably does not do entirely the same thing as one who tithes it as a token and reminder that all her wealth, all the world's wealth, is at the disposal of the divine. Losing that sense of religious duty changes the act, even if the outward results remain the same. Accordingly, the believer does not simply have an extra supposed reason for doing the very things that decent unbelievers do: she does different things, and her failures are correspondingly different. Believers sin, but unbelievers only err.

Before examining that distinction more carefully, a third reply to the thesis that religion is only morality with a disposable top-dressing should be outlined. Is it actually the case that religious rules can even be mapped into secular morality? It may seem that secular moralists do acknowledge the force, for example, of promise-keeping, in a way that mirrors the religious observance of an oath. It is certainly assumed that decent atheists can be expected to speak the truth in court without being literally on oath. Decent and high-minded atheists regularly insist that obedience to the moral law is something for which they need no extra religious motive, that true morality is even incompatible with acting in obedience to the Lord. But believers in an absolute, atheistical morality are perhaps rarer than they were. An atheistical life project may include a determination to live peaceably, consistently, temperately, and this project may be justified as likelier to lead to happiness than the alternatives, or as more consistent with the rational nature of humanity. But it is very unlikely that such a project will require, or be able to support, an absolute and undeviating obedience to any rule at all. It is only generally true that perjury, theft, murder, corruption, bring a net disadvantage to the agent and any group with which she identifies. There will always be occasions when, so far as we can see, such acts would be decidedly advantageous: death-bed promises, unpleasant misers, lustful teenagers may be ready temptations to one breach of moral law or another. A traditionally religious person may conceive that these rules are to be obeyed as being God's law, not merely as rules that usually bring a temporal advantage. The times when a breach of law seems likely to be advantageous are temptations in a religious context, and simple exceptions in an atheistical. The irreligious moralist may, of course, remind herself that her judgement is very likely to be adrift, that it only seems a good idea to break a general rule. But there will be occasions when, as far as temporal advantage goes, it really is, and the unbeliever, knowing this, is likely to be less securely armed against temptation even than the believers.

Whatever life-project an irreligious person establishes for herself, or accepts from others, can only be a make-shift, a way of getting through the day with as much delight, as little despair as possible. It will usually be obvious that one might have adopted a different one, or might adopt one yet. It will always be obvious that the general rules are only rules of thumb, to be followed (at best) until there is a strong temptation to do otherwise. Only the religious, who acknowledge an eternal significance in what they do, have much hope of holding to an absolute refusal of temptation – not that they necessarily do much better in practice. Believing that the voice of honest indignation is the voice of God, the Lord of Hosts, an agent has reason to think that fair-dealing will at last be vindicated. Believing that the laws of justice are only (excellent) devices for keeping the peace between quarrelsome humans, an agent must acknowledge that injustice will sometimes pay. A decent atheist has no good reason not to torture innocents if this is, humanly speaking, the only way to break the terrorist's will (the innocents are her young children) and discover where the atom bomb that will otherwise level London is. We can take it for granted that no-one brought up in a society influenced by religious tradition or even decent humanism would find it easy to torture the terrorist's children till she confessed. Only the conviction that it is the Lord that forbids such dealings could give us reason not to force ourselves to do the deed; that, or the conviction that such deeds live on in worlds beyond the present. The rules of *karma* may secure us against temptation, almost as well as the Lord's command: but in either case it is supposed that moral laws will in the end turn out to be the laws of nature, and not merely rational devices to secure a temporal advantage.

The religious may think more rules are absolute than do the irreligious, and acknowledge duties that the irreligious do not. Part of the confusion in twentieth-century moral theory is that respectable moralists are constantly groping for good reasons to adopt the rules and practices we have inherited from more religious ages. Filial duty, marital affection, patriotism, keeping one's word cannot really be deduced from rationally self-evident principle, or made to seem (in the abstract) more conducive to general 'happiness' (as if we knew what 'happiness' could be, abstracted from all the rules and practices it supposedly justifies). Such duties as these make sense as the require- ments on us of a supreme benevolence that would fit us for its service, or as the noble eightfold path to deliverance from all ordinary, temporal concerns. If there is no such supreme benevolence, no such deliverance, then these supposed duties can at best be culturally determined guidelines, of no force to guard or guide our souls. It is not surprising that so many practical politicians in the past have insisted that religion is necessary to preserve social harmony: in its absence people in the end do only what is right in their own eyes, only what they themselves imagine to be advantageous. A sword-age, an axe-age, before the world's ruin. Without religion, order is maintained by force, and that is itself an encouragement to others to try and impose their will by a similar use of force.

Purity and Pollution

In suggesting that religious belief makes an absolute rejection of injustice, whatever the apparent consequences, both reasonable and psychologically possible, I do not imply that all the religious would accept such absolutes. Obedience to God, or dedication to the spiritual way, may not be well expressed as absolute obedience to a set of prohibitions and injunctions. The Augustinian aphorism, 'Love God and do what you will', can be understood to mean that the believer should, in every situation, act out of a God-directed love: what she does may be generally describable as not telling lies, giving to those in need, and the like, but there will be occasions when love demands a lie, a theft, an uncommon act. Such 'situationist' ethics is, in practice, difficult to distinguish from a secular utilitarianism, the doctrine that one should so act as to maximise the 'happiness' of those affected by one's action and inaction. As such, it has all the usual problems of utilitarian morality, and conveys no distinctively religious meaning. But there is nonetheless a point to be made about the difference between 'God-directedness' and the rule-governed moral life.

What a secular morality advises against as moral error, religious doctrine treats as sin. Or rather the religions of the Book, and of the Vedas, do so: English-speaking Buddhists may use the same word, but 'sin' here means demerit, not a deliberate straying from the straight way that awakens the fountain of wrath against us. Religions of the Book and the Vedas typically treat the penalties of sin as the response of a 'personal' god; religions of the basket typically treat them as effects of 'impersonal' law. The distinction is not, perhaps, as clear as commentators suppose, and I shall have occasion later to dwell on what the difference between the personal and impersonal might be. All sides agree, at any rate, that it is a little death to stray, and that mere obedience to external laws is no guarantee that one has not strayed, technical disobedience no final proof that one has.

Sin, guilt, pollution are ideas that draw their strength from recognizably religious contexts, even if they survive into a secular society. The notion of 'clean hands and a pure heart' is one to which the most secular of moralists can respond. But the description originally refers to one who is fit to stand in the holy place (Psalm 24:3 f), one in whom the Lord has created a pure heart, and to whom He has given a new and steadfast spirit (Psalm 51:10) that she may stand in the Lord's presence. Pollution, uncleanness sets one apart from the Lord's presence, and it may be incurred by acts and accidents that secular moralists would not always recognize as involving moral error. As the religions of the Book developed, their doctors came to distinguish between the 'moral' and 'ceremonial' law, and came to set aside those elements of the tradition that seem to imply the existence of objective liability. Sophisticated moralists would deny that any blame attaches to one who did, in ignorance or by accident, something that it would be wrong to do deliberately (unless she were herself culpably responsible for being ignorant, or being in a case where accidents occur). No moral blame attaches: but religious pollution may. One may inadvertently be polluted, be rendered unfit for the holy place, and have to undergo a cleansing if one is to stand there again. Oedipus did not mean to kill his father and marry his mother, but he is a bearer of pollution even so. Sophocles causes the aged Oedipus to argue that he wasn't 'really' polluted because it was not his fault, but this is clearly a revolutionary doctrine, not a truism. What we now distinguish as ritual or ceremonial uncleanliness, as if it were a pretended pollution, is the original context within which 'moral uncleanliness' takes shape.

So what is pollution? What is holy? In an earlier chapter I characterized the sacred, aphoristically, as the awe-inspiringly useless, and profanation as the attempt to use that sacred for lesser ends, and on terms not dictated by the sacred. The holy is not quite the sacred, nor is pollution quite the same as profanation, though it may be doubted whether the average English-speaker makes much distinction. The words, at any rate, are available for use. Ritual purity and ritual pollution are linked opposites in a way that the sacred and the profane are not. The sacred is what may not be used, except on its own terms, and it would make sense to say that everything was sacred, even if it were very difficult to act on that assumption. The ritually pure is what has shaken off or will not endure the presence of pollution: the 'awful purity' which older hymns attribute to the divine has to be understood in opposition to the unclean. If everything were 'clean' there would be no filth from which we might be cleansed. Conversely, there is nothing finally objectionable about the profane. Though everything could be sacred, religious tradition usually allows the existence of some things that are profane. The existence of pollution or uncleanness, on the other hand, is an offence to purity: it could not be that everything was pure, but nothing *should* be impure (or impurity should be cast off into nothingness). Finally, whereas the sacred has no special link with what we know as moral goodness, the holy or pure has, at least in Western tradition, such a link. A supposed 'holy man' who was demonstrably a thief, liar, pimp and multiple murderer could only be a fraud – though his followers might find fault with the supposed demonstration.

The quality of holiness, as it is embodied in ritual and moral purity, is such as to exclude pollution. If the unclean approaches, the clean departs, but is not destroyed. An individual may cease to be holy, but the holy itself cannot be touched. The temple may fall, but the Lord that is above the temple cannot fail. To appreciate some individual as holy is to be made aware of something that only rests upon or in that individual or place, something that will depart when ritual or moral impurity damages its vessel. The quality of that presence is outlined for us by our sense of what it will not abide, what it will seek to burn up or abandon. In early Hebrew tradition it was blood and semen and discoloured skin that rendered individuals unclean, unfit to endure the presence of the Holy One of Israel. Later developments, while not denying that these were unclean, insisted that the Holy One became a flame and pestilence in the presence of all wickedness and injustice. False witnesses and money-grubbers and idolators were the unclean who must be purified by fire, cast out from the holy congregation or purged of their sin. The sinners whom Jesus consorted with were not so much people who had made 'moral errors' as people who felt themselves outcast from Israel, people who had incurred pollution by associating with the Gentile rulers, eating the unclean or failing to do their ceremonial duty. His promise, which was also that of the whole prophetic tradition, was that the doors were not yet shut, that the sinner could leave her sinning and be reunited with the Holy One (Derrett (1973)). Pollution, in short, is not always conceived to be absolute or ineradicable: the same system of belief and practice that labels someone as unclean also establishes the way in which the pollution may be washed away. Similarly in Hellenic lore: it is not that Orestes has done what, in the abstract, he 'ought not', but that he has incurred an appalling pollution which may spread to all those who grant him hospitality. Where a modern secular moralist might seek to persuade Orestes that his special, accidental tie with Clytemnestra ought not, rationally speaking, to count against his duty to restore legitimate government and punish a murderess (or else, of course, that he ought not to have let his equally accidental tie with Agamemnon lead him into private vendetta), Aeschylus sees that Orestes must be really cleansed, that the force of the pollution must be recognized, and civil ways of reattaching its victims to the holy congregation. Even in South-East Asia, governed by popular Buddhist tradition, where sin is no longer experienced in terms of angry divinities, but as a weight upon the soul's rebirth, there is a similar pattern of possible restoration, a similar sense that pollution does not have to be only a matter of deliberate intent to break 'the moral law'. Sin is the departure from the right way, the creation of barriers between the self and the holy, particularly as that is embodied in the congregation.

Looking outward from Western tradition, we encounter the Hindu: here pollution is pushed outward to the untouchables, and each caste identifies itself as more or less pure than another (Dumont (1972)). Untouchables bear the burden of association with human excrement, slaughtered cows and the like: others may purge their impurity, but the permanently casteless cannot. They are the sink of India's pollution. In this context Mahatma Gandhi's obsession with enemas, defecation and properly constructed latrines makes both practical and symbolic sense. By striving to make it a personal and social duty to keep oneself and one's surroundings clean, turning excrement into usable manure, Gandhi hoped to bring the untouchables into the holy congregation. True pollution was hatred, lust and hopelessness – as Jesus and Gautama had tried to make their people see. 'Wicked thoughts, murder, adultery, fornication, theft, perjury, slander – these all proceed from the heart: and these are the things that defile a man; but to eat without first washing his hands, that cannot defile him' (Matthew 15:19 f.).

Inescapable pollution, the kind that causes its victim to be seen, even by her own self, as dirt, has – regrettably – become an established part of Hindu tradition. But Westerners should not hold themselves entirely guiltless. Notions of purity and pollution are easily developed into social forms that require a visible, indisputable vehicle of pollution. Other members of society can then define their own freedom from pollution by keeping their distance from those perceived as filthy, and (correspondingly) immoral. British society has analogies with Hindu society, though we do not have as rigidly schematized a system. Few members of the professional or monied classes can ever conceive that they might be expected to do those jobs which we conceive to be filthy. Jobs or lifestyles that confict with the proper duty of class-conscious householders, or that have characteristically been done by migrant or minority groups, are relatively polluting. It is one of the usual ironies that, for example, the Rom (commonly called 'Gypsies') and the settled British regard each other as ceremonially unclean. Immigrants of distinguishable racial and cultural stocks are regularly perceived as bearers of ceremonial pollution, carriers of ritual meaning – though this perception is usually rationalized in merely 'hygienic' or 'economic' terms. The realization that the Rom regard 'us' as intolerably dirty (for using the same bowls to wash our dishes and our bodies, or allowing cats and dogs within our homes) is a salutory reminder that much of what passes for rational hygiene is really a concern for ritual purity, for the life of the congregation.

'Immorality', so conceived, is often sexual, at least in traditional British society. To be 'immoral', in ordinary language, is to have formed an illicit sexual union, or to have engaged in 'self-pollution'. Such language is now frowned on by both secular and religious moralists, as implying that sexuality itself is somehow defiling. Whatever moral wrong is done in fornication or adultery must be understood as some form of injustice, a matter of having wronged one's partner, spouse or child (present or resultant). Doubtless this is the proper attitude. But it is worth, briefly, considering what strength there might be in the older view. Crucially, of course, sexual immorality was, for males, a matter of 'defiling oneself with women': to do so was to be ritually impure, to have desecrated the temple of the Holy Spirit. Married couples might, for the sake of procreation, bear the pollution, and aim at last to live 'as brother and sister'. The unmarried, or the wilfully sterile, had no such excuse. Being holy was a matter of being pure, of not letting one's substance flow out into sexual activity. This might be rationalized as a recognition that sexual activity is a tiring distraction from other and perhaps more important (male) activities. It does also, fairly clearly, embody a characteristic male nervousness about too close an association with women.

This syndrome was not, as popular writers sometimes imply, the invention of St Paul, or of the Christian Church. It could with some plausibility be argued that Paul himself wrote against those extremists who thought it better 'not to touch a woman', and that Christian tradition, in approving virginity for women as well as for men, made the first steps towards recognizing females as children of God in their own right, as something more than vessels of pollution to be saved by child-bearing. But there is some truth in the view that popular Christian tradition has often suggested that it is chiefly by sexual irregularity that we are rendered impure, that the only real occasion to excommunicate someone is that he or she has committed 'an immorality'. Few, if any, serious theologians would ever openly have agreed that masturbation, fornication, adultery or sodomy were worse sins than murder, theft, usury or false witness, but it is usually the sexual sins that are taken to render a man unfit for priesthood or other high office in the church, or to be a cause for scandal should the sinner(s) seek to take communion. Anyone who writes to a church newspaper to suggest that it may not be entirely wicked to live together 'without benefit of clergy' can still be sure of a vitriolic response – though it is significant that the argument offered will usually be in terms of the supposed miseries that pre-marital sex occasions, and not (as once it was) in terms of the pollution incident on all sexual activity.

Quite why sexual morality, so called, has come to loom so large in popular Christian religiosity is a puzzle. Some of the blame may rest on St Augustine's identification of the root of sin with 'concupiscence', and that with lust: lustfulness is perhaps the best-known form of that desire to have more which conflicts so strongly with the virtues needed for a sociable and peaceful life. Part of the explanation doubtless lies in the simultaneous growth of 'family life' as one of the central themes of that religious tradition (a topic to which I shall return) but it may also be founded on a realization of the 'idolatrous' potential of sexuality. 'Holiness' is a certain single-mindedness and dedication to that life which is not confined within the circles of this world: sexual desire is one of the most obvious distractions, and one that seems to bind its victims more closely to ephemeral pleasure. Aphrodite was feared, and mocked, in Olympian tradition for similar cause, that she summoned people from their places in the Zeus-defended social order. That religious tradition's view of holiness was not so strongly directed toward 'eternal life', and Aphrodite correspondingly honoured as well as feared. Where the pious expect their holy life to continue into eternity, everything that is conceived to be 'of this life' is perceived as polluting, as barnacles upon a smoothly running ship. Fences are then set about the law to guard, as believers suppose, themselves against the chance of slipping. Such regulations, at best, are guards; at worst, occasions of sin. The motive of the religious quest for purity is not to obey these regulations, not to maintain social conventions nor maximize happiness, but to embody the holy life, the life demanded by the God of their devotion. Its price, all too often, has been a lack of regard for lesser values, and a projection onto others of the filth it fears.

Devotion and Atonement

If holiness is a sort of single-mindedness, and sin is all that leads us from the one straight way, the general goal of religion is *moksa*, deliverance from evil, from all the things that 'get in the way'. The first notion of *moksa* is probably obtained in a social, ceremonial context. Pollution and impurity are the things that make it impossible, or illegal, to join in the ceremonies of our tribe, to experience a sense of community as that is embodied in ritual. Those rituals serve partly to protect and partly to constitute the way of life which is required of us in a cosmic context. Pollution prevents our participation in a cosmic project, and purification joins us to the holy congregation once again.

Because religious ritual does purport to be more than the embodiment of human togetherness, power politics or aestheticism, it is always possible for believers to conclude that the very rituals which have hitherto defined purity and pollution have themselves become obstacles to the cosmic project. "New moons and sabbaths and assemblies, sacred seasons and ceremonies I cannot endure. I cannot tolerate your new moons and your festivals; they have become a burden to me, and I can put up with them no longer" (Isaiah 1:3 f.). When this happens, the very thing which existing rituals define as impure becomes the vehicle of a new covenant: just so, Gandhi tried to make the task of clearing up human excrement a sacrament, and Buddhist commentators fiercely locate the Buddha nature in ever 'lowlier' and more ritually impure exemplars. The historical dialectic that creates rituals to define purity and pollution, and then transcends those rituals to find a higher purity in the very thing that was defined as dirt, constantly reverses the values of 'cleanliness' and 'dirtiness'. So in our own, partly secular, tradition the usual conjunction of 'holiness' and dirt was cancelled by the aphorism that 'Cleanliness is next to godliness', which has in its turn gone so far toward idealizing the ritual antisepticism of the world of white-coated doctors, plastic-wrapped meat, and vaginal deodorants as to elicit a youthful rebellion in favour of 'naturalness', a largely romantic effort to be at one with the usual processes of nature. In all these changes something, whether it is dung or plastic, is defined as pollution, and those in search of holiness must dissociate themselves from the ritually impure. The hygienic or economic rationalizations of their chosen way do not altogether conceal the 'religious' motive, the wish to be part of, to be animated by a wider life than 'one's own', to be 'all right'.

Hindu tradition, very usefully, has distinguished three characteristic paths to being 'all right': the ways of knowledge, works and devotion – the three ways of chapter 4. 'Works' constitute the duties of one's station, both 'ritual' and 'social'. By doing what is laid down one may at last be so assimilated to the action as to be conscious of no spot or stain. But this path, however appropriate to diviner ages, is neither wholly practicable nor wholly desirable in this age, the Kali Yuga, when there is no agreed or honourable social system and it is not clear even what one's 'station' really is. When a modern Arjuna doubts if he should wage war, it would no longer be enough to say simply (as Krishna does in the *Bhagavat-Gita*) that it is his job, as a *kshatriya*, to fight in defence of the established order, at whatever cost. Not that Krishna's argument is wholly irrelevant to the modern soldier or statesman, but that we are inevitably more conscious that the established order may not have all right on its side, that it can be no-one's duty to do 'the duties of her station' without asking whether it is really God's will that she should occupy that station.

In the Kali Yuga, the way of knowledge is also not entirely appropriate. In this age we can rarely do more than preserve the ancient bodies of religious knowledge, and not advance them or set them on any mere secure theoretical footing. We do not have the equipment or the technique to uncover the real nature of the divine, and must content ourselves with rote-learning of the sacred texts. The ways of work and knowledge being effectively closed to us, the way of devotion constitutes the principal route to liberation. By devotion to the god of our individual vocation we may be released from all impurity into the perfect single-mindedness of the divine. Hindu tradition is more open than some others in allowing that people are not temperamentally equipped to worship the same god, or to worship the divine under one guise only. Vishnu, Shiva and Kali (in their various forms) are the chief cult-objects for Vedic religions; assorted Buddhas, each at the beginning of a devotional genealogy from master to disciple, play a similar role in the religions of the baskets; those whose religious traditions are of the Book are usually less willing to concede that the One God may be known in many, seemingly incompatible guises, and that religious devotees may rightly and honourably pray to apparently distinct divinities, but even they do in practice revere different saints and images and may sometimes acknowledge that there are as many theophanies as there are worshippers.

Whatever the eventual solution of the quarrel between dogmatic monism and pluralism, we can at least concede that one very common way of acting on the impulse to holiness is through devotion to an intensely imagined deity, conceived as the founder of an historical community, as the source of purification, as the one by whose merits our wounds are to be healed. Sometimes the devotee experiences the presence of her god at a crucial moment in her religious development; sometimes she knows the god only through the texts and rituals of her community, but hopes one day to 'know as she is known'. One of the things that devotees have in common is that they conceive of their purification (whether instantaneously or gradually realised) as consequent upon their god's action, not their own. It is through the grace of Kali, or the good outpourings of the Buddhas, or the grace of our Lord Jesus Christ, that the devotee finds a new life, cleansed of past pollution, and given the strength to rejoice in future danger.

It is the Christian variant that has, amongst religions of the Book, made most play with the notion of redemption by faith. Personal devotion to the intensely imagined Christ has even, in some sects, taken the place of sacramental participation in the church's yearly round or God-fearing struggle against social evil as the one permitted medium of salvation. Even those Christians who would deny that a 'direct, personal relationship with Christ' was necessary to redemption, usually retain at least the conviction that they ought to believe that Jesus Christ, his death and resurrection are central to the possibility of living a life 'pleasing to God'. Studies of 'atonement theory' record a variety of models that have served to encapsulate the doctrine, or excite the religious imagination. Christ's crucifixion was a conquest of the powers, leading them captive in his triumphal procession. It was the payment of a debt owed by all humanity to the Lord of Justice and Mercy. It was a sharing in the worst that sin could do to its helpless victims. It was a propitiatory sacrifice to turn away divine wrath. It was a last-ditch attempt by the One God to show His adulterous beloved how much she was loved. Theologians usually conclude by refusing to rule any of these models out of court, and reasserting that, they know not how, Christ's crucifixion somehow put God and humanity on a new footing. Atheistical critics generally have no difficulty in so describing the supposed event as to make it unbelievable, or immoral, or both. Are we to suppose that a loving Creator is moved to show mercy that He would otherwise not show, by the spectacle of innocent, voluntarily undertaken agony? Or that God is divided against Himself? Or that the devil is deprived of his rightful prey by a cosmic conjuring trick?

Modernist theologians usually prefer some version of the 'subjectivist' solution. The crucifixion did not alter the 'objective' relationship between the Lord and the human soul: the Lord is always ready to forgive, and to give new life to the penitent. Rather it alters the 'subjective' relationship, how *we* see things. Our minds and perceptions are turned around when 'we survey the wondrous Cross': if that is what scholarship and patriotism and sound statesmanship did, we can no longer think them quite as godly as we did; if that is what human beings can go through, with their wills untarnished, we can no longer quite so readily excuse ourselves for not obeying our vocation; if God's Anointed can be mocked, and scourged and hung upon a tree, 'abused by all men, scorned by the people' (Psalm 22.6), then God's image is not to be seen only (or at all) in the prosperous and contented rulers. More traditional theologians may instead hark back to the theories of pollution that I have already sketched: by becoming a curse, accepting the utmost of pollution, Jesus Christ purged the ancient curse, and made true the Psalmist's dictum 'darkness is no darkness for Thee, and night is as luminous as day' (Psalm 139.12). The Christ is found even in Hell (1 Peter 3.19), just as the figure of the Buddha can be seen in all six worlds of Buddhist cosmology, amongst ghosts and hells and demons as well as animals and gods and people. The Lord demands that impurity be cast off, that iniquity be fiercely rejected, but chooses to bear the chief part of that symbolic rejection Himself, so that His creation may be brought into a new and deeper association with His Spirit.

The theological intricacies of this debate are not my present concern – except to remark that all these models are of value, in religion, only insofar as they excite a lively devotion, and not as reporting upon things simply as they are. What is of importance is that, although Christian theologians often talk in legalistic or moralistic ways of 'the atonement', the essence of the doctrine is a denial of the merely moral. It is in the more ancient and widespread notions of pollution, purity and new life that vicarious atonement makes sense. In morality no-one is to be blamed or punished who is not personally responsible for a crime, and no amount of vicarious suffering can remove another's guilt, or appease an honest judge. Innocents may pay another's fine, but they cannot bear another's guilt or punishment. Pollution, on the other hand, is only partly deserved, and may be removed by another's action. What matters in religion, one might exaggeratedly conclude, is not the moral wrongs that have been committed for which someone must bear the blame, but the state of the wrongdoers' souls. In believing that the god was ready to share our lives, bear our infirmities, we can grasp that we are not excluded from the divine. In believing that the holy congregation is such as we would wish to give our unquestioning allegiance, we must also believe that we could not easily be members of it: 'I wouldn't want to join a club that would have me as a member'. The spectacle of an archetypical member of that congregation, the epitome of holiness, Himself associating with outcasts and enduring apparently final abandonment, casts a new light on the pride which keeps us from realizing that 'the Lord is greater than our hearts, and knows all things' (1 John 3:20).

Imagining the figure of a god who hurries to share our manifold impurities, and welcomes all those who turn from their wickedness, is a way of restoring to oneself the conviction that one is not excluded and cast off forever. We do not need to make ourselves clean before we approach: the approach itself is enough to establish us within the kingdom. The thief need only call upon Kuan Yin; the desperate invoke the name of Amida Buddha; the prodigal return apologetically to her Father. All those who carry that image of the loving god in their hearts are essentially pure.

Selfhood and the God Within

In speaking so carefully of 'imagination', 'image' and 'imagined deity' I do not imply that the truths of religion are merely psychological, that Christ or Krishna or Kuan Yin only exists as the mental image of His or Her devotee. The relationship between 'reality' and 'imagination' is a more complex one than naive realism supposes. Whatever the ontological status of a devotee's god, it is clear that the devotee must 'use her imagination' in conceiving that god, though it may sometimes be more accurate to say that imagination uses the devotee: the god's presence is not exactly something that she summons, but something that imposes itself on her. That truth of experience may reflect a metaphysical truth, that the god is real, and has real effects. It may not simply be the believer's belief in her god that changes her life: it may be the god that does so. But the question whether the god is 'real' or merely 'ideal' is one that merits later clarification and discussion; what concerns me here is the god as phenomenological reality, Krishna as His devotees encounter Him through the religious imagination.

What concerns me especially is the relationship between 'self' and 'god'. Any gathering of concerned Christians that touches upon the 'other religions' is certain to throw up the indignant assertion that Hindus have no proper grasp of the 'otherness' of God, that their mystical tradition suffers from the megalomaniac conviction that the Human Soul is identical with God, that everyone (on Hindu terms) is the same as everyone else. A similar gathering of concerned Hindus probably conceives that Christians treat God as one object amongst many, that they identify only one man with God, that they insist on preserving their own ephemeral personalities to eternity. Both sides, in almost perfect ignorance of other traditions, probably conclude by complimenting themselves that theirs is at once the most spiritual, and the most materialistic of the great religions. Christians think Hindus and Buddhists are either crude idolaters or cowardly escapists; Hindus think that Christians are egomaniacs. Both sides are usually very unwilling to be educated, though they may be prepared to be tolerant of each other's supposed errors. But what matters more than tolerance is understanding. 'Being tolerated' is about as insulting as being publicly forgiven for what one has not done.

What is going on when Paul declares his conviction that 'the life (he) now lives is not (his) life, but the life which Christ lives in (him)' (Galatians 2:20)? What is going on when the Upanisadic writers speak of *moksa*, liberation, as the discovery of the divine Self in all things? What, for that matter, is going on in cases of spirit possession, and why are these not interpreted as discoveries of the devotee's true self? These are not metaphysical questions, but phenomenological ones, attempts to understand what people mean by what they say, attempts to enter their experience in imagination, and to try and understand our own. It is imaginably true that, for example, such visionary and mystical literature 'really' stems from the difficulties occasioned by having a brain composed of two hemispheres, each capable at a pinch of serving to control the body. It is imaginable (more or less) that early records of gods' speech to mortals are relics of a time when information processed in the right hemisphere was conveyed to the left hemisphere only in hypnagogic visions and mysterious voices. It is also imaginable that certain religion crises, 'outpourings of the Spirit' or 'prophetic visions' are similarly dependent on right-left brain interaction. Such a discovery would not settle the metaphysical question, whether these cerebral events were or were not mirrors of metaphysical reality, but it might assist with the solution. It would be entirely beside the phenomenological point. What concerns me here is not what physical or other processes might be supposed to produce these experiences, or these dicta, but what the experiences are, what the dicta really mean. Even if it were true that, say, baptism in the Holy Spirit was accompanied or even caused by a temporary surge in right-brain activity, that is not how the devotee experiences it, not what she imagines in the event. What, phenomenologically, occurs?

There are modes of purification which raise no special question of identity: the believer is polluted, undergoes the correct ritual and is pure again. A religious crisis occurs when no ordinary ritual can wash deep enough to change the underlying sources of pollution: we may wash the outside, but cannot wash the inside. When this becomes evident, when 'the whole heart of man is evil from the beginning' we need a new self, a new life, not just the old refurbished. At the same time it is not enough simply that one creature cease to be, and a newly created creature take up its proper task. Maybe it would be better for the world at large if this occurred, if I were instantaneously replaced by 'someone else', with access to my memories but free of the impurities that make it impossible for me to live a devout and holy life. It is not unimaginable that it would be better for me if I ceased to exist, but it would surely be better still if the new creature were in some sense really I (or if I could conceive that it were). But what is it to be 'me', and what am I requiring that the 'new creature' be? If we have no clear or coherent answer to that question, can we be so sure that we understand what is at issue when one believer denies that the self can achieve eternal life, and another asserts that it can? When Gautama refused to say whether 'the soul' was mortal or immortal was he not wise, in view of the difficulties attendant upon saying what it is for a soul to be, or not to be, at all?

The psychological and social fact is that people do convert, some people several times. In moving into a new life which they perceive to be radically discontinous with the old, a new ego-ideal is posited. Part of what it is to be 'one and the same' is the ego-ideal, the comprehensive image of what one would wish to believe oneself to be. It is in terms of that ego-ideal that individuals act, and the moment when it is revealed as foolish, flawed, wicked or otherwise tarnished may be the beginning of despair, or of a new beginning. Paul's ideal had been the up-and-coming Pharisee, the colonial boy made good: when that ego-ideal was shattered he was set instead to embody the new ideal, the resurrected Lord. For the single-minded, such an ideal is not simply a pattern that they strive to realize; it is a present reality that acts through their bodies, to which they give their acquiescence. Christ survived in His apostles because those apostles so internalized His words and deeds that henceforward they lived by a new ego-ideal. In living for that ideal, from that responsive presence, they escape from past pollution.

The panic that most of us feel when we contemplate the possibility of such single-mindedness, as well as the obvious fact that I have had to distinguish Paul himself from both his earlier and later ego-ideals, serves as a reminder that ego-ideals are not all that count for questions of identity. Is there some other sense in which Paul might claim that it was Christ that lived in him? What is it to believe, contrariwise, that what lives in me is not what lives in any 'other', is wholly and exclusively Me? The teaching of recent moralists, working outside the religious tradition, has tended to emphasize the radical irreducibility of My choices, that I am an individual beholden to no-one, maker of the laws of My own being, a world in Myself. Some have gone so far as to suggest that a belief in 'objective moral law' is a surrender of personal autonomy, that the Ego is and must be the sole rule of any life. Not all moralists of this stamp are ready to admit that what they are praising is the kind of person whom older or more ordinary moralists would describe as a psychopathic criminal. Not all are ready to draw the extreme anarchist conclusion, that the Ego must always act for Its own and never bow to any other will. Some have sought to evade the more outrageous consequences of egoism by following Kant's thesis that the Ego should, or can consistently, make only those laws for itself that it can conceive to be made, and followed, by all 'other' Egos. This move harks back to an older tradition, to the doctrine that what is to have the upper hand in this 'my' life is something present in all, not just in Me. I am my own Lawmaker only in the Pickwickian sense that the laws that govern (or strive to govern) me are those through which there is an understanding of my being as a rational agent. On this view my being is not a being separate and individual, but universal reason.

Despite these gestures toward an older rationalism, recent moral philosophy has been strongly egoistic, in theory if not in straight-forwardly criminal practice. What is odd about this is that the dominance of egoism has coincided with the rise of a naturalistic theory of humanity and the world that leaves little room for the existence of genuine individuals. The piece of living matter, the vehicle of the all-conquering gene, that is commonly identified with 'a human being' turns out, from an 'objective' point of view, to be an arbitrarily selected segment of biochemical process. The sheerly subjective being that has been taken in the past to be the 'real' self, associated with but not identical to the physical segment, has been disregarded or explained away. Even in the social sciences, which must take more account of subjectivity, the notion of 'individual egos' has been unfashionable: what people say and do and think is understood as a function of the whole social nexus that issues in particular utterances and acts. What popular thought considers 'I' turns out to be a function of the whole physical and social universe. Egoism, correspondingly, is not well grounded in a metaphysical truism (that there are many real selves), but is instead a particular social doctrine, a way in which the social universe organizes itself.

It is not a metaphysical truism that there are individual selves identical with the persons recognized in ordinary social life, such that those selves are the ultimate and irreducible subjects of ethical obligation and error. When it is decided that it shall be individual persons only who are answerable for 'their' faults, that no-one should suffer for 'another's' fault, this is not a simple deduction from a recognizable fact. The 'fact' of individual selfhood is constituted in that ethical decision. We can, accordingly, let ourselves consider what other policies might be, what other subjects or selves we might comprehend. The tradition of the baskets has had, as one of its central themes, that there simply is no such thing as an individual self. What there is is the causal chain of emotion and circumstance, the consequences of desire and wrong opinion. Individual persons now suffer the karmic consequences of acts performed and ideas entertained by 'other' persons, who have the same sort of relationship with those present events as do past moments of the present-day individuals. The child is father to the man: but some long-ago individual was father and mother to the child. By this account, when we say 'I' we might be referring to the whole chain of consequences that issues in the present, and will stretch on for ever unless some way is found of cancelling the cycle of disappointed hopes and indignant rage. Realizing that there is no substantial self identical with any bodily person or ghostly revenant is, perhaps, one way of achieving *moksa*, the end of all desire.

It is not a way that has had a friendly reception among Book-religious, who regularly declare that Buddhism is nihilistic, pessimistic and unaware of the real substantial existence of individual selves. But the tradition of the Book is at least as ambiguous in its treatment of personal selfhood. Whereas ethical individualists take it for granted that no-one may be justly punished for 'another's' error, and that other persons are indeed other ethical subjects, religious tradition is not so clear. Whereas in Adam all die, so in Christ all are made alive. The individual Abrahamic believer does not, or should not, conceive herself to be a separate substance, answerable to no-one but herself, accountable for nothing but the acts performed during 'her' body's lifetime, or her conscious adulthood. She is a member of the mystical Israel, identifies with her people's sufferings, answers for the right upbringing of children, accepts obligations not of 'her own' making. If the individual self is constituted in the ethical decision to prosecute and punish only those physical beings that have been consciously associated with wrong-doing – rather than (as most human societies have done) taking vengeance indiscriminately on family, children and associates – we can conceive that 'the people' or 'the mystical Israel' or 'humankind' is constituted in the ethical decision to abide the natural and moral consequences of bygone action. 'Original sin' is the weight of guilt that all 'individual' members of the human race must carry, simply as moments or elements of that on-going subject. On this account, the subject that was 'dead in trespasses and sin' was not the man Paul, the identifiable physical organism born in Tarsus and executed in Rome, but humankind, or even the whole created universe, that found one of its voices in that particular figure. Redemption, correspondingly, is the formation or revelation of a new organism, casting off its matrix in discovering itself as 'the new Jerusalem'. The Old Adam was dead: or rather, since its limbs and members continued to proliferate, each new believer was cut off from Adam, and grafted into the vine of the spiritual Israel. As believers, we share in the life that was from the beginning and was manifested in the man Jesus – on condition that, and insofar as, we (or our mortal desires and frailties) are 'crucified with Christ'.

Neither Buddhists, Hindus nor Abrahamists need deny that there are identifiable persons, who are born, mature and die. What none of them need assert is that these persons are real irreducible subjects, or 'selves'. When such persons speak, reflexively, of themselves or of their selves the speech is about the real subjects of the moral or religious quest, and these subjects may not be simply identical with the bodily persons concerned. That the Self is identical with Brahman, the true ultimate, or that the Self is the spiritual substance that reincarnates as 'boy and girl and bush and bird and a dumb fish in the sea', or that the Self is Christ, constitute alternatives to ethical individualism that may all, in their moment, be correct. On this account 'Christ' does not simply name the man Paul's ego-ideal, but rather the historical organism with which Paul identifies, in which he found a new life.

Sin, correspondingly, has as its general form the insistence on having one's own way which is equivalent to being 'a limb of Satan'. Those who refuse to understand themselves, the physical presences who are named in social registers, as parts of those wider wholes, commonwealth and church and God's creation, are expressions of a perennial revolt. In striving to be 'wholes' they only mouth the words of the Lie. Repentance is a matter of acknowledging one's place; redemption is being recreated as a member of that whole which may outlast all others. Religious piety consists in that lively sense of being one of the 'whole company of heaven', and impiety is pretending to a selfhood independent of that whole.

Religion as Psychosis?

Is there a third possible account of Paul's conviction, or the conviction of those who experience Brahman as their Self, or who (at a lower level of religious sophistication, or of lunacy) believe themselves to be Napoleon? Any of us may see a point of contact between our lives and situations and what we believe of some notable's life and situation. We may see ourselves as following in that one's footsteps, or as acting out a pattern heroically manifest in that one's life. Most philosophers strive to be Socratic, and do not mean merely that they want to be socratic: 'being Socratic' contains an implicit reference to the historical role-model, Socrates, who devoted himself to waking his fellow-citizens up from their dogmatic slumbers, and submitted to execution rather than betray his vocation. Similarly, any of us may recognize a metaphorical truth in the notion of death, decay, destitution as a description of acute depression. These metaphors and images do not exhaust reality for us, but for psychotics they do: psychotics 'seriously believe' that, for example, they are dead, or have been turned to stone, or simply are Napoleon, not merely that, in certain respects, they are *as if* dead, calcified, or Napoleon. Should we not consider whether the metaphorical image of being 'dead in trespasses and sin', or of being, in some respects, in a situation like that of Jesus, may not issue, in a suitably disturbed mind, in the conviction of being 'literally' dead, reborn, and animated by Christ's 'literal' Spirit?

 On this account 'non-psychotic religion' is an ordinarily neurotic expression of the realities of depression, exaltation, hero-worship. It becomes psychotic when the metaphors and imaginative symbols define an unordinary, logically incoherent 'reality' that shuts the believer out of any 'ordinary' living, prevents her understanding that it is in 'ordinary', person-to-person life that real possibilities exist. Ordinary (which is not to say trival) depression builds into a conviction of having 'really' committed 'the sin against the Holy Spirit' that is unforgiveable. An ordinarily reconstructed life, in which one has 'forgiven oneself' for past failures, issues in hero-worship of the new role-model (by which one will in turn be found wanting). Much of religion is the record of manic-depressive illness, and its main merit (that it does, in part, provide a usable framework, for such cycles) is perilously close to its main fault (that it gets in the way of genuine resolutions of the problem). On this account a sense of sin is neurotic guilt; a sense of new life mediated by an imagined deity something very like delusion, 'harmless' or otherwise.

This problem is simply one version of the general puzzle about religion and irreligion, lent a particular force by the phenomena of clinical depression. In this latter the victim may 'literally' perceive poison covering her hands and fear lest others be polluted by her touch; she may hear voices, and feel herself divided into two or more selves. Other abnormal conditions also reflect religious language to an alarming degree: 'multiple personality' cases, where two or more apparent selves inhabit the same body, sometimes in ignorance of each other, may seem to provide 'literal' examples of the religious belief that one's life is being lived by another, that one is not what one was. The sense of being an observer while some other personality acts is familiar enough, as well as the desperate internal cry 'what on earth am I doing?'. In openly psychotic cases this sense of alienation from one's public acts, or sense of not having lived up to some one of our ego-ideals, is manifested in multiple personality, or disassociations, or hallucinatory slime that can be washed off only with blood, or religious crisis.

The banal response to this is simply to agree that religion is sometimes psychotic, but that there is or may be a 'rational religiosity' that is indistinguishable from common secular decency (whatever that may be). As I have said before, what James called 'the religion of healthy-mindedness' was not in fact always as banal as he suggests: most of its advocates were aware of the horrors of depression, and sought a way out of them by mind-control and the techniques of meditative prayer. But some of the versions of common-sensical 'sanity' do ignore the depths too readily: 'depths', not because depression is a particularly profound or illuminating spiritual condition, but because the victim is, subjectively, in the pit. It does no good to tell the victim that she is 'mistaken', that her hands are not literally contaminated, that there are no literal voices. She may retain enough ordinary sense to know, or tell herself, that this is so, but the hallucinatory pressure to 'mistake' metaphors for reality remains as strong, and the metaphors do in any case express a real truth.

An older religious tradition, less concerned to assimilate itself to secular psychiatry, would have no difficulty in understanding these conditions. The victim of paranoia, depression, multiple personality is the victim of demons, and religion is the way out of the pit. Mythologically, to escape these demons we need the assistance of some stronger power that can open the way, bind the demons, heal the affliction. It is not enough for just anyone to try and bind or exorcise the demons: only those really endowed with power should even risk the attempt. It is indeed evidence, of a kind, for the literal and not merely metaphorical truth of demon-language that attempts at exorcism may go disastrously wrong. The demon affects not only its first victim – in which it operates as a psychosis – but also others involved in the story, and even (it is occasionally alleged) inanimate material in the vicinity. Secular psychiatrists who take such stories seriously have to speak of 'contagious' psychosis, psychokinesis and the like. It might be easier to agree that there are demons, spiritual presences who force their worlds on unwary mortals. The relationship between religious doctrines of sin, pollution, hell and redemption, and psychotic utterances is likely to be complex. The victim of psychosis, for example, is likely to have learnt a religious language in which she will express her sufferings, and do so differently if she is part of a different tradition. But the religious language, nonetheless, is used because it is recognizably appropriate, and seems to stem from just such experiences as the victim now endures. Atheists may, not unreasonably, conclude that religion is a mental illness more or less contained by ritual and imagination. Non-atheists may at least consider whether mental illness is not, after all, a real war, and religion, in its various and sometimes demon-ridden forms, a realistic response to the spiritual situation.

On this account, when Gautama broke past the demons of illusion, rage and greed, he did not merely 'conquer' his own tendencies but inflicted a genuine defeat upon spiritual forces really identical with those that prowl around and about our souls. That is why it does some good to call on the Buddhas: not merely that it gives us an inspiring role-model that may give us the courage to live through depression and temptation, but that the demons recollect their past defeat and the Buddhas lend their promised protection. The plausibility of this story depends both on the actual success of appeals to Amida Buddha (which might be explained merely psychologically), and on the possibility of giving a coherent account of such a spiritual universe. Whether it is believed or not depends also (and, maybe, chiefly) on whether our actual social and historical setting lets us find it a story by which we might live. It is not surprising that ages and nations which have an interest in believing that reality is manipulable by purely mechanical means are disinclined to recognize the force of the older vision. Both materialist and spiritualist can acknowledge that there are close ties between religion and psychosis: it does not follow that religious piety is a psychotic or neurotic compensation for felt inadequacy. That same charge, after all, could as easily be levelled at materialism.

Further reading

Derrett (1973); Dodds (1951); Dumont (1972).

Gandhi's concern with latrines is discussed by Mehta (1977). On 'Divine Command Morality' see Helm's useful collection (Helm 1981), and Gustafson (1982). I have myself attacked one very common argument against taking God's Word as Law in *Philosophical Quarterly*, 32, 1982. Secular moral philosophy is at present dominated by the clash between utilitarian theory (which takes acts to be right insofar as they promote, or are likely to promote, the general happiness) and various 'intuitionistic' theories, which deny that there is any one overriding reason for thinking any class of acts right or wrong: the secular equivalent of polytheism. Few secular moralists any longer feel the sacred awe that afflicted Kant when he considered the moral law – which is hardly surprising in a world perceived as godless. What is surprising is that secular moralists imagine that they still believe what god-fearing moralists do, that no-one ever meant more by morality than a quaint device for keeping the peace between contending egos. See Berger (1970), Macintyre (1981), Mitchell (1980). On the relation of religion and psychosis see Clark (1984), Drury (1973), Laing (1960), Wisdom (1953), Zaehner (1974).

7

Causality and Creation

The Argument from Design

Religious traditions, in addition to their social or psychiatric role, purport to offer a realistic explanation of how things in general are as they are. Not all religious believers are much concerned with this, and there is good reason to doubt whether it lies at the centre of the religious lives even of those who lay stress on religion's explanatory powers. It is for this reason that I have chosen to approach religion from within the complex of ritual and personal devotion, and not (as some philosophers have done) as if such things as 'the argument from design' could usefully be considered in the abstract. Another obvious reason for not beginning a philosophical study of religion by talking of the so-called 'Five Ways' (Aquinas's five arguments for the existence of God) is that not all religious traditions even include a reference to (let alone an argument for) such a Deity. Buddhist religious may agree that there is a being of vast powers, and more vast conceit, who was the first to fall into the realm of time-bound individuals, and absurdly believed himself the real maker of all later arrivals. But what keeps things going is not the action of an omnipresent subject, but the forces of greed, rage and ignorance. The Unborn and Indestructible is not well thought of as a single being, even one endowed with all imaginable perfections. Olympianism, from another religious angle, did not identify Zeus as the Ultimate Explanation: the order that Zeus sanctions is born of Chaos and Unfolding Time. Even the Abrahamic religions, which have been normative for Western philosophers, and which have always included creation myths, addressing the Lord as 'Maker of all things, visible and invisible', do not argue for 'God's existence' on the basis of information available to non-believers. They recognize His handiwork in the heavens, because they already recognize Him. It may even be that those who first said that their God was the Creator did not mean to offer a causal explanation of the world, but rather to insist that the presence known to them in cult and private prayer was bound to win His contests: the claim was about the future, not the past.

But although religion is not primarily concerned with explanations for the way things are, and may sometimes be deliberately scathing about those who seek such explanations (which is the real moral of stories about the earth's resting on a tortoise which rests on an elephant which rests . . .), it would be odd if religious tradition had no explanation to offer. Some believers try to formalize their recognition of divine handiwork by constructing arguments from design, and critics of religion regularly concentrate their attention on the adequacy of those arguments. Any introduction to the philosophy of religion must take account of this dialectic. Before trying to do so, I must re-emphasize that the arguments cannot be properly understood in the abstract, away from religious prayer and practice. We are not dealing with a maverick hypothesis, that the Tungulka meteor was a crashing space-ship manned by extraterrestrial explorers of whom nothing else has ever been heard. The spiritual beings who may be supposed to be the explanation of how things are have been encountered in ordinary life and ritual. The One Indestructible which is the unimaginable Beginning in Buddhist tradition is not an arbitrary postulate, but the Buddha-nature itself (not a thing, of course, strictly to be encountered or experienced as if it were a finite object). That the Lord is the Creator is a conclusion, not a definition. It is not just any imaginable Creator or Spiritual Cause that religious cosmology hypothesizes: instead it welcomes the discovery that the whole world can be explained by the same presence that is known in prayer and ritual and sacred text. In (supposedly) proving 'God's existence' from the existence of design, what I prove (if anything) is Her activity.

Despite all this, there can be no doubt that most ordinary Abrahamists are unnerved by claims to 'explain' the universe without recourse to divine creativity, and all ordinary believers (of whatever stamp) may sometimes feel that the only way to insist upon or to establish a realistic interpretation of their creeds is to emphasize their explanatory function. Real gods may be genuine explanations: merely ideal gods are only 'as-if' explanations, and sometimes hardly that. Believing in real gods seems to be rationally dependent on believing that they would be possible, reasonable or the best explanations of what happens. Is this last a reasonable belief?

What is being done when we 'explain'? What is to count as a good 'explanation'? What sort of 'explanation' would divine creation be? Or (for that matter) a spiritual fall that constitutes the world of temporal individuals? What is the relationship between 'global' and 'local' explanation, and which lies at the centre of the religious enterprise?

David Hume, in his magnificent 'Dialogues concerning Natural Religion' (1976), plausibly observed that unsophisticated believers use the gods to explain exceptional events, odd entities: more sophisticated writers insist that the gods are to explain the whole system of nature, that there is nothing especially god-given about bizarre events, that everything (properly understood) is a 'miracle'. This shift from local to global explanation goes hand in hand with a reduced appeal to 'miracles' as evidence for religious doctrine, and with a more universal conception of the divine. There have been critics who have suspected that these shifts have slowly emptied the gods hypothesis of serious content, that 'God as Universal Creator' differs hardly at all from 'Natural Law', except that we still retain old images appropriate to local godlings who keep the wells fresh, or panic the horses. This suspicion is confirmed when theologians increasingly deny that the universal creator can ever 'really' be understood as anything much like an ordinary person.

One response to these problems has been to withdraw the offer strictly to explain the universe. John Wisdom's classic story, 'Gods', tells how two travellers reach a part of the forest that shows some inconclusive 'signs of cultivation' (Wisdom (1953)). One insists that the plants are growing simply as they will; the other, that there is a Gardener, perhaps with slightly different horticultural tastes, invisible, uncatchable and quiet. Sometimes leaves are found disturbed from what might be theoretically expected: one traveller concludes that that is how those leaves grow; the other that the gardener's passage has displaced them. No test of the alternative hypotheses is mutually acceptable, but it is hard not to conclude, in the end, that the gardener is 'no explanation' at all, that she does not differ from a sheerly ideal gardener. What is at issue between the travellers is a mere 'attitude', that has no real explanatory significance. Some theologians, persuaded by this sort of reasoning, have retreated from the global claims of their predecessors. Religion is not concerned to explain the universe, but to enable us to cope with it, whatever it is. Extremists have abandoned all metaphysical pretensions, concluding that religion can never been more than a set of devices for structuring our personal and social lives, in the interval between darkness and the dark.

Wisdom's garden differs from the world we inhabit. Of the garden the travellers can at least agree that there are some plants which are not usually found to grow or flourish in uncultivated spots. One concludes that this spot is cultivated, though no other marks of the gardener's presence (no footprints, discarded tools, or horticultural labels) can be found. The other concludes that plants like that do, after all, grow and flourish in the wild. But when we consider the world as a whole we can no longer find out what would be the case: we have no access to a range of universes, some of which are divinely managed, and some are not, and so have no information on what things would be like if they 'grew by themselves'. Accordingly, we do not even have the beginnings of an argument, as the travellers do, for inferring the existence of a divine providence. If there is such a providential factor, nothing 'grows by itself'; if there is not, everything does. In either case, we cannot learn how to distinguish between what does and does not 'grow by itself'.

The so-called 'argument from design', indeed, can be expressed in such a way as to reveal a contradiction in its premises. Typically, we are asked to accept (i) that signs of goal-directed order (e.g. the inner working of a watch) only occur as a result of creative intelligence (i.e. a watch-maker), and (ii) that signs of goal-directed order (e.g. the inner workings of the vascular system, or the fitness of the cosmic environment for life) occur in the absence of detectable, finite intelligence. From this it is concluded that there is a non-finite creative intelligence at work. But the two premises are in danger of contradicting each other: if we have reason in experience to believe the second premise, we have reason to disbelieve the first. Apparently goal-directed order does occur in the apparent absence of creative intelligence. We might as well argue (i) that smoke occurs only where there is fire, (ii) that some smoke occurs without detectable fire, and therefore (iii) that there is an undetectable sort of fire in those latter cases. The best that we might manage along this line is that there is something *like* fire, in some indefinable way, in the apparently fireless cases, like fire in producing smoke and in some other respect which is the real causative property. Similarly, as Hume argued, we might conclude that there is something remotely and indefinitely *like* creative intelligence at work in the world – but it need not be so like as to deserve that title. The metaphorical extension of concepts learned in one area is sometimes a useful tool, but it can also be a barrier to understanding.

One possible reply to this Humean attack is that our ground for believing the first premise, that goal-directedness requires creative intelligence, is not that we have only experienced goal-directedness in the detectable presence of such providential action (in that case we could not accept the second premise), but that we can see, by reason, that no other account of goal-directedness will do. Things could not be expected to work towards distinct goals unless some governing intelligence required them to: the future event, the successful achievement, cannot itself act upon the past processes except insofar as it is represented in the foreseeing intellect. My getting home early tonight only explains my leaving the office early, or my travelling by car, insofar as it is an 'intentional' object, the object of my desire and forethought:

this is so both because the event has not yet occurred (and 'backward causation' is impossible) and because it may never occur (there may be a traffic-jam and I reach home late). But this too must fail. Even as stated, it only proposes a dilemma, that there is either a directing intelligence at work, or a mere appearance of goal-directedness. A good many biologists have sought to abandon explanation in terms of 'final causes' precisely because they thought it committed them to belief in just such an infinite providence. The apparent existence of goal-directedness does not require us to believe in such a god, even if real goal-directedness did. However, even the dilemma is a false one: Aristotle's belief that 'teleological explanation' of natural phenomena is appropriate did not commit him to belief in a creator-spirit. He distinguished 'four causes', four ways of explaining a thing. 'Why is there a statue there?' may get several answers: 'to fill a niche' (final cause); 'because the marble has the obviously artificial shape of a deer' (formal cause); 'because Pheidias took a chisel to the stone' (efficient cause); 'because marble doesn't melt at room temperatures' (material cause). The 'function' of an organ is what it is 'for', and we need to know what it is for if we are to identify it correctly. A heart, for example, is a blood-pump, and defectiveness as a pump marks it as relatively diseased or damaged. It is because most hearts, or at any rate our ancestors' hearts, functioned adequately that there are such hearts now. Accordingly, their pumping blood is at once the 'final cause' of their structure, and part of the efficient cause of there being such organs. Aristotle was also, not unreasonably, prepared to extend this functional analysis to whole organisms: the 'function' and final cause of, say, antelope structure is the characteristic form of antelope life, and identifying an organism depends on our recognition of the form of life that its structure more or less effectively serves. Even when Aristotle so far extended the analysis as to provide a final cause for the whole universe, and concluded that it was because an approximation to the self-sustaining life of God was maintained over time that there was such a universe at all, he did not do so to claim that the universe was designed or created or providentially guarded.

In brief, we can retain our allegiance to functional or teleological explanation without supposing that this establishes the existence of a creator-spirit, and the argument from the pervasiveness of 'goal-directedness' in the world of nature does not establish that it was consciously designed. It may simply be that this is the sort of universe that does naturally exist, as being the one that most effectively sustains itself. Other, non-self-sustaining universes may, as it were, have emerged by the million from the happy nothing, but been lost too soon for consciousness. Our world is the least self-sustaining universe that can sustain conscious life: it is hardly surprising that 'we' look out on a world fit for us, looking as if it were designed for the production of conscious life. This has been dignified in recent years as 'the anthropic principle': the universe is as it is because we are in it. There are indefinitely many other 'possible' universes, which do not allow for the emergence of conscious life. We do not need to suppose – though of course we may – that this universe was designed with us in mind. The 'anthropic principle' only explains the fitness of the universe we perceive on the assumption that there are or have been indefinitely many other 'attempts'. If this were the one and only attempt, it would indeed be slightly startling, in a way that is difficult to formalize, that it should have been quite so 'successful', but we might still, legitimately, shrug our shoulders and decline to suppose that even this suggested any real design. As far as we can see, things do not *need* to be as they are, but we may here simply have reached the limit of explanation. Maybe there simply is no 'ultimate' explanation, nothing that gives any reason to expect the universe to exist, or to be (in the sense that it is) functionally analysable.

If there is an explanation, we can agree that the hypothesis of a creator-spirit is not an entirely bad one. But the evidence does not require us to make that hypothesis, and it is not altogether easy to see what other consequences can be drawn from the hypothesis, so that it might be checked or used to predict. If the universe is designed with a view to producing or housing conscious beings, we might reasonably expect that there would be more examples of sentient existence than the terrestrial. If it is not designed, but merely 'as chance would have it', we have (perhaps) less reason to expect that life and consciousness are anything but a once-in-a-cosmic-aeon fluke. The discovery of non-terrestrial life of a kind with which we could communicate would be confirmatory evidence of a kind. But the inference is fairly weak: maybe the creator-spirit has other plans as well, and is content with merely terrestrial life and consciousness. Maybe there is some natural factor which we do not know that makes the emergence of self-replicating molecules more likely than it seems to us (maybe, for example, the universe is full of life-spores from the true once-in-an-aeon beginning).

One further argument in this area deserves some mention. Our very notion of causality derives, it can be argued, from our experience of volition. The only true causes known to us are our own wills. The events we merely perceive do not strictly cause anything: it is only that they are found together in regular ways. Striking a match does not *cause* the match to light, though it is an occasion when we may expect the match to light. It does not *cause*, because there is no necessary intelligible connection between the one event and the other – as George Berkeley argued before Hume, and theistic 'occasionalists' in Islam (who held that it was God alone who brought it about that fire follows the striking of a match) even before Berkeley. Accordingly, if we hold by the thesis that there is a genuine cause of events, that cause must be a creative spirit or will capable of upholding and enforcing the whole system of phenomenal ideas. God's relation to the cosmos is like our relation to the ideas of our imagination, and we as finite spirits move within the confines of the arch-magician's art. The plausibility of this view rests upon the prior plausibility of Berkeley's analysis of causation and phenomenal being. As an analysis of our experience it raises philo-sophical problems too large to consider here: what it chiefly produces in this context is an important distinction between two modes of 'understanding' phenomena. Where the currently popular modes of 'explanation' rest upon the model of 'mechanical causation', the Berkelian approach treats the phenomena as a 'text', a communication in the divinely ordained language of phenomena (Berkeley (1948)).

The inadequacies of formal cosmological or teleological argument for the existence of a creator-spirit have persuaded many commentators that the religious doctrine of creation should not be interpreted as a large-scale explanatory theory of the kind familiar to us in science. Pretending to 'explain' the universe by referring to the purpose of a creator-spirit may sometimes be an appealing policy, but it has no clearly demonstrable superiority over other policies: pretending to 'explain' things, for example, by referring to unknown, necessary, natural laws that turn out to be both self-explanatory and with enough content to dictate the emergence of just the universe we have, or (alternatively) abandoning all attempts at cosmic explanation. The phenomena do not require us to prefer the theistic to the naturalistic hypothesis, nor even to seek such ultimate explanations at all. If we have good reasons for accepting a doctrine of creation they are not simply or exclusively or chiefly 'scientific' reasons. Some commentators have gone further, and dismissed all thought that religious doctrine might help to explain the phenomena: 'the purposes of God' are moral or spiritual postulates, and of no use to explain why Israel rose and fell, or the universe was formed. There is some force in this thesis, and it may occasionally be worth emphasizing that 'God' emphatically does not name just any cosmic engineer of the kind that Hume's Cleanthes – the spokesman for a rational deism contrasted with Philo's scepticism and Demea's traditional theism – seems content to worship (Hume (1976)). But it must be doubted that 'ordinary believers' will be entirely happy to abandon all explanatory claims. Even those religious who make no mention of personal creation, depict the phenomena of our present existence as something arising out of a more 'real' and 'eternal' world which is not felt to be merely an expression of moral commitment on the part of believers. Religion may not be adopted because it is, in the abstract, a 'better' explanation than any other: it does not follow that it incorporates no distinctive explanatory theses.

Sectarians and Deists

If we suppose that the universe is indeed to be explained as a project of the infinite and unconditioned will, we have still not quite achieved a genuinely religious doctrine. Suppose that there was indeed a plan, but that the world as it is now is simply a forgotten (or disregarded) relic, left to chug its way to destruction. Whatever the First Will desired of its creation, it has long since achieved, or abandoned the attempt. What now is, was planned only in the sense that the Creator did not trouble to prevent it, and is now a matter of complete indifference to the First Will. This imaginable doctrine does not even allow, as certain religious traditions have done, that it might be possible to escape from an unsatisfactory universe, to meet the God beyond the Sky, who will not assist us, but will not ignore us if we climb up to Its level. The hypothesis I am exploring allows no such release. That the universe exists, and contains some traces of goal-directedness, is explained by its origin in a creative spirit, but that spirit is not our friend, not an object of worship for any but the self-alienated. As an explanatory hypothesis it may be preferable both to the hypothesis of infinitely many universes, and to the sheer rejection of explanation: as a religious doctrine it is unlikely to achieve much popularity.

Even as an 'explanation', of course, it is somewhat lacking. Things as they are simply do what comes 'naturally': they act of themselves and as chance would have it, even though the initial impetus, the bare fact of being, stems from a creative decision. Once the Creator is pushed that far back, It differs little from no Creator at all, and must be left out of account when we seek a rational account of the universe. The strength of theism, as an explanatory hypothesis and a religious doctrine, comes from the sense that everything has a part to play in a cosmic plan. 'God is working His purpose out as year succeeds to year'. This thesis too may come to seem ridiculous or superstitious: most of us are disconcerted by, even faintly contemptuous of, those sectarians who see the hand of God in every shift and turn of their personal lives. There is a strong emotional pressure, in us as in the ancient pagans, to think that God, the true Creator, must be above the minor details. It would be paranoid self-conceit to think that it is any part of God's plan that my shoe-lace should break, or the roof leak, or the land be swept by hurricanes, or the people perish. If we follow that path to the end, we shall be back with the indifferent Creator, which is indistinguishable in practice from the Indifferent Void. If we retreat from that irreligious conclusion, and let ourselves suppose that God's plan does include us, we may end up with the sectarians.

One reason why it might be unwise to allow Providence too much of a hand in the chances of this mortal life, and correspondingly wise to restrict Its operation to the realm of general law, is the puzzle created by the existence of evil, of events that no morally conscientious being could be supposed to approve or bring about. That problem I shall reserve for a later chapter. What concerns me here are the two opposed characters, 'deist' and 'sectarian', and what their respective emotions may show us about religion. It is necessary to add, given the powerful impulse in all of us to seek a compromise solution, that I do not mean to prejudge the issue in favour, as it were, of a Broad Church Anglicanism, that God is concerned with middle-sized issues, but not with every detail of our lives. It may be that the right way forward is to take account of both impulses, but we should not equate that synthesis with a murky and unprincipled compromise – unprincipled because there is no way of defining just why the Creator should be concerned with nothing below a certain 'size', with the problems of racism in the inner cities, but not with an individual's inability to make jam properly. How, in the light of eternity, can one problem loom 'larger', so as to catch the Creator's wandering attention, than another?

Deism is the explanatory element of religion in its most emaciated form. Things exist because there was a divine volition towards an unknown purpose, but nothing we encounter in the world now serves any particular divine end. If we give our worship to that imagined Creator, wholly indifferent to us and to our purposes as it is, we implicitly devalue all our present purposes, all other purposes we might ever have. 'Worshipping' such a one involves no service, not even service of a diabolical kind, but mere admiration of indifference, mere disloyalty to all our ordinary lives. It is an extreme form of that self abnegation, self-alienation that secular commentators see in all religion, a surrender of humanity before the Void. In practice, of course, deists do not worship their inactive Creator, but abandon 'religion' in favour of secular humanism or the like. They do sometimes retain the rhetoric of worship, or else attempt the 'God's eye view' of things: to see things as they 'are' is to see things without emotional effect or sympathy, as a 'lazy Creator' might. Such 'indifferentism' is not always couched in religious rhetoric, but it is nonetheless a recognizable 'religion', a way of relating human individuals to the cosmic whole, of validating one particular emotional perspective as that from which all things sprang, by which all things are judged.

At the other, and perhaps more traditionally religious, extreme, sectarian enthusiasm detects a divine meaning in the most seemingly trivial event. So far from ordaining merely general laws, the Creator manages every detail: 'general laws', indeed, are not even the instruments of the Creator, but only the record of Its consistent purposes. The sun will not rise tomorrow 'because it always does', and falling objects will not fall as they do 'because of the law of gravity'. These laws, or general descriptions of what has happened in the past and may be expected to happen in the future, are merely records of what God usually does, 'God's habits'. Not a sparrow falls to the ground without our heavenly Father knowing it: nothing is too trivial for God's attention, and nothing could occur at all without God's providential will. In brief, the Creator did not establish a universe of natural forces and then absent Itself, but rather acts continually. Every separate motion, event or change, is God's, and would not happen 'of itself' without God's care. The conviction that this is so does not rest on experimental evidence: it is not the observation that a distinguishable event, God's active help, accompanies all other events, all other conjunctions. We are in no position to make any such observation. It must rest instead on the theoretical conviction that 'true causation' is not to be found in the mere conjunction of events, and on the experience of feeling the phenomena to be the speech, the product of 'something far more deeply interfused'.

When we feel the universe to be 'created', our conviction is not well expressed by the doctrine that some other thing preceded the present universe, and is 'causally responsible' for it in just the same way as a human craftsman is responsible for a toy train. The point is rather that the events and conjunctions we experience seem to us like the fragments of a gigantic play, in which each event is an expression of the playwright's purpose – a play, moreover, which the author has not left entirely to others to enact. The universe has to be read as a fragmentary text, not explained as an artefact. Similarly, when a particular event (a stroke of lightning, say) is 'explained' as a bolt from the hand of Zeus, what is being discussed is not the mere 'natural event' (the event as described by a secularist) but the humanly significant, 'socialized' event. Zeus' stupendous intention is read in the downfall of the lofty. The sort of understanding that 'religion' offers is not of the 'scientific' kind: scientific 'explanation' subsuming particular events under more general laws, is no more than the grammar of creation. 'Really to understand' a text we need more than a list of its grammatical regularities and favourite expressions – the sort of list that computers can provide: we need to be able to enter the intention of the author as that is embodied in the text. The proof that we have read the text correctly does not rest upon our ability to find extra-textual evidence of the author's intention. Even with works of human art we cannot find such extra-textual evidence, but only other texts that need their own interpreter. An interpretation is to be preferred if less of the text is merely accidental on that interpretation, if it fits well with provisional interpretations of similar texts, if it can structure our own experience to good effect.

Human authors, obviously, make mistakes, ignore striking possibilities and fail to produce the ideal text that can, without fudging, be read according to decent hermeneutical canons. It is sometimes a waste of time to try and see particular meaning in the choice of one word rather than another, in a failure to resolve apparent contradiction, in a confusion of loose ends and entangled stories. In the ideal text nothing is superfluous; everything is taken up into a discoverable meaning whose perception alters the reader's perceptions of her own extra-textual experience. Everything, as it were, becomes a further episode in the story. 'Sacred' texts are just those texts that have struck generations as very nearly ideal. But the one genuinely ideal text, which we read only in fragments, is the speech of the divine spirit, the phenomenal universe. If we can once envisage that spirit, everything will be for us Its play.

If we understand the 'createdness' of things on this analogy, we can see that there is never likely to be any contradiction between 'scientific' and 'religious' understanding. Science, on this account, seeks only regularities and the cosmic grammar: religion seeks to read the text, guided by the conviction that nothing will in the end be merely accidental, that the world is not merely episodic (one damn thing after another), that we can, a little, see things as the universal speaker does. It is probable that science itself owes much to this conviction, that it could hardly have got started amongst a people who did not expect to be able to read God's play, or thought that most things were accidental, and beneath God's notice (see Jaki (1974)). On the other hand, science practises the self-denying ordinance that it is concerned only with generalities, with repeatable experiments and not unique events. 'Religion', dangerously, attempts to grasp particularities. Scientific inquiry cannot tell, does not even wish to tell, why this individual in particular has been struck by lightning: it can only say that electrical discharges between the sky and earth travel the path of least resistance. It does not see a general 'religious' truth in this, as that 'God loves to strike down the over-weening', nor can it say anything more about why this lightning strike killed just this man.

Two features of the contrast deserve particular attention. Firstly, the tendency of 'religion' to seek 'moralistic' explanations. Secondly, its concern with individuals. These features are not peculiar to ordinarily theistic religious traditions. Some traditions blame disaster on the spite of witches, or on ceremonial impurities that have left the way open to demonic incursion. Those traditions that conceive the spiritual causes of the universe as gods, or as God, see disaster as the fountain of wrath raised up against the evil-doer. Naively: anyone who suffers must have deserved it. Less naive traditions are less confident in claiming to understand the purposes of the Almighty. Thornton Wilder, in *The Bridge of San Luis Rey*, depicts a priest who seeks to understand the purposes of God in the collapse of a bridge, and persuades himself that the victims merited God's judgement more than others who escaped (in heretical contradiction of Jesus' words about the tower of Siloam: Luke 13:4). Wilder, less naively, tells the story of those victims' travel to the bridge so that the whole is 'religiously significant' without being anything as simple-minded as a judgement upon singular wickedness. There is, in the fiction, a completeness, a fruition about the individual lives that fits well with the religious hope that each life, each episode is significant.

Wilder's book is, of course, a fiction. Its religious merit is that it gives a fleeting sense of what the divine viewpoint might be like. To understand the universe as a text, or a fragmentary text, is to enter a little into the viewpoint and intention of its author. To be convinced of God is to perceive as God perceives: not the 'God's eye view' of cosmic aeons, in which individuals fall into insigificance, but the more divine outlook, for which nothing is accidental, no individual lost. Where this view differs from the typical sectarians', eager to see God in the downfall of an enemy or the success of a business venture, is that it does not contain God's purposes in ours. It is one thing to imagine that we see our secret purposes and desires at large in the world, 'to see a god on every wind & a blessing on every blast; to hear sounds of love in the thunderstorm that destroys our enemies' house; to rejoice in the blight that covers his field, and the sickness that cuts off his children, while our olive and vine sing and laugh round our door, and our children bring fruits and flowers' (William Blake, *Vala*, Night the Second, 410–13). It is quite another to believe that the cosmic play embodies a life founded in a divine purpose that we may at last appreciate, once we have learned to see things as the author does.

Predestinarianism and *Anatta*

That the phenomenal universe is a communication, a meaningful text, to be understood in the context of its complete unfolding, is a general statement that most religious traditions can accept, incorporate and qualify. To believe that this world is a play, whose grammar is discoverable by science, and whose meaning only by devotion, is compatible with many different views of the play, its genre or its value. Does it have a beginning, a middle and an end? Does it have a single climax, or a central plot? May we, as actors, interpolate fresh lines? What is the general relationship between divine action and the acts of finite beings? The notion of the universe as a text or intentional action is formed on the analogy of our own acts and utterances, and our own known causality. But since 'the universe' includes all the events that are our acts and utterances it seems that they are only elements in the divine act – in which case our own sense of agency is illusory. God, as it were, gives His creatures the mistaken sense that they are real causes, but all their doings are really His: they are hardly even observers, since observation as we ordinarily conceive it requires voluntary attention.

Notoriously, such an extreme doctrine, even if it is true, cannot be the creed we live by. We cannot conceive it to be the case that everything has its single source in the Spirit at the same time that we assess the apparent acts of others and determine on our own. The moral injunction, 'Do the best you can', dissolves into the inane instruction 'Do what you are going to do', and thence into the void. But though there are grave difficulties in taking any form of determinism as a practical creed, it cannot easily be dismissed: there is, at any rate, something to be learned from a comparison between theistic predestinarianism and the achievement of enlightenment in Mahayana tradition. Solidly based believers of either tradition will, of course, consider this comparison ill-founded, largely because they have gravely distorted notions of the other tradition. What follows may at least provoke such true believers into more accurate description. My point is not, of course, that these doctrines are 'identical': they are not. They do, however, play a similar role in their respective religious systems.

Buddhist tradition is almost unanimous in the claim that the Self does not exist. Whereas we are predisposed to think that there is in each of us a single, substantial being that has sinned and may yet be punished, or that may at last escape from all the changes and chances of this mortal life, most Buddhists (at least when speaking carefully) would say that the core of enlightenment is *Anatta*, the doctrine of No-Self. The illusion of separate selfhood is to be analysed away by attention to the passing moods and images of mental life, to the future decay and absorption of this mortal flesh. Only the chain of consequences remains, and *nirvana* is the ending of that chain. It is customary to insist that the Book-religious, on the other hand, believe in real, substantial selves, the souls whom God will punish or forgive. But predestinarianism is a constantly recurring theme, and by its standards – as I have already observed – there are no selves as they are customarily thought to be, no individual and independent causes of act and utterance. What looked like 'ours' is only God's, and there is no real volition but His.

Predestinarianism is the No-Self Doctrine of the Book-religious, differing from that of the Basket-religious in that the connections between successive mental and material events are merely contingent on God's unfettered will, whereas the law of *karma* pretends to a more 'necessary' nature. The identity of *nirvana* and *samsara*, conversely, is the Mahayana equivalent of the predestinarian doctrine of the Will of God. While some versions of Buddhist teaching make it sound as if the object of the Noble Eightfold Path were escape, for a Self that is said not to exist, to another realm in which suffering is no more and the Buddha-nature shines clear, this is not the only theme. Some of these religious hope for a rebirth in the heaven of Amitabha Buddha, conceived in much the same style as the heavens imagined by religions of the Book. But the dominant strand of Mahayana teaching, consistently with *Anatta*, is that *nirvana*, the state of desire's extinction, is nothing else than *samsara*, the realm of illusion and continuous change. Enlightenment comes with the realization that it is already there: the enlightened burst out laughing as they understand that everything already has the Buddha-nature. Similarly, the Book-religious pray for the coming of God's Kingdom, His will to be done: the joke, for predestinarians, is that it already is. We 'enter' the Kingdom when we see that we never left it, that the whole notion of not being under His command is vacuous.

The first stage of this doctrine is usually to try and make oneself, somehow, enjoy the world, to accept everything that happens as the Will of God, or as the unfolding of the Buddha-nature. One's own failure to achieve this goal is to be disparaged, the failures of others blamed. The second stage, achieved in Zen Buddhism and its relatives, and in occasional Quietists and Sufis, is to realize the incoherence of the first stage. If everything already is the Will of God, there are no failures. If the Buddha-nature is a leaking fountain-pen it is also the mind that sees and resents that pen, just as it is. We have no need to polish the mirror of our minds to see things clearly: everything, including us, is how it is ordained. As an abstract doctrine this is hardly adequate to moral, ceremonial or scholarly needs, and it is not taught as such to novices. Its force as an enduring theme within disparate traditions is in its occasional realization: one in whom the vision is realized, momentarily or over a long life, is so filled with joy as to be an easy image of the Buddha-nature. Those who realize it do not conclude that they will rape, murder and plunder (as one might who only heard the abstract message that 'whatever is, is good'), but act out of a new-found sense of confidence that does not need such props.

The Dragon in the Deeps

This predestinarian, pantheistic monism is not the only way of understanding the divine creation, nor is it likely to earn much applause among the ordinarily religious. Believing that, whatever one does, one is already saved, that the Buddha-nature is as much in treacherous thieves as in saintly hermits or honest farmers, is dangerous doctrine, however well it serves the enlightenment of the selected few. The other image of providential creation and continued care is the victory of light over darkness, order over chaos. The god has slain, is slaying or will slay the dragon in the deep. 'This most beautiful system of the sun, planets and comets could only proceed from the counsel and dominion of an intelligent, powerful being. This being governs all things, not as the soul of the world but as Lord over all' (Newton, *Principia* 544). The divine is not the only causal agent, and has endowed the other agents with a fragment or simulacrum of its power. Some mythologies, including the Olympian, propose that the god of human devotion arises from chaos, and then imposes his order on the dawning world. Zeus must battle with Titans, giants and Typhon, who in his multiplicity of forms and refusal of all discipline is a clearer image of the unfettered will than Zeus himself. Often such mythologies depict the chaotic origin, the enemy, as a female figure, and modern mythographers have seen this as a reference to some prehistoric battle between worshippers of the military sky-god and of the agricultural earth-goddess – a battle that ended by demoting Goddess to a demon, or carving up her functions amongst the daughters and wives of the triumphant gods. There may be some truth in this, though not one susceptible to archaeological proof. There is no clear relic, now, of any genuinely matriarchal, Goddess-worshipping era, though not all ages and peoples have been as dogmatically patriarchal as the Hebrews, or even the Greeks. Other mythographers, acknowledging that we can trace no connection between these myths and an historical overthrow of gynaicocracy, have preferred to trace profound psychological insights. Part of the process of growing up into an acceptable adult is the overthrow in each individual of the internalized Mother. All of us, whether male or female, begin our conscious lives as subjects of a mother, who is by turns comforting, restricting, terrifying. Kali, amongst Hindus, Coatlicue, amongst pre-Conquest Mexicans, and even Olympian Demeter (in her yearly separation from Persephone) are at once creatrix and destroyer.

Females may hope to escape subservience by incarnating the archetype, by becoming mother in their turn. Males must either capitulate or bind down that image. In some cultures male initiation ceremonies, involving agonizing surgery, seem designed at once to embody Mother (by creating the appearances of a vulva) and to make the novice into a new being, barred by traumatic memory from his woman-dominated past.

These psychologizing interpretations also, doubtless, have some truth. They go some way, at any rate, to explaining the panic that seems to overcome some believers brought up to acknowledge the Fatherhood of God when they are reminded that religious tradition also acknowledges the divine as Mother, and that women too are 'made in God's image'. Part of their religion, it can reasonably be suspected, is a rejection of Mother, as ancestral chaos and the enemy of individual life. It is similarly, perhaps, no accident that those who wish to revitalize ancient traditions of respect for Nature, and to play down the individualistic ethos of westernized culture, have used the image of Goddess as their guide.

But it is not enough to characterize the myth of Marduk and Tiamat, Yahweh and Rahab, as an historical cryptogram or psycho-drama. It expresses a serious cosmological option. Whereas the pantheistic strand of religious tradition understands the universe, as it were, as a poetic monologue, this other strand sees it as a drama or romance. There is no single cause of all that happens. The god perhaps has set the scene, but the scene is one in which many contending and co-operating spirits play. Not everything that happens is straightforwardly an utterance or act of the supremely worshipful. Whereas in the pantheistic model everything is already part of God's kingdom or an expression of the Buddha-nature, merely by existing, and enlightenment is an understanding of that fact, and consequent delight in things just as they are, this other model firmly distinguishes *dar al-Islam* from *dar al-harb*, the kingdom of God from the kingdom of the enemy. The enemy may be deluded, never realizing that the contest is not an equal one, that all its power is an echo or fragment of the infinite, but God's servants must experience the contest as real.

Insofar as God is conceived in opposition to 'other' wills, God functions as a finite spirit, whose volitions do not determine all phenomena. Insofar as God is God, the one true source of all power and might, God is infinite spirit, not to be encountered as one power, even the mightiest, among many. Mythologically, the divine is simultaneously conceived as a finite contestant, under whose banner we enlist against the world, the flesh and the devil, and as the infinite and inscrutable foundation even of our enemies' existence. Calvinist doctrine requires that God is causally responsible for sin, and rightly opposed to it. This is perhaps a particularly open case of the opposition (contradiction?) often found in religious tradition. Ahura Mazda, God of Light, is the twin of Ahriman, the Lie, and both are offspring of Zurvan, who is Time. The Word opposes the devil, or if the Word is too far assimilated to the Father the Archangel Michael steps in to be the agent of the infinite in the cosmic drama. These myths may be used to justify military adventures against the supposed enemies of the Lord, or else understood as metaphors for the bloodless strife with vengefulness and dishonesty. What concerns me here is the metaphysical puzzle they suggest.

How can anything not be subject to the all-powerful origin? How can there ever be a successful rebellion against the source, or a fall from the happy nothing? 'Creation as conquest' requires that there be something other than the divine which yet owes its duty and hope of happiness to the divine. The divine is not literally the creator of everything, although it must somehow cooperate with any other local creator, local actor. Or rather, God may make every *thing*, but not every act or happening: what He makes are individual substances with powers and purposes of their own. If this is so, then my earlier counter to the argument from design should be reconsidered. It is not everything that is 'explained' by reference to God's creative act or the effluence of divine light: we can distinguish in experience between what is not of God and what is. 'Chaos', 'disorder', 'grasping individualism', 'decay', 'impurity': all these things betoken God's (relative) absence, and their opposites God's presence. God (or the gods or the Buddha-nature) is what we must suppose as the single cause of stable being, tidiness, concern for others, growth, purity and the rest. There are places from which God has withdrawn, at least as active presence, and persons whom God has disowned.

It would be entirely wrong to suppose that this view is peculiarly 'Western', and the pantheistic model 'Eastern': wrong both historically and methodologically. The God revealed to Job is one that holds all things in His hands, that gives each created thing its nature and its time, however horrific it may seem to us. Hindu gods are set against the demons who corrode the cosmos. Division between 'west' and 'east' is methodologically useless, since there are no such simple divisions in humankind, nor any explanatory advantage in invoking them. The opposition between monism and pluralism seems endemic in religious tradition. If the socially dominant myth is that of the Conquering Sun we can be sure that the claims of Mother Night, for whom all things are equally Her children and agents, will be pressed. If the dominant myth is that all things are God, we can be sure that there will be some godly person to oppose the creed maintained by those who do not see the divine unity.

The conquest model envisages what would happen if things were left 'to themselves', to their implanted powers and individual wills, and concludes from the fact that this is not what always and entirely happens that there is 'a power, not ourselves, that makes for righteousness'. In this it resembles Newtonian science. Whereas Aristotelian science understands 'what naturally happens' as 'what observably does usually happen', Newton followed a more Platonic line. In Aristotelian terms it 'naturally happens' that heavy things fall, light things rise, and nothing but circular motion can go on for ever. In Newtonian terms everything would 'naturally' either stay still or go on in a straight line for ever. The fact that this is not what observably happens, leads to the hypothesis of an interfering force, gravitational attraction. We can find approximations to the Newtonian 'ideal' of unending linear motion, but there is always some interference. Correspondingly, whereas the pantheistic model understands the divine as what observably goes on, the conquest model imagines what would go on without God's mastering presence, discovers approximations to that abandoned state, and posits the interfering factor of divine agency as an explanation of why total ruin is not reached. Left to themselves, individuals naturally act in such a way that disorder grows; if there is not now the maximum disorder it is because a power interferes. Left to themselves, individuals cannot reach beyond the boundaries of their own selfhood; if there is not now the maximum of violence and grasping individualism, it is because a power interferes. It is to that single interfering power that we give the title 'God' or 'Buddha-nature', and we can to some extent measure the degree of its influence on recalcitrant material.

The Real and the Unreal

Our view of what would happen if God's guiding hand were even a little looser rests not on immediate observation (any more than Newtonian mechanics does) but on a theory deeply influenced by past religious speculation and present political practice. God as Conqueror, all too often, is an image of invading king or authoritarian government. The God of Israel leads genocidal armies against a land whose inhabitants he no longer favours. Genghis Khan claims the Mandate of Heaven. Sectarians like Thomas Muntzer urge their followers not to be moved by pity as they wield God's scythe (Cohn (1970) p. 247 f). The Book-religious have been particularly inclined to identify themselves with

God's purpose (or God with their purpose), and alien peoples and the non-human environment with the Enemy, owed no courtesy, mercy or fair dealing. This way of reading the cosmic drama is as an epic, complete with heroes and justly assaulted villains. The more subtle versions also embody the discovery that even we, the heroes of our psycho-drama, have sinned and fallen short of the glory of God. The wrath of God might justly be visited on us – partly for our failure to assist God's vengeance on rebellious spirits (witness King Agag's fate, and Saul's: 1 Samuel 15:9 ff.).

An alternative reading, which still treats the divine as something that might be escaped, that is not already embodied in the world, assumes that the righteous sovereign will not control or destroy apparently rebellious nature, but rather remove impediments to let all things develop as they 'naturally' would. The divine order is immanent in the cooperative motions of elements, natural organisms, people, but not fully realized because of 'unnatural' appetites and egotisms that the sovereign, like a gardener, must direct and prune. Such sovereignty, exercised from an imperial centre, would be superfluous if so many did not already choose to 'get in nature's way'. The Yellow River must be allowed its nature, to flood, but that flooding may be directed into water channels prepared for it. God the Conqueror might suppress the river, dam it back or break up all its waters. God the Gardener shows it how to be itself, clears it of the illusion (so to speak) that there are individuals atomically distinct from one another.

The softer-seeming 'Confucian' model leans toward the pantheistic, but does not suppose that all things as they are reflect the way of Heaven. There is distortion, fragmentation to be remedied. But whereas the Israelitish model understands the cosmos as an epic drama, moving from creation through apostasy to final judgement and the dawn of a new heaven and earth, the Confucian reads it more as an unending romance, whose resolution lies in the continual return of momentary balance. Like Aristotle's, the Confucian model sees a universe perpetually approximating to, and falling away from, what is natural, the best reflection of the way of Heaven. God does not act upon it as a warrior or craftsman might, but as a goal and immanent power. Romance, of course, which postulates a cosmos where no real and irrevocable change occurs, may dissolve at times into lyric poetry. If things will always be (or appear) very much the same, despite local disturbance, non-action seems the best rule, a refusal to engage in long-term projects for the betterment of this or that. Better to think it all a passing show, a dream, and so avoid heartbreak.

That the world is a dream is the final model for the relationship between 'creation' and the absolute, a model which is (in a sense) implicit in the central doctrine of religion, that phenomena are to be conceived as the sport of the divinity, and we the wanderers in the Red King's dream. It will concern me again in a discussion of immortality, the life after death. Here it is necessary to spell out what the doctrine of *maya* implies, and why some moralists have resented it. Our present phenomenal existence is *maya*, illusion, and the devotee must know it. God creates by world-wide hallucination, or (equivalently) the world emerges through the self-deception of beings who would otherwise know (and once did know) the truth. It is the most pervasive of human delusions to believe that I am here, and you are there: really, there is no distance. To the Waking One all that we now experience is a shadow-play, a dream, and nothing in it matters all that much.

That is sufficient reason for moralists to blench. Even if we cannot be 'absolutely' and 'ideally' certain that being boiled alive is a considerable evil, the rules of decision-making under uncertainty make it clear that it would be a worse mistake to boil someone alive if it were than not to do so if it weren't. Those who have passed beyond uncertainty into conviction that this life is but a dream may justly be feared (though how they can be controlled or punished is difficult to see). But though the criminal conclusion from the doctrine of *maya* has occasionally been drawn, we should perhaps allow its spokesmen some credit. It only seems that no real evil can be done, whatever we do, if we are 'only dreaming', because we concentrate our attention on the phenomena. If the phenomenal world is *maya* it is the direction of the *self* that matters. Waking from illusion is coming to know who we are, and evil is the willed absorption into dream. The Waking One appreciates and pities those still involved in *maya*, and dedicates itself to waking them up.

Those who prefer this model of the relationship between phenomena and the spiritual reality tend to regard the cosmic coming-to-be as a grand mistake, from which we ought to awaken. Immanentists regard things as they are as just what they ought to be; transcendentalists who follow a conquering divinity think that they may eventually be as they ought to be; 'Confucians', amongst whom most traditional African religious should perhaps be counted (as well as most mainstream Jews and Christians, who have quietly abandoned any expectation of a definitive end to phenomenal history), are content with the occasional emergence of the divine, when real nature is allowed its say. Illusionists think that the self-styled creator, Brahma, is only the first individual to 'fall' into spatio-temporal, individualist existence, or that the Demiurge is a misguided child of a momentarily distracted Sophia, the divine wisdom. Liberation comes by remembering our secret identity. Careless comparison between traditions then suggests that warrior-transcen-dentalists are the misguided servants of a deluded godlet, or that illusionists are the deluded victims of the Enemy, who scorns the Lord's creation. More careful comparison may suggest that the 'Fall' into *maya* (the conviction that I am here, you there, that we have opposing interests, that God is to be known as an object) is recognized as a fault in other traditions than the openly illusionist. Whatever the images of creation the religious use, it is clear that the divine is not known as an object, that reality is the divine, that there is a real synthesis of all apparently opposing interests, that it is an error to imagine evil as something beyond us in which we have ourselves no part.

When we explain the universe of our experience in religious terms we understand it as a text whose spirit we can enter, through which we grow. Whether it is an epic drama, a romance, a lyric poem, a bundle of love letters, it is at least not something 'making no sense at all'. If it were, if things arose as chance would have it, there could be no privileged position for the 'little agitation of the brain called thought' (Hume (1976) p. 168). It would not be enough to brace ourselves against the 'triumph of omnipotent matter': we should have to acknowledge that there was no secure or reliable tie of any sort between our speculative myth-making and the way things are. A romantic despair may be a pleasing posture: real despair is not. The doctrine or doctrines of creation are not so much explanatory in their function as anti-depressant, though it must be admitted that when they are abstracted from their religious context, the life of piety, they can be made to seem themselves the most depressing of news.

Further reading

Aho (1981), Berkeley (1948), Clark (1984), Hume (1976), Jaki (1974), Mackie (1982), Wisdom (1953).

Swinburne (1980) offers a more sympathetic account of the arguments from design; see also Macpherson (1972) and Hooykass (1972). Atkins (1981) argues that a 'lazy creator' need do almost nothing to allow the universe to emerge.

The Buddhist doctrine of Anatta is expounded by Rahula (1967) and discussed, from somewhat different perspectives, by Gudmunsen (1967) and Parfit (1984).

Pure faith indeed – you know not what you ask!
Naked belief in God the Omnipotent,
Omniscient, Omnipresent, sears too much
The sense of conscious creatures to be borne.
It were the seeing Him, no flesh shall dare.
Some think, Creation's meant to show Him forth:
I say, it's meant to hide Him all it can,
And that's what all the blessed Evil's for.
Its use in Time is to environ us,
Our breath, our drop of dew, with shield enough
Against that sight till we can bear its stress.
Under a vertical sun, the exposed brain
And lidless eye and disemprisoned heart
Less certainly would wither up at once
Than mind, confronted with the truth of Him.
But time and earth case-harden us to live;
The feeblest sense is trusted most; the child
Feels God a moment, ichors o'er the place.
Plays on and grows to be a man like us.
With me, faith means perpetual unbelief
Kept quiet like the snake 'neath Michael's foot
Who stands calm just because he feels it writhe.
Or, if that's too ambitious, – here's my box –
I need the excitation of a pinch
Threatening the torpor of the inside-nose
Nigh on the imminent sneeze that never comes.
'Leave it in peace' advise the simple folk –
Make it aware of peace by itching-fits,
Say I – let doubt occasion still more faith!
(Robert Browning, 'Bishop Blougram's Apology', 647–75)

8

War and the Problem of Evil

The Problems of Evil

If the general character of religion is the discovery of humanly significant meaning in the world, the one problem which all religions face is posed by the apparent meaninglessness of suffering in particular, and evil in general. If 'all things come from God' can God be the sort of thing that we can sympathize with, or praise? If there are things that do not come from God, what assurance have we that the other origin will not prove the mightier?

The 'problem of evil' is really at least three problems. The first is one that all of us, religious or irreligious, have to face: how can we summon up the energy and courage to cope with a phenomenal universe that so often works against us and our ideals? Things are not as we would want them to be, and all of us can be sure that we ourselves, or else those we care for, will be subject to disappointments, agonies and failures of a kind that any 'reasonable' person would have to agree were, to put it mildly, depressing. Some of us, like the dying Keats, find the world 'too brutal for us', and hope to escape into illusion or into death. Those who do not succumb to suicidal depression are usually kept secure by resolute attention to immediate duties, refusal to burden our imaginations with the unspeakable horrors that lurk around and within the sunlit pastures of civil society. Despair is not wholly unreasonable, but its peculiar evil is that giving way to it exacerbates the problem, for ourselves and others. Those gifted with equable temperaments find it difficult to conceive how all occasions conspire to afflict the depressed, and may unthinkingly imagine that such despair is a fuss about nothing. Robust 'healthy-mindedness' is one response to the existential problem, but it is not one that is always in our gift, and those who have managed it should not boast too loudly.

The second problem faces the religious. Those who have despaired of humanly significant meaning, and reckon everything a 'cosmic accident', must find their own route to courage and equanimity, but do not have to make themselves believe that there is anything – apart from the courage with which they face the world – deserving of their devotion. The religious reckon that they have found, in themselves and in the rituals and texts of their tradition, something that holds dominion over all the world, and that requires their duty. Their problem is: how shall they remain loyal to a power, a principle that manifests itself in so disdainful a form? How may we serve the gods from any motive but ignoble fear?

The third problem faces the Abrahamic theist. Other religious may fall in love with Kali, Mother and Murderess, and see no oddity or contradiction in the game She plays. Those who are committed to finding the divine in our experience of an indignant love, in the cry of the oppressed to an almighty saviour, cannot so easily set the question aside: if God is all-good He desires an end to evil; if God is all-powerful He can secure what He desires – whence then is evil? It is this third problem that has exercised most philosophers, sometimes with the unspoken assumption that if only this form of theism can be refuted all religion can be abandoned – a somewhat parochial thesis.

The simplest versions of the atheistical argument attempt to express these three axioms of Abrahamic theism as an 'inconsistent triad', any two of which are incompatible with the third: (i) God is all-good; (ii) God is all-powerful; (iii) there is evil. If God wants there to be no evil, but there is, He cannot be all-powerful. If God could make an end of evil, but hasn't, He cannot be all-good. If God could and would eliminate all evil, there can be none. Critics argue that abandoning any one of the axioms must alter Abrahamic theism to destruction, but that they cannot be coherently maintained together. With the added proviso that even 'God-talk' must be subject to the rules of logic, the conclusion follows that Abrahamic theism cannot be correct – though some mutation of it may find favour.

These simple versions, pretending that there is an easy contradiction in the axioms, do not really work. Does God's all-goodness really require Him to eliminate all evil? Is tolerance no virtue in the divine? Which sovereign would we more respect? One who prevented everything that did not fit her plan, or one who allowed her subjects to make their own ways? Does God's almightiness extend to performing logical impossibilities? If it does, then Abrahamic theism does not have to be coherent to be true. If it does not, then we can reasonably suppose that, for example, God Himself cannot *make* His creatures good – since 'being good' requires an unforced motion of the will. Is local evil always universal evil? Are we sure that when the last account is cast it will prove impossible to say 'Well, it was worth it'? If we are not (as who could be?) is it reasonable for us to set limits on the local evil that an all-powerful, all-good divinity might allow for the sake of ends quite unobtainable through any other means?

As a knock-down argument, in short, the third problem of evil is a non-starter. There is no necessary contradiction in agreeing that many things are, in the abstract, not as God or any divinely motivated person would wish, but believing that God's purposes are good and His power infinitely adequate to bring them to completion. Even the apparently complacent doctrine that this is 'the best of all possible worlds' is not the inept and sterile fiction that Voltaire taught Europe to suppose (by confronting the innocent Candide and his tutor Dr Pangloss with all the horrors of civilization and the natural order). It is the claim that even the all-powerful cannot wholly prevent all suffering, all wrong, without at the same time preventing the moral and personal growth of His creatures. We may not be able to trace any particular advantage from any particular horror, and it would be presumptuous to try, but it does not require any very robust faith to believe that the omniscient has ordained the best world possible for our moral endeavour, with no enemy entirely beyond our strength as that is supplied and reinforced by the almighty, but with no easy and immediate victories.

This theodicy, the so-called 'free-will defence', presents at least two further problems: firstly, it has often been expressed in distressingly anthropocentric terms; secondly, it seems to require us to accept one particular metaphysical thesis, anti-determinism. Neither seems entirely necessary. The anthropocentricity of the defence lies in the claim that the sufferings of sentient creation have been necessary, as means and inevitable byproduct, for the production of free moral agents. There seems no good reason to accept that God is so limited in His choice of secondary causes: He did not need to create so many years of agony – He could have done it all in six days. Some theists have replied that God's goodness does not require Him to be concerned about animal suffering (Geach 1977a)) – a reply that also reduces the amount of human distress that God needs to mind about, but which sits very ill with the Abrahamic conception of a loving God. What sort of love is it that does not mind at all about the sufferings of the beloved? Others have held that all individual souls need 'something to shove against' if they are to grow, that God's purposes extend to non-humans also, and have set the scene for their own flowering. The world, mythologically, was as God wanted it before the emergence merely of our human kind.

The free-will defence also seems to require the falsity of determinism in all its forms: if we could be moral agents, personal beings, despite being exactly determined in all our doings, why could not the all-powerful have determined us to act 'correctly' on all occasions? One response, revealing an ambiguity in this theodicy, is that a world of beings who acted 'freely' (in that they did what they chose to do) but who were so made that they always chose the right course, would lack the experience of self-wounding repentance, of ineradicable dependence: never having sinned nor seemed to themselves to sin, they could not distinguish what they would 'naturally' do from God's own grace. The only method of allowing finite spirits a way of recognizing their own finitude and dependence is to allow (or determine) them to 'make mistakes'. A world of 'natural saints' would be no breeding place for true religion.

It would not, of course, be 'fair' of God to make His creatures 'make mistakes' and then 'punish' them, though there might be no unfairness involved in choosing this way, of seeming error and painful repentance, of making Himself new creatures. God's justice is better served if His creatures are made genuinely independent sources of action, such that God Himself does not interfere or determine their choice – He could do so, but at the price of abandoning His purpose. Such anti-determinism is not the thesis that free action is entirely random, and consequently unpredictable, but that created individuals are true causes, not merely moments in a causal chain. On this account, God's goodness and power are not incompatible with His creation and maintenance of a universe in which creatures are to be confronted with occasions of stumbling, with evil in themselves and in the natural order. Even if we do not altogether understand just why God permits just what He does, we have no right to insist that there can be no satisfactory reason, on the lines that I have sketched, for a universe of change and chance and seeming tragedy. The strong atheistical challenge therefore fails.

Rewriting the Abrahamic Axioms

But though attempts to refute Abrahamic theism by proving a logical inconsistency in it are certainly failures, that hardly ends the argument. The real problem of evil is not the third, but the second. How can we find it in our hearts to worship

> the unfamiliar Name
> behind the hands that wove
> the intolerable shirt of flame
> which human power cannot remove.
> (T.S. Eliot, 'Little Gidding', IV, 9–12)

Conversely, how can we believe that the thing we truly worship has the upper hand? Are we not continually shown that love, humane civility, the best that we can imagine in society, has no greater strength or permanence than lust, brutality, corruption and the mere accidents of change and chance? There may be some reason why the almighty Lord of love and justice lets a child perish in bewildered pain rather than revoke His gift of liberty. There may be some reason why the almighty Lord allows a cloud of lust, hatred and confusion to obscure the thought and corrupt the action of the child's killer. The child may wake to life eternal and know that her 'last moments' were no more than nightmare. The killer may in turn have been the victim of a rebel angel, allowed its prey by a deity that does not protect the innocent. It may be that His creatures must have problems, must have genuine liberty: but need there really be so much unrequited agony? Do we really find it easy to think that the Chief Power is one that shares anything of our values, or that the idealized bearer of our values is really the Chief Power? We cannot absolutely exclude the possibility, but what reason could we have to think it real? There have been moments, it is true, when all seemed well, but those moments pass, and we are lost once more in the terrified suspicion that the powers-that-be are not our friends. Chronic depression is at once the name for an extreme despair, and one argument – by its very existence – for the thesis that the powers are not what we could rationally love. What we love and worship is not in command; what is in command is not what we could worship.

The Abrahamic tradition is no more homogeneous than any other: many answers, of a kind, have been propounded. Some worshippers have been content to remind themselves of the absurdity of striving to judge God: not simply the impiety, but the grotesque contradiction involved in saying, of the only source and sustainer of one's life and thought, that It is not to be approved. A shorter, but no more real a contradiction is to say simply 'Nothing that I say can be trusted'. We cannot turn upon the origin of all our life, our thoughts and values: accordingly, the first message of any sane doctrine must be 'Honour the Origin'. We must believe of God that He is good, or else abandon all attempts to talk sense, in this or any other field. The pot cannot argue with the potter: what God purposes, however ill it sits with our first preferences, must be our prayer. His goodness does not require of Him what goodness requires in us. We must take care, must not think ourselves divine, must not torment or kill: God is not subject to these rules, which He enjoins on us. Though good, He need not care; although He cares, it may not be as we do.

This reply amounts to a re-reading of the first axiom. God's goodness is not quite what we imagined, but is not something that we can coherently deny. A second reply amounts to a re-reading of the second axiom. God's power is not displayed in domination and control, but in perseverance and gradual persuasion. The worshipful is not to be found among the rulers of this momentary world: they have their reward, and can work their will on all that seems and is most helpless. God himself is subject to the whims of His own creatures, and His best image and embodiment is in the helpless victim, 'the worm that is no man' (Psalm 22:6), who yet outlasts the kings. God is almighty, not in the sense that He can unmake nations and worlds at will, but that there is no power strong enough to overmaster Him, and make Him what He is not. God, the true and abiding God, is not in command, but one day all the gods shall bow to Him, conquered at last by His unfailing love. Those filled with the Spirit of God, who know God (as it were) from inside, may speak with authority, but it is not the authority of one who can destroy at will. God's omnipotence, in these religious terms, is the promise of eventual success in turning the hearts of all to beat as one.

This reply has much to commend it. By Jesus' account – at least as it is traditionally interpreted – the greatest in the Kingdom is a child, one entirely vulnerable to violence, without any 'weapon' but the capacity to awaken love. Only those who strive to be like their heavenly Father in perfect submission can hope to avoid destruction. Those who hope to defend themselves and their interests by increasing their armies and their armouries lie at the mercy of a stronger army: it is the meek who inherit the earth, although each new generation of would-be rulers forgets the fact. The crucifixion is what we do to God. So Edwin Muir conceives an entirely unequal fight between 'the crested animal in his pride' and 'a soft round beast as brown as clay' that somehow is never quite killed:

> And now, while the trees stand watching, still
> the unequal battle rages there.
> The killing beast that cannot kill
> swells and swells in his fury till
> you'd almost think it was despair.
> (Edwin Muir, 'The Combat')

The Prince of this world is not God, and the divine is seen and understood only in the entire absence of temporal power. This is not simply a Christian theme, though that tradition carries a crucifixion at its heart in constant reminder that God's power is not like a prince's (a reminder constantly ignored). Vivekananda (1959) spoke fervently of 'the beggar god', known in the poor and oppressed, and offered as part of *bhakti-yoga*, the way of devotion, the worship of God in the form of a child – a worship, as he said, more familiar to Christians (who have the baby Jesus) and Hindus (who have Krishna) than to Muslims. Folk

Christianity, among its many contradictions, has managed to create a largely un-biblical Nativity, and Adoration of the Shepherds and the Wise Men, whose message is that the worshipful is not experienced as dominating power, but in helplessness. That is the power that Jesus preached: the soft answer, the smile, the willingness to yield and to endure.

But though this answer is commendable, and even traditional, it is certainly not the only answer given. The baby Krishna can tease his mother by showing her the cosmos in his mouth, and grows up to be the warrior who drives Arjuna to put aside his pacifistic qualms and destroy the enemies of good order. The boy Jesus, in apocryphal writings, cheeks his teachers, and in the canonical, ignores his parents' cares. He grows up to drive out sickness, utter vitriolic attacks on 'scribes and Pharisees, hypocrites', announce the coming of God's dreadful judgement (mercifully delayed for one last season) and curse the fruitless figtree to destruction. The figure hung upon the cross will judge the nations. God's power, now manifest in human weakness, will one day cast down the mighty, and exalt the weak, in fact as it has already done in idea.

God is almighty, absolute sovereign. That is why there is a thrill of religious excitement in the paradox that the eternal Word is a baby, and why the Christmas legend imposes its own logic even on Abrahamic believers who would rather think of Jesus as a Galilaean holy man, not as the incarnate Lord. Even if it weren't true, somehow it ought to be: the object of our worship ought to be both genuinely almighty and genuinely feeble. That he was virgin-born is no greater paradox. That the story is to be believed cannot be shown by demonstration from known truths: its 'proof', so to call it, can only be in the quality of the piety and devotion it incomprehensibly evokes. That may indeed be the only final answer to the problem of evil: not that we have any rational solution, but that religious love is somehow raised up in us despite the enormities of natural existence. It may be the only final answer, but philosophers may perhaps be allowed to struggle with the paradox.

A thorough-going re-reading of 'God's omnipotence' as simply the enduring power of submissive love is hardly true to the tradition (though it may usefully remind us of elements in that tradition). A thorough-going insistence that 'God's goodness' is simply His being the First Cause and Constant Sustainer of all thought and being (so that 'God is not to be trusted' is pragmatically absurd) is also not entirely true to the tradition. The pot constantly argues with the potter: though Job is proverbially described as 'patient' or 'uncomplaining', the biblical Job in fact complains constantly and eloquently that he does not deserve his troubles. It is Job's *impatience* that the Lord approves, his refusal to accept the rationalizations of his friends. Job does not agree that he is somehow 'better off' because he is ruined, nor that it is enough to say that God cannot be defied. He demands an answer, though he knows that there can be no judge to decide between God and himself.

The answer he seems to get – though it must be admitted that the Book of Job has almost as many interpretations as interpreters (see Glatzer (1969)) – amounts to a re-reading of the third axiom of Abrahamic theism, that there is evil. The voice from the whirlwind shows Job what he had known intellectually but had not appreciated: the Lord gives everything its season, whether it be antelope or lion, coney or hippopotamus. Everything has its turn, and pays its price for being. A similar idea crosses the Hellenic mind: all things make restitution to Persephone for their mutual injustice. Even Satan, by implication, is permitted to be himself, and Job is positively praised (at the same moment that he is silenced) for maintaining his integrity. The Lord sets limits on all things in the act of creating them as what they are, and His objectivity, His divine impartiality, breathes life into ostrich and crocodile and the smallpox bacillus. On this account much of what we think evil, whether personal disaster or malevolence, is such as we (being what we are) should rage against, but which at the same time we must acknowledge as the byproduct of some other creature's good. It is, as the Book of Job makes clear, not an answer that is likely to satisfy those who merely hear of it: they must be shown the glory of the Lord in the created universe of manifold and mutually dependent being before they understand their place.

Punishment

These variations within the Abrahamic tradition do not respond to one pervasive thought – that we deserve our troubles. It seems difficult to see how any Abrahamic theist could believe this, in view of Christ's sufferings, or those of the Jewish people, or of an abducted, raped and murdered child. It is also difficult to see how such a theme could be compatible with the central theme of most religious traditions, that we are to understand ourselves to be forgiven. If God has forgiven us, or all that lives is holy, or the Buddha-nature is made known in what is most despicable, how can we also see our trials as *punishment*? If we are still being punished, we have not been forgiven. If we are forgiven, then our troubles, however great, are not punishments. Indeed, most priests who have had to comfort the bereaved, especially those brutally bereft of children, make it their task to contradict and drive away the thought that God is punishing them, or that it is in some way their *fault*. It is a release, even a religious revival, to understand that the trouble is not punishment, nor something with which God wanted to afflict us.

But though this is now (and doubtless rightly) what priests say, it is not what religious tradition has decreed in the past. Some of my troubles (by the older account) are the reward of my own sin (whether imposed by God, or by the impersonal operation of the law of *karma*). Others are 'rewards' of my people's sin: the sins of the fathers visited on the children, or the sins of some past life brought to fruition in this. Others are part and parcel of the universal sin, the 'original sin' of disobedience or egoistic greed. There may or may not be some way of escaping, or at least alleviating, the punishment, but only if we admit that we did deserve it. This moralizing approach to trouble is set against an alternative model, in which trouble is breathed on us through the irrational malevolence of witches: then there is no need to think ourselves at fault, but only to hunt down and defeat the alien evil-doer. The malevolence of demons (particularly against the righteous) may serve a similar purpose: it is not our fault if things go wrong, but the devil's – though we may surrender to the devil in our heart, and so deserve the final punishment.

The anthropological distinction between witch-hunting and sin-confessing cultures – the two main ways of moralizing diaster – is doubtless a real one. What they have in common is that someone is blamed. Certain modern fashions in psycho-therapy have a similar effect. Neurotic or even psychotic patients are encouraged to believe that it is their family which is to blame: parents especially are encouraged to blame themselves. The apparently humanistic impulse to take neurotic declarations seriously, and not resort to drugs, electric shocks or other ways of 'beating the devil out', sometimes issues in a thoroughly oppressive and cruel manipulation of the guilt-feelings of those who are most emotionally tied to the unfortunate patient. In this context the declaration that psychosis means nothing, that it is an affliction to be driven away and not a symptom of moral evil in the psychotic or her family, may be a necessary and liberating one. Encouraging people to blame their families is merely pandering to an age-old human failing.

At the same time, one route to maturity does lie through a recognition of one's own error. When a demonic Yahweh seeks to kill Moses and is appeased only by his first-born's circumcision, or an angel wrestles Jacob's hip out of joint and gives him a new name, the phenomenon of radical repentance is acted out in melodramatic terms. Witch-hunters and family therapists put the blame elsewhere, and encourage an irrational and destructive resentment. Those who preach the need for repentence may themselves be hunting witches, but what they preach (the need of each soul for radical self-appraisal and repentence) may be a necessary element in religious maturity. Each soul can say of herself that she deserved no better, that there is a wound at the centre of her heart that has not healed. Recognizing this may issue in excesses of self-flagellation – a matter, maybe, of taking one's own littleness too seriously, and despairing of God's power to amend.

Four attitudes to one's own distress can be distinguished. The first, that it is entirely random, that the universe (or at least this earth) is ruled by Luck alone. What happens is not wished for by any God worthy of our worship, nor is it causally related to our supposed wrong-doings (though we may, of course, increase the burden by foolishness). The second attitude, insisting that it is part of true religion to oppose the world's evils, makes an enemy of evil, whether by positing a horde of disconnected spirits or of diseases (consider here 'the war against disease'), and blames what happens on the indifference or malevolence of other creatures. The third attitude acknowledge our own identity with the enemy, that we are of just the same indifferent or cruel kind, and that (by our own standards) we deserve as much. The fourth, passing through self-torture, can accept and give forgiveness: after which what happens is not punishment, but only the working out of what went wrong, and there is always hope of a new beginning. The newly named Israel is reconciled to Esau; Orestes is restored to civil life; Gautama abandons his extreme austerities and sees the law of *karma* and the real purity of what cannot be named.

The recognition that one is oneself to blame (and to be forgiven), however important as an element of the religious life, cannot easily be transposed into a general 'explanation' of apparently innocent suffering. I may say of myself that I deserved no better, may 'circumcise my heart' or accept a spiritual 'flaying' (as the symbolic language of Middle America proposed), but to insist that this is true of all of us leads to the useless moralizing of 'Job's comforters' ('if *you* are suffering, *you* are to blame'), and to still worse places. Instead of being 'spiritually flayed' ourselves (to uncover the new life), we turn to flaying others, and covering our sins with the mask of their skin (a horrible practice to which Central American civilization descended). As an abstract thesis about the origin of evil, 'individual blame' may have a very bad effect, as well as being empirically unverifiable (or even false).

The two main ways of rendering the acceptance of guilt and repetance a humane endeavour have been, as I have already suggested, the doctrines of original sin and of reincarnation. Both doctrines cast doubt on one of the central liberal contentions (that there are discrete individually responsible selves readily identifiable with bodily persons), a doctrine that I discussed in chapter five. Coincidentally, this doctrine has come under forceful attack in philosophical circles in recent years, and moral philosophers are not longer as certain as once they were that 'self-interest' has any obvious or determinate sense. Correspondingly, it is no longer obvious that 'my' guilt must be related to the acts performed by or in 'this' body. What 'I' am, what I realize myself as, is related to what 'I' feel guilty about, what sins 'I' take on myself. In identifying himself with Israel, and accepting what happened to him as 'what Israel deserved' (if this is a true account of Jesus' psychology), Jesus was not committing an obvious logical or moral error. Israel was what he was, or Adam. Similarly, I may acknowledge as 'my' sin the sins of all 'my' ancestors and conspecifics: 'we were all that man when we were all in that man' – a doctrine made slightly easier, no doubt, by the now fanciful notion that all human beings began as pre-formed homunculi stacked up, as it were in Chinese boxes, in Adam's loins. What happens to this body must be accepted as the just punishment of my species-sin. If individual, personal identity is not an absolute (but only a particular social form) how can I resist the doctrine that I and all 'others' suffer now as Adam? Does it matter that rewards and punishment are distributed unevenly across the species? It is we or I that have deserved it all.

Similarly, the standard doctrine of reincarnation blames my present sufferings on the sins of past persons that were the former lives of the Self now embodied here. All apparent cases of 'innocent suffering' are the consequences of sins in an earlier life, and gradual release from this cycle of self-hatred, blame and vindictiveness must come through acceptance and repentance. The 'ontological' implications of reincarnation-theory (what it implies about the sort of things there are) will concern me in a later chapter. I mention it here only as a widely spread attempt to rationalize evil as a just punishment for past offences. Its drawback may seem to be that it gives us all less reason to assist the oppressed and ill: whatever happens to them they deserve. This callous conclusion may be muted in practice by the thought that damage to our own future prospects follows from our failure to relieve suffering or our insistence on acting as agents for another's punishment. Even if a given person 'ought' to suffer, it does not follow that any other has a right to make her suffer.

As a way of articulating a sense that what happens to me is somehow deserved, even though 'in this life' I have done nothing to deserve it, the theory of reincarnation has merits. Although there are occasional pieces of evidence that one person may 'remember' an earlier life, may 'remember' dying and finding herself embodied in a new infant life, the main force in inducing people to accept the theory is clearly that it seems to render the universe just. Nothing happens that is not an expectable and proper consequence of our past action. Nothing is final, and all error may be atoned for and amended in a future life. Western spiritism differs from Hindu or Buddhistic versions in emphasising the hope of a gradual progression within this world, rather than a final release from the wheel. The gods themselves are only elder siblings, and the eventual ideal is a community, and not a return to the One. It is an undeniably attractive creed. But does it really explain 'evil'? Some theorists relapse upon the Buddhist conclusion that temporal, individual being is a sheer absurd mistake, a fall that is undone when we realize that the eternal One cannot be escaped. Where could we have fallen? The dominant theme in Western spiritism, however, seems to be the same thought that has comforted some modern theists: if there are to be finite intelligences capable of maturing into true companions of the gods, they must, as it were, be planted 'a long way off' and told to make their own way 'back'. God or the gods must be around them all the time, but cannot make it too obvious. There must be puzzles and challenges and possibilities of failure. There must even be the possibility of giving up, of seeking a return to the primordial, undifferentiated One. 'Augustinian' theodicy, so called, blames imperfection and evil on the mere fall from Heaven (though Abrahamic believers have usually denied that Creation itself was a mistake). 'Irenaean' theodicy insists that God Herself could do no other than create imperfect beings, if they were to mature as quasi-independent beings (Hick (1966)). Spiritists have an advantage over this latter form of theism in this, that they think the gods themselves have grown up in the same way. If there could be an infinite joy and wisdom that did not need to mature through opposition and challenge (i.e. if the god of theism and his angels exist), why is it necessary for mature earthly beings that they grow up through such horrors? Could not God the Omnipotent make beings immediately fit for heaven? Is there not a powerful tradition that He did just that? 'Augustinians', on the other hand, whether they be literally Augustinian or professors of the other Buddhistic or Gnostic gospel (that all Creation is absurd) have the advantage over spiritists in this: if the world is simply such that new selves are constantly maturing upwards through the lives of earthworm, fish, eagle, human, god, why *is* it that the world is like that? Unless there is a pattern, established in the providence of God or the Buddha-nature from eternity, there seems no good reason to expect this spiritual progression. Perhaps instead all selves will regress or stay much the same. Why not accept the ancient image of the wheel from which we seek release? If there were no Unborn and Indestructible, as Gautama said, there would be no release.

Accordingly, despite the strengths of spiritism, we may reasonably doubt that it solves the problem of evil. Either temporal and individual existence is an error, and spiritism has the same problem as more familiar creeds (how could such an error happen?) or evil is a necessary concomitant of progress to maturity (in which case we have no assurance that such progress is to be expected). We need to hypothesize an Unborn and Indestructible if there is to be real progress or release. If we do hypothesise that Eternal Being we cannot say why or how we do not experience things as the Eternal does.

War in Heaven

One further, and very popular, response to the first and second problems of evil is through the passion of war. We are so used to deploring violence, and to persuading ourselves that 'no one really wants wars' except the military-industrial complex or power-mad politicians (and even they would rather not shed their own blood and brains), that we tend to ignore the cult of military violence. If we notice at all that many peoples are extremely warlike, the blame tends to be put on 'our animal nature', and ethological records searched for apparent analogues of human war, in 'slave-raiding' ants, or squabbling chimpanzees. These analogues are usually not very close, though there is doubtless some truth in the notion that evolutionary forces make it likely that we shall seek to promote the interests of our kin over those of strangers, resist incursions into land we call our own, and struggle for the upper hand by violence when the usual system of finding out who would probably win in a straight fight (display and bluff and counter-bluff) has failed. But our wars are not the relatively casual, episodic squabbles of competing males, competing clans. It is not true that we only fight wars in order to protect ourselves and our material interests. Human beings frequently organize their societies around the sacred duty of military violence, and rejoice in slaughter. Even when we justify war by extrinsic goals (the conversion of the heathen, or the liberation of the holy places) the means chosen are not necessarily those that might be chosen by beings not emotionally involved in the art of war. We apparently need to prove ourselves to our enemies, and to ourselves, and war is an essential element in the demonstration of moral purpose. If we can't risk our lives, our people's lives, how seriously do we care? What is not worth the price of a human life is really trivial.

It may be that our evolutionary past has set the scene for this. The chief problem facing social mammals is that of the surplus male, and many primates have evolved a system that flings the young males out to the edge of the clan, there to bear the brunt of predation and to forge alliances and rivalries that will at last allow a few to return to the clan's centre, the continuing lineage of mothers and daughters. Young male humans can easily be organized into gangs, packs, armies, which maintain group solidarity by the experience of shared hardship, delight in rough and tumble. It may well be that young males also suffer from a desire to prove themselves as tough and bloody as their sisters. War is to males what childbirth is to females: a proof of courage, a pledge to the future, a bond of shared experience. Those who cannot fight, or will not, are cheats, achieving a stay-at-home existence among the women without paying their male dues. The god Hephaistos, the lame smith of Olympus, has married Aphrodite only to be cuckolded by Ares.

In warlike cultures there can be few males who *will* not fight, even to the death, any more than our own young males are much concerned about the hidden risks of bike-riding, smoking, drinking, climbing rocks. These are the ways they must live as good pack-members (quite apart from any illusions they have about getting girls), and the way in which the conviction of immortality takes shape in them. The opposite conviction, that it is wrong to hurt, injure, kill even those of alien kinds, and that it is wrong to take pleasure in killing even when we 'have' to kill, amounts to a religious revolution. The Olympian religion may regard Ares as the most hateful of the gods, crass, bloodthirsty and stupid, but warriors still delight in their prowess, in tricks and treacheries as well as open contests. They fight to defend their people, and to enforce the laws of justice and hospitality, but also to live as fiercely and nobly as they can, 'not like a stall-fed ox'. The Hebrews' God is, originally, unashamedly a god of battle, and his people are enjoined to fight without mercy, trusting in their Lord, to enforce his ways. Hebrews and Greeks may, in some moods, agree that war is for the sake of peace, that God 'maketh wars to cease in all the world' (by destroying his enemies). Other traditions make war itself their aim: the 'flowery war' of the Aztecs was continued, according to strict rules, to maintain the supply of living hearts for Tezcatlipoca or the Sun; our own Northern ancestors expected to avoid the drab halls of the dead by dying in battle, and waking to fight their days away in Valhalla. Even in this century, and the settled West, it was not only Nazi barbarians who found their highest life in killing.

> And life is colour and warmth and light,
> and a striving evermore for these;
> and he is dead who will not fight;
> and who dies fighting has increase.
> (Julian Grenfell, 'Into Battle')

When liberals fail to take account of this terrible fact, that war is exciting both for non-participants and for the embattled warriors, they run the risk of irrelevance. Liberal attacks upon 'war-mongers' on behalf of their dupes sometimes sound like sermons against fornication by preachers who assume that boys only want to do it because they think it will win them kudos with their peers, and girls don't want to do it at all. Such sermons have minimal effect, because the preachers show themselves entirely ignorant of emotional realities. Really to preach against fornication is to try and tame an Olympian. Really to preach against war is no less a tour-de-force. Contrariwise, those conservatives who allege that human beings are 'naturally' and irredeemably warlike all too often sound like those who preach against all modifications of pure patriarchy, mistaking a particular cultural tradition for the ineluctable truth. Worship of the war-god is not the only possible religious form, though those who would renounce him must understand the costs, and the trials.

The long religious effort to tame or exorcise the god of war, the berserk fury that can fill an army or a nation, has issued, most notably, in Just War Theory, a topic which I must defer. Here my concern is with this religious answer to the first and second problems of evil. Where most of us cringe at the thought of suffering and slaughter, and think that how the world *should* be is quite at odds with the war of each against all, more robust or cruder spirits place their trust in War. Life is at its richest when it is most at risk; creatures are most themselves when they are tested against their rivals; war-making is a sort of love, a relishing of the enemy's virtues even as we strive to defeat them.

> Yea, I will bless them as they bend and love them as they lie,
> when on their skulls the sword I swing falls shattering from the sky.
> The hour when death is like a light and blood is like a rose –
> you never loved your friends, my friends, as I shall love my foes.
> (G.K. Chesterton, 'The Last Hero')

It is in this ceaseless war that honour and courage grow, and without it we could only sink down into complacent dullness, cringing from the minor pains of life, afraid to take any risk lest we lose a fragment of our useless lives. This is a religious doctrine, a way of passing beyond immediate fragmentary concerns by submitting ourselves to a passion, a continuing way of life that may demand our lives or those of others. If we can exalt and summon up this spirit in ourselves we may be better able to stand up against the world's brutalities, and not regard them as evils incompatible with honest worship of the powers that be. Outsiders and unbelievers, of course, will regard this theme with horror, its devotees as grinning murderers, or devil's dupes.

My own temptation is to think this final judgement is correct. Whatever is true and holy and of good report, it surely cannot be the joyous evisceration of our fellow creatures. When the Aztecs ripped out living hearts, or the Vikings cut their captives' ribs and pulled out their lungs to make a 'spread-eagled' gift to Odin, or Zen adepts boiled men alive, or Christian priests burnt suspected heretics and witches, they were devil-worshippers, and the only spirit that delighted in their work was Satan. But horrible and perverted though its manifestations are, the religion of war must still be considered as an image of the truth, a need to be acknowledged and a clue to one more theodicy. Failure to realize that it is a religious form leaves us with no protection against it, no answer to give its devotees. In seeking a 'moral equivalent' to war William James at once acknowledged the values war may protect, and pointed to alternative, more convivial modes of realizing these values. A similar transposition can help with the problem of evil.

The standard theodicies share an attempt to render apparent evil into something meaningful, appropriate and necessary, as punishment or instrument of growth. The archaic vision much more often was of an unmeaning chaos and darkness ordered and illuminated by the god, at war eternally with shapeless possibilities. Our role as the god's worshippers was 'to fight manfully under His banner against the flesh, the world and the devil'. God was realized in our hearts in that contest. Whence then is evil? It does not exist for a purpose, still less for God's purpose: it is rather the mass of possibilities that omniscience must know as possibilities, and heroic goodness strive to realize and redeem. Our world is the arena of that contest in which God meets the possibilities that (in some sense) God *might* have held secluded in His mere intelligence. Hebraic legend, as interpreted by Christians, has suggested that the Adam somehow chose to know both good and evil, 'the secluded vision of battle in the law' (Williams (1938) p. 10), and that the second Adam's action is to turn the known evil into an occasion of good. This account is dualist in this sense, that there are opposing principles: God, the good, 'might' have have made only worlds where things go easily, but has instead realized other worlds, opposed in their essence to the eternal light. Creation was not straightforwardly a mistake, though Adam and Brahma alike may be thought rash in encountering too easily the secluded terrors. What we do not need to suppose is that a child's murder is somehow a good, even a good too raw for our digestion. It is an evil, but the divine life will – we may believe – bring good from it, for parents, child and fuddled murderer. In bracing ourselves for this spiritual conflict we may learn a little from the war-god's worshippers: our joy must be in fighting what is incompatible with joy, but we may do so without hatred, and delighting in the partial virtues of our foes. It is in that fight, and not in abstract reasoning about the problems, that we may find assurance of eventual victory.

The notion that there are two sides, that there is war in Heaven, is one that modernists have hidden from. Although the quarrel between light and darkness is a recurrent theme in religious tradition, there has also been constant pressure towards a monistic view of things. Even in those cultures that have emphasised the war, it has often happened that the war itself has become the end of action, and the single source of good. In Norse religion the god Thor is the protector of humane society against the giants of cold and the great serpent, but there is very little to choose between these ogres and the Aesir. It is Odin who claimed the Norsemen's devotion, the god of oath-breaking and slaughter, and their fantasized ideal was to die the last death at Ragnarok, when the world went down in flames. Those, upon the other hand, who have held to the hope of a good reconciliation as the outward sign of an underlying unity that cannot ever 'really' have been infringed, have been chary of any suggestion that there is any other power in the world than the divine.

Whether it is war that, paradoxically, sustains all things, or the unchanging One that stands impartially above and within *maya*, the message is the same: whatever is, is good, and 'true religion' is to do as one must. Chesterton, in his greatest poem, 'The Ballad of the White Horse' (1911), caused Alfred to warn of the old barbarian:

> When is great talk of trend and tide,
>   and wisdom and destiny,
> hail that undying heathen
>   that is sadder than the sea.

Against that tyranny Chesterton's Alfred drove:

> Follow a light that leaps and spins,
>   follow the fire unfurled!
> For riseth up against reason and rod,
> a thing forgotten, a thing downtrod,
> the last lost giant, even God,
>   is risen against the world.

It was perhaps in similar vein that Zarathustra proclaimed Ahura Mazda, the giant (or *asura*) against the lie that there is no real contest – though later variants of that tradition swayed backwards to the dream of a single Absolute for which evil and good were twins.

The dualistic vision of a real contest, of God against the world, has its own problems. The Devil cannot really be the equal opposite of God: how could there be a single cosmos within which these embattled powers contend if there were no single source of both these powers? The Devil can only be the opposite of St Michael, and have drawn Its power, somehow, from God's permission. As a general, abstract solution to the problem (can the divine be uniquely of one nature with Michael if the Devil also draws Its power from the Divine?) the dualist hypothesis is difficult to state. It may also be dangerous: what is inconvenient to us, or at odds with our plans for the Plan, gets counted as a creature of the Evil One, to be opposed by all possible devices. It does not seem to me, however, that there is any coherent way of avoiding a degree of dualism. Every attempt to say that belief in an irreducible conflict is an error simply defines a new conflict: between those who do and those who do not see a real identity between St Francis and Caligula. If it is wrong to take sides, it is right to take sides against those who take sides: it is, accordingly, right in principle (or at any rate, 'not wrong') to take sides. There are few modern moralists quite as opinionated and judgemental as those who fondly assert that it is wrong to be judgemental: it seems that the one unforgiveable sin is to think that anything is really sinful.

Dualists do not need to think that things now are as they should be, or as the divine requires, though they may recognize that one way to realize the divine is to see its echo even in our enemies, and to heal divisions not by the way of slaughter but of unsentimental love. 'Love' in a monistic world-view is simple recognition of the unity, and indistinguishable from any other unifying passion. In a dualistic world-view love implies care, unwillingness to let the beloved suffer or become evil, respect for the real difference between creatures, determination to live one way and not another. Humane religion rests on the conviction that the world is not *one* in all possible senses, that there are things worth opposing. We may pray that God arise and that His enemies be scattered: He may be doing so, but the battle is not over.

Further reading

Aho (1981), Head & Cranston (1977), Hick (1966), Stevenson (1974), Turville-Petre (1964), Wilhelm & Baynes (1951), Zaehner (1974).

Glatzer (1969) is a collection of essays from various perspectives on the Book of Job: several authors opt for what might be called the Buggins' Turn theory – the divine providence is revealed in Job's, and Satan's, freedom to be themselves. Recent free-will theodicies have centred on the question whether God might not have created a world in which people freely did only what was right (see Mackie (1982)): attempts to unravel this require a sophisticated analysis of 'possible-world' theory, on which see Plantinga (1975), and his other, more technical works. Geach (1977a) is a forceful statement of a more Augustinian view of the matter than Hick's.

9

Prayer, Sacrifice and Time

Before All Worlds

Once upon a time there was a people who believed that the world was
sustained by the blood of a divine sacrifice, that they could share in the
work of sacrifice through repentance, self-torture and a holy death, that
those who died for the cause had gone to be with God. They expected a
second coming of the god who had died, and thought of themselves as
living in the last age of the world. At the same time they practised
brutalities and treacheries upon their enemies that still appal us,
reckoning that no treaties or rules of civility prevail against God and
their destiny.

My description is, deliberately, vague, and so recalls both European
Christendom and Aztec civilization. When Europeans encountered the
Aztecs, they recognized that here was a people, like themselves, who
feared the judgement, hoped to share in the Sacrifice, and practised
austerities in fear and hope. They recognized also the triumphalism of a
people who deliberately sought occasions for war: a neighbouring king
was asked for his daughter (supposedly in marriage); on arriving at the
celebratory feast he was greeted by the royal suitor wearing his
daughter's flayed skin. It is hardly surprising that those first Europeans
concluded that here was a devil-worshipping people, their hearts
corrupted and controlled by a diabolical parody of Christian faith.
Repentance and self-sacrifice, which are themes in most religious
traditions, were acted out in the most gruesome forms. Metaphors took
control of Mexican society to the point where an entire people seem to
have been living in a sort of psychotic hallucination: the sun set, quite
literally, in blood, and was reborn from blood.

What is worth discussing here is the notion of sacrifice that lies
behind Aztec and European practice. Most philosophical commentary
has been concerned with the idea that we may, and should, 'give things
to God', or else with the more general question whether those rites that

we naturally count as sacrificial are really all of the same form, undertaken with a similar intent and effect. These questions are entirely apt, but it is perhaps better to begin from the Divine Sacrifice. It takes a god to perform the act of self-giving that makes general life possible, or a god to destroy Chaos. Does the world begin from Marduk's destruction of Tiamat (as the Babylonians said) or from Purusa's self-fragmentation (as early Hindu speculation suggested)? The Lamb that was slain 'before all worlds' is the very priest of the sacrifice, and the god.

What is involved in this thought that the universe is founded on a death, a dismemberment, whether that is followed by a resurrection or not? One response is to suggest that the myth-makers were speaking of the universe in a language of symbol derived from their experience of social order. Just as a social universe is, at least in archaic society, established and maintained by a sacrificial rite that binds participants together, so we may imagine that the world itself, in which we all participate willy-nilly, must have been established in like manner. Just as a city is marked out from chaos by digging a ditch and establishing the centre and the four gates of the city, so the cosmic city – the universe understood as a city – must have been laid out by an effort that required a god's power. The earthly city is then understood as a copy of the celestial, which is itself a projection of the earthly. Where our ancestors explained their social practices as a re-enactment of the gods' original ordering of the world, we (believing that their story about the gods is merely a projection of their own practice) must then find some other explanation for the common human habit of marking out such cities, such enclaves in a fearful world, and of paying for their foundation with blood. It is not necessarily a hopeless task. But if Aristotle was right to suspect that myths and old wives' tales are relics of some past philosophy, we might ask whether there might not after all be some sense in the ancient explanation. Why must we suppose that the universe was not founded in something we can represent as blood-sacrifice? What might that real foundation be?

Mythologically, blood-sacrifice is a payment or bribe or bait to induce the demonic powers to allow the establishment of a humanly significant universe. Or else it is the only way that the created world can have any share in the divine power of independent action. God permits the powers (those principles and forces that govern the world under God, and which are characterized mythologically as titans or demons) to feed on Him so that a world may come into being. The demons suppose Him vanquished, but His fragmented self (the sparks of the divine) works in the lump, until the universe (ruled by powers divided from the God) itself becomes God's outward body. That image is mythological because it relies upon concepts and images drawn from within the created universe to describe an unimaginable and unique event. It is mythological also in that it may move us in ways that we do not altogether understand, and may not be easy to translate into the relatively abstract terms preferred by modern philosophers. But it is not entirely without intellectual content. If we suppose that there really was a 'time' when the infinite and eternal was the only existent, how can we conceive that anything 'else' began, except by God's deliberately allowing other things to use God's power? So long as God does not 'surrender' real power to His creation there *is* no genuine creation, for the imagined creatures exist only as fantasies, that make no real demands and impose no real burdens. If creation is to be genuine, the essentially unlimited Creator must limit himself, must become as-it-were a finite being, even if it is with a view to a re-integration of the fragmented deity, or a taming of the rebellious creation.

Any divine Creator may therefore be considered as a self-immolating, sacrificed god. Anthropologists who fancy (though the fashion is perhaps past) that every dying god must be a representative of the seedling corn or the dying year, have things the wrong way round. That the seed must 'die' in order to come alive again need not be the first thought of religious metaphysicians: it may represent a deeper truth, that the Creator must 'die' in order to create. One particular modification of this may make sense of Christian orthodoxy (though it is perhaps not usual to connect God's 'self-emptying' with His creative work): God becomes a finite being, a fellow-member of the community He empties Himself to make. God Himself is sacrificed for us, and we share in that surrendered life by eating the god. This story, and its concomitant rituals, may have greater resonance than the abstract assertion that creation requires self-fragmentation or self-surrender, but it should not therefore be regarded as intellectually null. The abstract assertion, after all, is probably true, and not beyond the intellectual grasp even of our benighted ancestors.

Sharing in the Feast

Finite individuals exist by the weird withdrawal or self-immolation or self-finitization of the infinite and eternal. We are all bought at a price, ransomed from the limbo of mere possibility by God's readiness to place His power at our disposal, to be bound by our decisions. Those who profess belief in an omnipotent God are often asked whether He could create a stone He could not lift: it is presumed, illogically, that a contradiction follows whether He could or not. The correct answer must be that He could (i.e. He could cease to be omnipotent), and that the really interesting question is: 'would He?'. It may be that what He creates is not entirely beyond His power to control or redeem (so that He has not ceased to be omnipotent), but if He creates at all it must involve some readiness at least to postpone the full use of His power. He creates by self-surrender, self-limitation. Consider Ernesto Cardenal's extraordinary and splendid thought: 'the mere fact that we exist proves His infinite and eternal love, for from all eternity He chose us from among an infinite number of possible beings' (Cardenal (1974) p. 40). 'God' stands both for the one original, infinite and eternal substance, and for the divine leader of the dance He has set in motion. Paradoxically, both stories of God's embodiment and death, and stories of the forcible parting of Earth and Heaven point the same moral: finite individuals can only really exist when Heaven does not permeate existence; they can only really exist when Heaven has put its power into their individual lives. Our sacrifices are reminders of that first surrender, and awakenings of the first great light as it is dispersed among us: 'Christ our Passover is sacrificed for us: *therefore* let us keep the feast'.

But this is not now the most familiar aspect of sacrifice. A sacrifice, to contemporary Westerners, is a loss, a price paid for something else. We 'sacrifice' our health and happiness for the sake of an imagined security, or we 'make sacrifices' to send our children to schools of our own choosing. Sometimes we can trace causal pathways that give us reason to suppose that the loss will be made good. Sometimes we 'make the sacrifice' only in the superstitious fear that the gods do not allow too much prosperity. A 'sacrifice', in any case, is something surrendered absolutely. Such absolute losses are not the religious norm. In Greece it was only the 'chthonic' deities (those who dwelt below, in contrast with the Olympians in heaven) who demanded the total loss and destruction of the object sacrificed. Amongst the Hebrews sin-offerings were surrendered whole. Other sacrifices were intended to be shared by the worshipping community. Indeed, it was the official rule amongst both Greeks and Hebrews that no farm animal was killed for food except 'in sacrifice'. That is why Paul has to tread very carefully when discussing whether Corinthian Christians should eat meat: the animals had been dedicated to a pagan god, and eating their flesh was, at least for the scrupulous, a sharing in a pagan communion. In most cases the animal was not conceived as identical with, or possessed by the god, but she did belong to him.

Most sacrifices involved dedicating something to the god, and sharing in the resulting feast: they were not simply 'sacrificial' in the modern sense. Whether the gods needed their share, or were merely insistent on being recognized as the source and protector of their people, seems to vary. Philosophers and prophets alike have insisted that God does not need such sustenance, nor our aid in providing it: 'if I were hungry, I would not tell thee: for the world is mine, and the fulness thereof' (Psalm 50:12). It is very likely that those who first killed animals on God's altar merely sought to return the life of the animals (which they identified with the blood) to God who gave it, in the hope of being allowed to eat the flesh. It is a custom and belief which we have done ill to forget about, imagining that animals are entirely 'ours', to do with as we please. But though there is good reason to insist that God does not need the flesh of bulls, or the blood of goats, it may also be well to wonder whether there is some more serious meaning in the practice of 'giving things to God', as if He needed them. What possible truth is imaged in the practice of inviting God to our feasts, and are there better ways of doing it?

In what sense might the Omnipotent need our help? The answer is implicit in the thesis that creation involves self-abnegation, a readiness to allow created beings a real choice about what goes on. If that is really what God allows, so that the tapestry of time is woven, in part, by those finite choices, then what He makes of that tapestry must depend, in part, on us. Of this the supreme example in orthodox Christian tradition is Mary Mother of God: 'The incarnation was not only the work of the Father, of His Power and His Spirit . . . but it was also the work of the will and faith of the Virgin' (according to Cabasilas, active in 1350: Ware, 1963, p. 263). Her '*fiat*' (let it be so) inaugurates the new creation, as the Creator's setting light apart from Himself (and so voluntarily accepting limitation) inaugurated the first. If God's will is to be done in the world, then He needs our cooperation (even if that cooperative volition is only a slight movement of the will, and its effects owed wholly to God). The sacrifice we owe to God is 'a pure heart and humble voice', or else (that not being obtainable) 'a broken and contrite heart'. Every ceremonial act worth reckoning an act of piety is an expression of that repentance and determination to 'do justice and love mercy and walk humbly with our God'. It is as we slip into believing that the metaphors and symbolic acts are to be understood 'materially' that we head towards Aztec psychosis. Each new victim trudging up the bloody steps of Tezcatlipoca's pyramid was met by the headless, heartless corpse of his predecessor, tumbling down the slope. The very flesh of those captured warriors who were appointed as a god's *ixiptla* (divine representative) was eaten by leading Aztecs (not, one may confidently insist, because they were short of protein). God wished us to 'feed upon Him in our hearts, by faith with thanksgiving'. Correspondingly He wished the devotion of our hearts. Demon-inspired psychosis takes these twin dicta 'literally'.

Contemplation and Worship

If what God desires and needs of us (now that He has put Himself at risk in creating a universe of potentially rebellious individuals) is a readiness to join His project, doing justice and loving mercy, can anything 'distinctively religious' be required of us? What difference should there be in outward act between a decent humanist and a devout believer? They will say different things about their purposes, and the believer will have a clearer reason for what looks like a necessary presupposition of moral action (that the Good will, in the end, prevail), but must the believer think it necessary to join in explicit praise and thanksgiving?

One constant theme in religious tradition is that the 'contemplative' life is superior to the 'active'. This distinction and preference seem to have several possible meanings. One interpretation, significant for our understanding of political philosophy, is simply that the spiritual welfare of humanity is of more importance than political security. Gautama might have been a *chakravartin*, a world-monarch, rather than an enlightened saviour, but chose rightly. Even the noblest and wisest of earthly rulers (name three) can count on no great success, no great influence on the populace, no assurance that their names and projects will be long remembered. Even the noblest and wisest of rulers (or they especially) must know that they cannot secure spiritual goods for their subjects – the goods of honesty, courage, temperance, compassion and piety. In that sense the life of political action can never be more than the constantly renewed attempt to secure the framework within which people may 'work out their own salvation'.

Another sense of the claim that the contemplative life is superior to the active rests on the superiority of its object: it would be ridiculous, said Aristotle, to suppose that human beings were the most important, most worshipful things in the world. God (and the whole cosmos) is more deserving of our admiring contemplation. This sort of life has been neglected by much recent moral and political philosophy. It is certainly easy to let oneself be persuaded that such theoreticians must be blind to the happiness, the felt contentment of human beings. They must obviously be cold and alienated personalities, incapable of the warm human relationship that modern moralists admire. On the other hand, it is not obvious that people who think 'warm human relationships' are the things most worth admiring are themselves especially admirable or successful lovers. Even human love is perhaps the better for a certain astringency in the lovers, an admission by each that they do not really 'live for' each other, or for the pleasures of companionship, that the world will go on well enough without them. People with no other interest than their relationships with others are not especially interesting people!

Such theoretical 'worship', however, may not be quite what, for example, monastic apologists have had in mind. A contemplative prayer that is embodied in ritual observance (e.g. the celebration of the eucharist) has been regarded as a better thing than an active concern for the welfare of our fellows because it is directed toward God, and because all other creatures are better served by such worship than by direct action. But even monks are not as eager as once they were to contend that praying for one's neighbour is a better help than merely visiting or feeding her. Common sense suggests quite strongly that God wants us to help each other and that we can do so by direct means better than by praying to a deity who is (presumably) already doing all that He consistently can to help. Common sense can believe that, by praying, we may ourselves acquire such virtue as will help us to help others; it does not so easily believe that petitionary prayer or contemplative prayer gives any direct aid to others. The point is not that we see no direct causal connection (that could be managed via the prayer's 'influence' on God): it is that it seems absurd to suppose that God's willingness to help Tamar could possibly be conditional on Zachary's prayer. It seems one degree more absurd that the aid should depend on Zachary's celebration of the eucharist in accordance with canon law. Such a theory seems merely magical.

Although God 'needs' (or has chosen to need) our practical help in ordering His world, this does not itself explain why He should require our ritual worship, or make His aid conditional on the efforts of a few to praise Him satisfactorily. Attempts to express the thought that He does usually end by making God sound like a finite egoist, the sort of tyrant who dispenses aid only when flattered by his favourites, or else like an easily manipulable dotard. A purely impersonal model has sometimes been preferred for just this reason: until Tibetan civilization was forcibly dismembered, and subject to *diaspora* (like the Hebrew before it) its monasteries were held to be power-houses, keeping society and the world upon a relatively even keel by the accumulated prayer-power of the monks. Just the same has been believed of Christian monasteries and hermitages. In Judaic tradition the world is sustained only for the sake of the fifty-six just men (a number kept constant through birth and death), who are individually ignorant of their own role. The 'theistic' and 'Buddhistic' traditions are perhaps not as far apart as they seem.

But suppose that the phenomenal world really is the effect of a spiritual reality, the stamp of an eternal Logos (of the kind that I described in chapter 4), in which all 'essences' (not only what it is to be feline, or human, but what it is to be Zachary or Stephen) are perfectly realized. We who seem to ourselves to live 'in time', as separate individuals, may choose either to insist upon our egocentric being, or to accept ourselves, the creatures we now experience ourselves as being, as elements or shadows of the divinely ordained community. The 'angels of the children' (that is, their real and eternal selves) stand by the throne of God (so Jesus said: Matthew 18.10). If this is so, then it is perhaps not quite impossible to believe that by concentrating on remembering our secret identity, who and what we 'really' are, we may become, as it were, the place where Power enters the web. Any other place would do as well, but the Power that sustains things has to enter somewhere. This model does to some extent reflect what contemplatives claim, that their prayer is both their own, and also God's free choice of them. When they celebrate Mass, priests of this persuasion believe or even feel it to be God-in-Christ who celebrates. What He celebrates and offers is His own eternal and unrepeated sacrifice.

Ritual worship and personal prayer alike may be understood as occasions when we share, symbolically or literally, in the divine sacrifice by which the world is made. In one sense the divine could get on perfectly well without it; in another, it is foolish to say so. For though the divine need not create anything, its doing so (with a view to sharing its felicity with genuinely other beings) requires that it need those others to join in, by 'giving up themselves to its service, and by walking before it in humbleness and quietness all their days'. Maybe after all the chief end of humankind is not merely to preserve political harmony for the sake of human happiness (as if we knew what that was, independently of our religious judgements), but to learn to share the feast.

The Eternal Return

On this account our sacrifice of praise and thanksgiving is not a technique for securing favours from an egomaniacal tyrant, but a way of sharing in the divine life, and perhaps allowing it an entry into the world of our contrivance. There may even be something to be said for chantry priests and multiple celebrations of the one Mass. It is worth mentioning in this context the ancient idea that such ritual observances are not merely memorials, and certainly not repetitions of a previously concluded act. They are the human entry to That Time, the time before time, the beginning. Protestant progaganda and Roman folk-religion notwithstanding, Catholic dogma of the Mass emphatically denies that a priest offers any new sacrifice: he only shares in the one sacrifice. The same has been said of ritual observance in other religious traditions.

Sharing may be analysed in some such way as I have described: participation in a wider identity, a glimpse of the divine self-giving. What shall we say of the myth of the eternal return? I suggested in chapter 3, in line with anthropological information, that rites of passage seem designed to draw attention to the logical impossibility of time, the existence of something that transcends past and future. What concern me here are not those rituals (which mark off before and after), but ones that purport to be the very action of the eternal, ceaselessly renewed. The celebration of the eucharist does not divide time (though a believer's first communion may) in the way that a marriage or a baptism does. It is an action performed in time, but one that purports also to be outside time. My attempt to make sense of this doctrine, and to expound its underlying metaphysic, will involve a digression, into the metaphysics of astrology, that may puzzle some readers. Those who wish may simply skip this section.

Not all pious believers, after all, see ritual observance as something that stands, or looks, outside time, outside our ordinary daily lives. Piety is often shown in a dislike of any ritual that seems to coerce or confine the gods. Those whose chief religious experience lies in the dedication of the individual conscience to the One, and who live in relatively unstructured societies, may regard the ritual observances of their neighbours with amusement or scorn. For them worship must be entirely 'this-worldly', a matter of communal hymn-singing or reading of the scriptures to provide the individual with such force and learning as she needs to cope with time. This may so far degenerate as to be no more than an exchange of moral aphorism, the sort of social reinforcement that all of us (even the most firmly individualistic) sometimes need. We need to confirm to ourselves that any reasonable person may think that, say, capitalism is the cause of crime, women are hard-done-by, and the millenium will come by class-solidarity. The smaller the sect, the more intense the slogan-chanting and rhetorical argument. In this situation it may be as well sometimes to recall the merits of religious ritual, as an opening into a world that does not feed upon our current preoccupations, that is what it is and not just what we would have it be.

So how can we make sense of 'religious services', those careful structures that stand outside our everyday perception of temporal process? What, for that matter, is temporal process? Two features stand out: first, that times change; second, that the past is lost to us. Times change. Our present situation, though it may be like indefinitely many past situations in indefinitely many ways, is not what the past situations were. We are constantly confronting new occasions. The natural world, at least in equable climes, does give us a constantly renewed sense of meeting with 'the same situation' again and again: spring returns, and the swallow. It is as if we were walking round the seasons' track, meeting 'the same' seasons. In the merely temporal order they are never the same seasons: the spring of 1984 is not the same spring as the spring of 1489. In extreme cases one might say that the rising sun (or the sun's rising) of 23 July is not that of 24 July – a thought that seems to have nagged at the Aztecs. Of the rising sun we can say that there is one sun and many risings, whereas there is not one spring that rhythmically returns (except in poetic fiction). But though common sense insists that the sun is a substance (an individual bearer of properties that can be reidentified through many manifestations and under many names) and spring is not, the poetic fiction is very powerful. It remains possible that our readiness to see phenomena as the result of occasionally present real powers should be taken seriously. Maybe Spring is real after all, and even the thirty-six decans of the mediaeval zodiac (three strange figures to each zodiacal sign). These latter were intensely imagined forms, employed in the art of memory and in magical rites: as the decans of Taurus, 'a man ploughing, a man bearing a key, a man holding a serpent and a spear' (Yates (1966) p. 210). Our system of 'returning' seasons, months and festivals is crude by comparison with Renaissance zodiacal magic (a movement inextricably bound up with the growth of modern science), or the fifty-year calendars of Central America. Wheels within wheels rotate down time's highway, constantly reintroducing us to old friends and enemies: the intensely imagined forms that are the sun's passage through Scorpio in conjunction with Saturn, when Mars is in Taurus, and the like. Serious astrology is founded on the conviction that time is not merely linear, an endless motion from one state to another: instead it involves passage beneath the sway of a finite number of abiding powers. That is why the occasional attack of a professional astronomer is beside any sensible point, and further evidence of the indomitable ignorance of specialists! Astrology is not refuted by naive reminders that the planets are a long way off, or that the constellations from which zodiacal figures take their name are arbitrary aggregates of unconnected stars, and no longer occupy the parts of the sky where popular astrology places those figures. Astrological conclusions about the character to be expected of entities or projects begun 'when the sun is in the House of Scorpio' do not rest on any theory about the immaterial influence of the light of the stars in the constellation Scorpio. They are instead an attempt to reach behind the phenomena by intuiting the imaginative unity, the ever-recurring entity that is one House, one decan, one planet or another. The heavens, as seen from earth, are a decodable representation of a cosmic dance. That they are also the phenomenal effects of planetary orbs that move in accordance with the Newtonian laws of motion is not in conflict with this astrological view – any more than the fact that these shapes here-now are produced in accordance with complex laws of physics, chemistry and biology in any way conflicts with the certain fact that they are a decodable representation of my meaning.

The astrological structure whose debased form still fascinates the general public (confess: have you not read your 'horoscope' in this last month?) is not the only possible one, and is probably nothing like the truth. It serves us as an example of one constantly recurring response to our life in time: we would like to have the same things back again, and will not readily submit to a merely linear count of arbitrarily long moments (as one might say it is now 10^{57} chronons since the Big Bang). The round of months and festivals represents to us a truth: that we are always walking round an eternal order, that we are not getting further away from it with every passing chronon. 'Ceremonial time' does not change. Our ceremonials are greetings to the particular power or energy whose rule is upon us. Occasions that we thought were new are only unfamiliar permutations by the standing powers, and when we look 'back' we find that we have met them all before. A reasonably intelligent forty-year old has seen, so the Stoic emperor Marcus Aurelius said, the whole past and future of the universe (*Meditations* 11.1). The author of *Ecclesiastes* felt much the same.

The comfort provided by ceremonial time can, of course, turn sour: the thought may grow that we cannot escape, that all our thoughts and doings (including this) are fixed by the celestial game our betters play. That is why the pious have usually insisted that the astrological powers were not God, that God could yet make all things new, that God had delivered His true friends from the grasp of celestial demons. We are not tied to the wheel, though the wheel rolls on. Anthropologists who have uncovered the almost universal tendency to belief in 'cyclical time' (which is to say, our walk around the fixed stations of the zodiacal powers) therefore do wrong to think that this is all religion is, the service of these intensely imagined presences that manifest themselves as springtime and harvest, or the first third of March. In theistic and Buddhistic tradition alike, such presences are servants of the enlightened one, not masters.

The eucharistic ritual (to return to this one example) may be celebrated in accordance with the Church's Year: Advent, Christmas, Epiphany, Lent, Easter, Pentecost and

the passionless Sundays after Trinity,
neither feast-day nor fast.

The familiar collects are prayed, the cycle of readings heard, but something is also going on that reaches past the wheel. A pagan religion which has forgotten the One behind the gods may be content to see Christ born at Yule, dead and raised at Easter, as if he were indeed the Year-Daimon whom an earlier generation of anthropologists detected in all myth and ritual. True piety remembers that Christ is to be born in our hearts always, that his resurrection (which is not simply his bodily revival) is a 'present' fact.

Cyclical or ceremonial time, although it partly answers the helplessness sometimes engendered by the thought that times change, does not preserve our past for us. Although the yearly reappearance of the green leaves and the swallow may be understood as our encounter with an abiding Spring, it does not return our past encounters. We remember very little. The earth itself 'remembers' very little, since the effects of every past event are slowly lost. Things would be different now if some other man had been the Kaiser, or if the Tungulka meteor had struck New York instead: so our present-day situation can be regarded as a kind of memory of the actual events. But whether things would be very different now if Alexander had lived on a year or two, or Helen resisted Paris, is quite obscure, and what Caesar (let alone an anonymous soldier in his army) had for breakfast by the Rubicon is wholly undeterminable. The anti-realist philosophers, with whom this book is an oblique debate, would have to say that Caesar's breakfast and his servant's name are now figments, that historical 'truths' last only as long as the 'evidence' for them. Arthur Prior, a logician and philosopher who died untimely, found this concept consoling, in that many truths we would be glad to forget will in due course cease to be truths at all. Even those of us who hold to realism, to the vulgar belief that Caesar either had porridge or he didn't (even if we never know which), can agree the past events are constantly, though erratically, slipping out of effective reality, and that this is often a consoling thought. What has happened will not determine the world for ever: what we do now does not usually, if ever, swing the universe from one potential future to a radically different one. Cleopatra's nose does not really determine destiny, a parent's cross word does not really bring a nation to its knees.

But consoling though this limitation on our powers, and on the longevity of the causal daisy-chain, may be, it also constitutes a loss. What are lost are not only the memories and effects of what has happened, but also the probabilities that were not realized, the lives we did not live which hang around us all like ghosts. Some speculative philosophers have suggested that all possible worlds are realized in the multi-dimensional matrix of which 'our' world is a segment, that all my decisions and indecisions have, somewhere, gone all possible ways. This extraordinarily unpleasant thought implies that decisions never matter, as things will go all possible ways in any case, but does not actually solve the existential problem posed by the loss of our potentialities. That there is a parallel world in which I, or my doppelgänger, chose to be a monk or an actor, to settle in Japan or accept an offered friendship, may be of minor psychological interest, but does not alter the fact that this world's Stephen cannot now have done these things. What is really required to satisfy us is that there be a store in which all that is good and worthy of remembrance still exists, and in which unrealized potentials it were well to realize are teased out. This perhaps is what Purgatory has been supposed to be, the discovery of unrealized good, the memory of what is worth remembering. Dante, at the top of Purgatory Peak, drinks first of Forgetfulness and then of Good Remembrance.

The eucharist, whose believers are 'one bread, one body because they all partake of the one bread', has been understood as an offering of the whole body of the faithful. There all lives meet, and all participants in every age are 'contemporaries', remembered in their and our eternal forms. There is, on this 'high' view of the sacrament, only one celebration of the eucharist, endlessly mirrored or transmitted in this world of time. The science-fiction writer, James Blish, probably without quite intending it, offered a secular metaphor: an imagined Dirac transmitter whose transmissions are received at every receiver simultaneously, and so (it turns out) at every moment. To speak on a Dirac transmitter is to speak to all times, because it has only one eternal time. In Blish's story, 'Beep', an elite and esoteric group grows up to use and protect that knowledge.

On this interpretation, sacraments such as the eucharist are viewed as transtemporal exchanges. Those for whom this is merely a rather strained metaphor may agree that a ritual known or believed to have been performed over the centuries does give a sense of contact with an otherwise forgotten past. This is merely subjective, and must be sustained by whatever device will give us that 'historical sense'. If it is more than a metaphor, and the eucharist a single celebration scattered over time, the precise 'accidents' of its scattering matter less. It is the same body whatever bread appears, and (within reason) whatever words are said. It is the Divine Man's sacrifice.

Humility and Self-Sacrifice

The tradition of sacrificial prayer seems to require both that it is we, as individuals in linear history, who act, and also that we are thereby at one with a presence and action that is not subject to 'linear history'.

History is linear, rather than cyclical, if every event happens only once, and is preceded and followed by indefinitely many other such events. However long we live, or however far we travel, we shall never again encounter the lost years of our innocence. But although the divine sacrifice gets further away in linear time, it is always just as present in the world of prayer. Religious error, correspondingly, comes in two forms: on the one hand, some devote themselves to what goes on in the world as we ordinarily conceive it, the world of linear history, and imagine that God's Kingdom is not yet established, or even that God needs our assistance; on the other, some contemplate the eternal as a refuge from history. The first group gradually become indistinguishable from secular millenarians; the second are in retreat.

Sacrificial prayer, the offering of one's heart through the mediation of God-in-Humanity, was once the core of piety. Ancient and medieval religious literature was concerned with prayer, not with social justice or even sacramental theology. The necessary virtues that we must attempt to bring to prayer include humility, charity, simplicity, generosity, courage, patience and desire (though the 'desire' in question must include a willingness not to receive: the Spanish mystic, St John of the Cross is almost Buddhistic in his rejection of anything that we would ordinarily call 'desire'). Of these the most peculiar 'virtue' to the ordinarily pagan eye is humility. What is it, and why have the religious usually thought it so necessary?

The claim that they have, of course, is questionable. It is frequently alleged that serious pagans, well-read in the great Greek philosophers, found the Christian concentration on humility repugnant, that they admired instead those 'great-souled' and honourable persons who had an accurate perception of their own high worth. Truly virtuous persons knew that they were virtuous, and reckoned themselves as admirable as any other. Protestations of personal sinfulness, whether accurate or not, reflected ill on the speaker's character. How could God prefer a 'broken and a contrite heart' to a heart rightly convinced of its own virtue? It could not be that God should take the weak, the sinful and the foolish for His friends: the wise were His friends, and all things belonged to them (since all belonged to God, and friends have everything in common). Christians by contrast followed Judaic precedent in reckoning that 'all our righteousness is dirty rags', and that God made His friends wherever He chose. It was not by our independent merit that we might hope to please Him, as if there were some other eternal source of virtue than Himself.

The contrast is a real one, but we may doubt that the disputing parties quite understood each other. Serious pagans, on the one hand, were as convinced as Hebrews of the unwisdom of *hubris*, arrogance.

Even the noblest, most virtuous and most successful – especially they – must remember their place, that they are not gods, nor God. Popularly conceived deity was jealous of human prowess, and ever ready to strike down the presumptuous. The philosophers' god was not so grudging, and welcomed the truly virtuous. But, even so, virtue was displayed in submission to the Law. If everything 'belonged' to the wise, it was not for them to use in any way that anyone might imagine. Conversely, the Judaic and Christian tradition did not require that saints should cringe before just any self-styled Lord: on the contrary, obedient submission to God required a real independence of mind and action. Those who know their own smallness and insufficiency may be released from worldly fears.

Not all 'self-sacrifice' is godly. Popular secular morality has inherited an approval of 'altruism' and 'self-sacrifice' that may justly be questioned. 'Living for others' is not a project that can be enjoined on all ('what puzzles me is what the *others* are for'), nor one that the others are always likely to approve. Those who self-consciously 'live for others' are, it has been claimed, either seeking to make the others into what they think worthy, or else are living a contradiction. How can I really say that I will not seek out what I conceive to be good, but always let my judgement and purpose be overruled by another finite being, doing what *they* want rather than what I would want? Trying to live like that is surely an abnegation of personal responsibility, in favour of slavery, and is also very likely to be hypocritical: what it really amounts to is striving for peace and quiet at whatever cost. Being what we are, it may be well for us to praise 'altruists' (those who act to secure another's good) even when they achieve no greater good than 'egoists' (those who aim to secure their own): but if these altruists are genuinely moral agents they should rather be described as people who find their own good in helping others. Such a 'sacrifice' does not involve loss, but gain: the decently self-sacrificial are those who share, not those who let someone else have the burden of deciding what is to be done.

Those who sacrifice themselves for others – in the popular sense – are slaves; those who sacrifice others to themselves are despots. Those who have woken up to freedom know, however inarticulately, that there are other forms of companionship. Friends do not slavishly 'give up' their own purposes so that the other gets her way (what then gets done?). Neither do they insist on their own way at whatever cost to their friendship. Instead all take as their chief goal and good the maintenance and increase of their friendly association, and their common ideal. From the point of view of such friendship, any insistence on always being the one to 'sacrifice' rather than accepting the other's service is recognizably egotistical, an arrogant assumption that the other has nothing to contribute. 'Genuine' humility and love accepts an equality of effort.

Friendship – which is to say, love purged of concupiscence (the desire to possess and dominate) – constitutes an Aristotelian middle path between slavery and despotism. It also serves as a model for genuine humility. What the hymn calls 'true lowliness of heart, that takes the humbler part and o'er its own short-comings weeps with loathing' is an inch away from arrogance. The truly humble do not distrust the divine forgiveness, nor imagine that they have somehow managed an irrecoverable fall. The obverse fault, of supposing that one's faults are venial because they are one's own, is as comic. The pious know that they live by God's mercy, and are content to do so, not supposing that they can compensate for their sins – any more than friends need to keep an exact account of who owes what to whom. If they do keep such a tally, they are not *friends*, and will not be so as long as they make such divisions.

When religious tradition advises humility, it is not the sort of slavishness that cringes now in hope of gradually accumulating credit till we end as 'equals' or 'superiors'. If religious tradition advises an awareness of our identity with the Divine, or the presence in us of the divine spark or the divine image, it is not the sort of humanistic arrogance that reckons others are not so 'divine'. Humble obedience 'even unto death',| accepting every supposed humiliation as| something that involves no outraged dignity, may seem very different from the alternative response to disaster, which reckons such outward events as of no account. There is indeed a great difference between one who has abandoned a sense of dignity (like St Francis) and one whose dignity, whose own feeling of personal worth, is impervious to the judgement of those he reckons his inferiors. But the ideals are not, perhaps, all that far apart. St Francis's humility, his willingness (even his eagerness) to be 'made a fool of', to be stripped of all social status and graces, was conjoined with a sense of being personally loved – not for anything he did (and might fail to do), but as a member by baptism and vocation of Christ's body. A sense of being infinitely loved, and a sense of infinite personal worth, not dependent on our having achieved any special status, but on our mere existence, are not all that different. To be properly humble is simply to accept one's own being as something that God, inscrutably, wills to preserve, on His terms and not in virtue of any spurious social status.

Humble obedience to the law and our vocation, animated by friendship, constitutes the sacrifice that piety demands. All other material and social 'sacrifice' is only vulgarly so called. We think of it as 'sacrificial' because we think of it as a loss, even though we know that we did not ourselves create it, and 'give it to God' only by ignoring the fact that it is already at His absolute disposal. 'Mine are the cattle on a thousand hills'. The one thing that is not, under the terms of the game, at His absolute disposal, is the tiny movement of the heart that sets us towards humility rather than ignorant pride. That motion is our only sacrifice, for only that can make us 'sacred', part of His network rather than a self-deluded would-be-individual, divided in imagination from the very system that gives us life.

According to Toynbee, 'every living creature is striving to make itself into a centre of the Universe, and in the act, is entering into rivalry with every other living creature, with the Universe itself, and with the Power that creates and sustains the universe and that is the Reality underlying the fleeting phenomena' (1956, p. 2). Whether this is true of literally *every* living creature is more than I know; even the thought that any creature can really rival the Universe and *Natura naturans* (i.e. Nature conceived as the Power that sustains, rather than as the complex of things sustained by that Power) seems a little extreme. We certainly imagine ourselves as if we were such individual divinities, and the sacrifice of prayer and thanksgiving, if it is anything, is part of our road back to more realistic imaginings.

Further reading

Aho (1981), Brundage (1979), Cardenal (1974), Clark (1975), Stace (1952), Toynbee (1956), Yates (1966).

On the concept of worship see Smart (1972). Prayer is discussed from an anti-realist standpoint by Phillips (1965), and more realistically (but with less philosophical sophistication) by Bloom (1980).

The virtues, especially those of humility, are discussed by Geach (1977b). The criticisms of 'slavishness' made by moralists like Nietzsche and Ayn Rand are echoed in Machan (1975).

Time, and especially the eternal return, is described by Eliade (1959). See also Fraser (1968), Gale (1978) and King-Farlow (1978). Prior (1967) provides tense-logics for several non-ordinary conceptions of time.

We have done with dogma and divinity,
    Easter and Whitsun past,
the long, long Sundays after Trinity
    are with us at last;
the passionless Sundays after Trinity,
    neither feast-day nor fast.

Christmas comes with plenty,
    Lent spreads out its pall,
but these are five and twenty,
    the longest Sundays of all;
the placid Sundays after Trinity,
    wheat-harvest, fruit-harvest, Fall.

Spring with its burst is over,
    summer has had its day,
the scented grasses and clover
    are cut and dried into hay;
the singing birds are silent,
    and the swallows have flown away.

Post pugnam pausa fiet;
    Lord, we have made our choice;
in the stillness of autumn quiet,
    we have heard the still, small voice.
We have sung *Oh where shall Wisdom?*
    Thick paper, folio, Boyce.

Let it not all be sadness,
    not *omnia vanitas*,
stir up a little gladness
    to lighten the *Tibi cras*;
send us that little summer,
    that comes with Martinmas

when still the cloudlet dapples
    the windless cobalt blue,
and the scent of gathered apples
    fills all the store-rooms through,
the gossamer silvers the bramble,
    the lawns are gemmed with dew.

An end of tombstone Latinity,
    stir up sober mirth,
twenty-fifth after Trinity,
    kneel with the listening earth,
behind the Advent trumpets
    they are singing Emmanuel's birth.

(John Meade Falkner, 'After Trinity')

10

Household, Sex and Gender

Due Order in Society and Cosmos

Religious understanding of the cosmos is closely related to religious construction of household and society. In the first place, we understand the cosmos in terms of the emotions, characters and wills that are our first environment: we socialize the whole cosmos, as it were, in accordance with the first pattern of childhood experience. Just as children have to learn their adults' whims and meanings, so we learn to recognize the 'expression' of the cosmos, to respond to it as friend and enemy and concerned outsider. Some of what we say about the cosmos may even look like coded utterances about family and social order. The image of 'Nature Red in Tooth and Claw' is not just a report on the way *animals* behave: it is a way of talking about how we might behave. Our wish to dominate or defeat 'Mother Nature' may say a lot about our patriarchalism. In the second place, the pattern we discover in the cosmos may be embodied in our regular 'personal' relationships. If the cosmos is governed, as we suppose, by the Father of Gods and Men, a patriarchal order is embodied in the household, not because each individual male can hope to enforce his will by his own strength and force of character (gorillas may manage this, but the human male is not so much bigger and stronger than the female) but because he symbolizes the Father. Where the circle of influence begins, of course, may be obscure: social order and imagined cosmos are mutually responsive. Older thinkers tended to assume that social order was founded on a recognition of the cosmic; modernists tend to assume that the way we imagine the cosmos is founded on 'natural' social order, and even that our religiosity is a distinctively mammalian response, the fantasy induced by a prolonged infancy and parental care. Would turtles, supposing that they could articulate their response to life, be likely to conceive a protective deity, or any meaning in the newly hatched turtle's dash through danger to the sea?

Both sides have a point. The way we are born into the world presumably has some connection with the way we think of it. At the least, we could hardly 'read' the cosmos if we had no experience of 'reading' each other. But too ready an assumption that we can identify certain 'natural' social orders, and explain our religious feelings on the basis of these other, social feelings, is probably misguided. Most of us inhabit 'houses' or 'flats' – groups of rooms, each with a different function, separated from other such houses by lockable doors and windows. We may no longer have hearths, but we have thresholds, and it is still a fairly distinctive event for someone to cross that threshold. Most of us, even now, expect to live in family households, with a husband and a wife, children and perhaps an elder relative and a pet or two. The pattern, to be sure, is changing in the settled West, and the changes may draw our attention to the artificiality of these arrangements. Family houses, it has been argued not implausibly (by Lord Raglan) began as little copies of royal palaces, and these of temples. We make a division between household and outside, family and non-family, that reflects the ancient division of sacred and profane. Each male householder, not long ago, could hope to be king and priest within a settled realm, between threshold and hearth. Other forms of household (e.g. the Hellenic) were differently arranged: male householders did not themselves live in the inner rooms, the women's territory, the sanctuary from which non-familiars were excluded. Other households (perhaps the global majority) do not inhabit groups of rooms or enclosed territories at all, or have clearly mapped out cosmic roles for men and women to play. The Forest Indians of South America live in federated communities of from forty to several hundred persons, sheltered when necessary in a communal house. Our form of family and household is a religious option, not a natural necessity. Accordingly, if our vision of heaven and the divine looks like an image of the earthly forms, we should ask whether the vision of heaven might not have come first.

It is a feature of ideologically motivated structures that they seem merely natural and obvious to their inhabitants. Obviously we have houses to keep out the rain, and keep our possessions secure, and provide private rooms for our families. Obviously we have families because males and females like each other and want children. Obviously Father, Son and Holy Spirit are a cosmic reflection of the ideal love, and the church's main function is to preserve the proper forms of family life. Future archaeologists will doubtless explain the 'Easter Gardens' constructed in Christian churches in the spring as celebrations of British floralism, the 'natural' passion of householders for a patch of green and flowering stuff around their houses. Though maybe by that time the archaeologists will have more occasion to know that it is not a natural necessity that we live in houses with gardens, with Mummy Bear, Daddy Bear and a line of growing Baby Bears. They will have their own hangups.

If houses and families are not first causes of religious symbolism, we can hardly explain religion by reference to such artificial facts, although it will be true that byproducts of the social system will alter our religious system. Despite Freud there is no compelling reason to believe that human beings 'naturally' establish patriarchal families, isolated from non-familial influences. But if they do establish them, in combination with a tangle of sexual moralisms, it is hardly surprising that adolescent males become impatient with the Old Man and seek guiltily to overthrow him and enjoy the taste of his wives. Nor is it then surprising if their religious world-view is distorted to the point that they must think that 'God is dead' if they are ever to grow up. Oedipal atheism, so to speak, can be understood in part as a response to the intolerable strains of Austrian patriarchy. The moral of this is that stable religious and social systems must bring up the young in such a way that the system is not subverted by its own byproducts: a patriarchal and repressive order founded upon a religious perception of the cosmos as governed by a jealous *paterfamilias* (tormented by the sinister suspicion that someone somewhere is happy!) is likely enough to maintain itself in the hearts of the young – unless they break away. Oedipal atheism, the rejection of divine authority and a wish to take 'God's place', may be an historical effect of a decaying patriarchy. As less repressive social forms take shape, a new religiosity, centred perhaps upon 'good fellowship', emerges.

Of these twists and turns there is perhaps no end. What is of more philosophical interest is the way that a cosmic vision has been used to back up social order. The Way Things Are, or the Way they would be if there were no interference or disobedience, is of a piece. There is an order of things within which human beings have their place: they play a part in the natural order, and they have different parts to play in the detailed social order. As human beings, we exist to serve the gods by sacrifice, or to tend the garden, or to contemplate the divine, or to serve as an exit from the wheel (for only as human beings can souls be liberated, not as animals or gods). As males we exist to use weapons against game or warriors, or to beget children, or to maintain social ceremonials, or to build temples. As females we exist to bear children, or to cultivate gardens, or to obey our husbands, or to manage households. Even within a single life our roles may change: from child to student to householder to *sannyasin* (renouncer), or through manifold layers of ceremonial initiation. In confused and polytheistic ages we may lose all sense of single identity through the transformations society requires (and invent philosophers who will deny that there is any single self to be concerned about). In the first confusion, people who can now imagine not behaving as their sexual role requires, confusedly believe that they are 'homosexual' or 'transsexual', instead of realizing that they are free to devise a new way of living. In the backlash, those who still hold by the older ways (or what they think were the older ways) insist that all experiments in living are treasonable, that there is one true order endorsed by the divine (and usually no older than a century or so).

The notion that there is a 'proper order' in terms of which we have functions has not been popular among moralists. Their claim has been that human individuals are not valuable merely instrumentally, and are independent choosers: there is nothing I am 'for' until I decide to embark on that particular project – to think otherwise is to suppose that I have standing obligations not of my own choosing. Put like that, the notion is a very peculiar one. What morally responsible person doubts that she may have obligations 'not of her own choosing'? Could I have obligations at all if I had no standing obligations even to keep my word, or abide by tacit compacts? Modern moralists talk a great deal about autonomy, the supposed duty of each individual to make her own decisions, her own promises. But why exactly should other individuals respect the absolute autonomy of any one individual? To do so, after all, is to allow their own autonomy to be restricted. Historically, the claims of absolute individualism are relics of three great movements: the first, a conception of divine reason as embodied equally, as the 'inner light', in all; the second, an insistence that political authority comes 'from below' (from the consent of the governed) and not from 'above' (from divine establishment); the third, a preference for 'impersonal' justifications on the part of a socially mobile, intellectual elite. The first movement developed in two directions. Some concluded that it was *reason* which spoke in each individual only when it said the same as it would in every other individual – the only obligations were those that could be conceived to be binding equally on all. Others preferred a more romantic creed: each individual self was queen of her own property, no matter what others might say, and her 'obligations' only what she chose to do. The second, explicitly political, movement also divided: was the necessary consent of the governed real or ideal? If it was the real consent that counted, government had only such authority over anyone as that one gave, and no more than the most minimal of states could be approved. If 'consent' was ideal, then the state could claim (and did) all such authority as the intelligentsia agreed would 'rationally' be consented to by reasonable people (even if ordinarily reasonable people did not in fact consent), and there were no practical limits to state authority (bound no longer by any sense that it owed its authority to its function in an already established order). The third movement is part of the apparatus of class-division: the upwardly mobile middle classes characteristically use 'impersonal' explanations of the behaviour they expect of their children; less socially mobile parents use 'personal' or 'functional' modes of control. Where the one parent says that it's wrong to pull your sister's hair because it hurts her, or because 'you wouldn't like that if I did it to you', the other says that it's wrong because 'good little boys don't do that', or 'your father said so', or 'I'll box your ears if you do it again'. As most professional moralists are drawn from the upwardly mobile classes (who must deal with people from many backgrounds and localities, and so cannot rely on a sense of fixed status), it is hardly surprising that they have neglected such local and personal rulings.

If these are historical movements, and if history shows that many societies have taken it for granted that there is an established order, that human beings do have functions, that 'the individual' is not the only arbiter of what one should do, what can we say about the arguments usually used in favour of moral and political individualism? Why has it been thought wrong to suppose that human beings 'have functions', and even different functions? More worryingly: is it possible that such individualism, once established in a religious respect for personal salvation, has begun to subvert the social order which gave rise to it? The spread of creeds which deliberately erode individual autonomy (requiring their followers simply to obey) at the same time as there is taking place a decline in the philosophical and social security of the 'personal self' is not encouraging. Decision-making becomes a function either of the sect-leader (who may order his followers to shave their heads, get married, beg in the streets or kill themselves), or of the momentary will. At the least, if liberals do not understand the challenge, they cannot adequately answer it.

Sex, Families and Phalansteries

Amongst the recurring forms of relationship that have been used to symbolize the relationship of mortal and immortal, and that have in turn been affected by beliefs about that relationship, are the following: male-female, mother-child, father-child, and to a lesser extent the relations of brothers, sisters or friends. The first three constitute (along with the master-slave relationship, which I shall ignore) the basic structure of the simple family, as described by Aristotle. In various combinations they provide a code for discourse about heaven and earth. Correspondingly, heaven and earth provide a code for discourse about the relations of male and female, parent and child and kinsfolk. Current fashion in anthropology is to interpret religious ritual and doctrine as a set of coded statements about family and state. Half a century ago there was an equally pervasive assumption that they were about seed-time and harvest, and the weather. It seems likely that current preoccupations will seem just as laughable a century hence, but there will doubtless still be a deep-seated unwillingness to think that religious ritual and doctrine are actually about the gods.

Male and female are standardly related in two ways, as lovers and as parents. Parentage is a social concept, not a biological one, and the two who have joint care of a child may be brother and sister, not lovers, and there may, in some cultures, be no tradition of joint 'parentage' at all. The two relationships that no human society can entirely escape are those of sexual partnership and motherhood. Everything else is indefinitely manipulable, and even these are very diverse in form. If we think of all such relationships as available for use as a language, each continuing tradition has a different dialect: we can convey information to each other (and perhaps especially to our children) by the way that we try to arrange our families. We convey information when what we do (or say, or write) is different from what we would do under other circumstances. My doodles do not mean very much, because their character does not vary with the situation in any systematic way. It is at least widely held in anthropological circles that family arrangements are more like words than like doodles: our stereotypes of Mother, Father and the Children carry implications about the rest of the world we inhabit. There will be some things that people within any given tradition will hardly be able to avoid 'saying' (unless they opt out of the system entirely); other things that they may find it very difficult to 'say' or even to think. Current fashion amounts to the belief that such statements in 'social-ish' are about nothing but themselves. It seems an unnecessary and pointless assumption. When Paul defended strict monogamy against advocates of divorce, adultery or remarriage by referring to the great mystery of Christ and His Church, he clearly believed that monogamous relationships made a statement about cosmic reality, not that mystical theology was a covert way of speaking about marital relationships. The idea that our ancestors were too devious or too embarrassed to speak openly about such things is about as silly as the older suggestion that they told tales of gods and dragons because they wanted to say that the sun would rise on time. Perhaps some did see the old dragon, Night, slain in the redness of each succeeding dawn, but if they did it was because they saw that story told in the sun's rising, not because the story only meant that the sun rose. Similarly, if people so arrange things that male and female wed, and dress them as gods for the occasion, it is because they want to 'say' and 'hear' a claim about the universe – for example, that the Divine will one day be united with His Beloved.

Either both male and female stand for the divine, or one does not. If both stand for the divine, the claim is made that, for example, Shiva and Shakti dance at the world's heart, the god and His power, or Yahweh joins with the Shekinah (the glory of God) in the Temple. Marriage and copulation are to be a way of saying that there is this glad duality in the divine, that 'God Themselves' is not alone. The merely 'secular' use of the symbolic apparatus is accordingly blasphemous, a 'taking of God's name in vain'. Marriage and copulation may even be more than a symbolic utterance: the partners may not merely believe some such doctrine, but experience its truth, may feel themselves to be taken up into a divine exchange. Male and female are possessed by Shiva and Shakti in the act, so that they find themselves doing or having done things that they would not have planned. If what they do (or the gods do in them) is not what orthodox believers can conceive the gods to do, it is an easy step to conclude that this copulation at least involved possession by fake gods, or demons. Only copulation that does not betray the faith is divinely blessed and ordered, for it cannot be that the gods would contradict themselves. Accordingly 'improper copulation' is possession by rebel spirits.

What does this polarity of male and female in the divine amount to? Doubtless trisexual beings would have reason to imagine God as Three-in-One, but it seems likely that more is intended than a mere insistence (sound as that insistence is) that neither sex is without its divine archetype. The philosophy of the Upanisads insists that the original self-knowledge of the One must, logically, involve it in duality: this is not a historical point, as if there was once a time when the One did not know itself, but a logical one. Subject and object, the knowing and what is known, are logically distinct, and when one knows itself, the self it knows is generated as something 'other' than the knowing one. The One becomes Two, and all self-conscious life thereafter knows itself as in a mirror by knowing its other half. Understandably enough, the 'Other' is usually female, the 'One' male (since it is male theologians who wrote down their musings).

Sometimes only one sex symbolizes the divine. If male and female stand for Christ and His Church, or Yahweh and Israel, adultery is a symbolic apostasy, and obedience to the husband, self-sacrificing care for the wife stand for the proper religious duties of Israel and God. Alternatively, if it is the female that stands for the divine, a lover's loyal service of his mistress symbolizes the soul's attempt to reach out to the One beyond all categories, the flight of the alone to the Alone. In

Western tradition it is noticeable that matrimony goes along with a masculine divinity, and a feminine divinity with more romantic liaisons. Whereas a God-fearing woman is expected to find God in her one man, a Goddess-loving man is allowed to see his divinity in successive mistresses (whether or not they consummate the match). This may be merely another rationalization of the sociobiologically explicable observation (or socially induced delusion) that females are likelier to stick by one mate, males likelier to prefer variety. In the absence of any genuine proof that this observation is correct, it seems preferable to ask instead what theological point is made in the difference.

Monogamous orthodoxy and the creed of romantic love embody different attitudes to the divine, and are hardly comprehensible outside this context. Monogamy requires the husband to care faithfully for his wife and raise a people from her, maintaining due order in the household, rebuking sin but never locking out the penitent. It requires a wife to obey her husband and not be diverted from her sworn oath by romantic temptation and entanglement. The divine that both must serve requires good order in the community, and reliance upon sworn loyalty, not romantic passion. The cult perhaps spread by the troubadors, upon the other hand, requires the lover to abandon or betray all other delights and duties at the arbitrary appearance and command of erotic beauty, and never to transform that beauty into the mere friendship and shared duties of a household, but to follow the divine embodied in his lady where it leads. It may even be unwise to consummate the affair, as that begins another cycle and may cool the passion. It is better to burn than to marry. Romantic love requires the lady to receive and gratify that passion (short, perhaps, of consummation), and be forever one that must be courted and won again, never taken for granted, never merely mortal. The recurrent evocation of this theme, in the poems of Robert Graves or the fantasies of E.R. Eddison or in popular song and romantic fiction, is not merely founded upon 'natural lust'. The whole system is profoundly 'unnatural', and only with difficulty are traces of it found in other cultures. Sexual attraction is a fact of human life: romantic love, of the kind that I have just described, is a religious invention. Its theme and centre is a rejection of mere sociality in favour of a transcendent ideal, mirrored evanescently in time's moving mirror. The spirit it awakens is an individual passion that makes a new creature of the lover, an enthusiasm that makes of him a god of peculiar kind – a god in need. He is possessed by, or is, a god, because he is suffused with an immortal passion which would vanish if consummated: he is a god because he is not perfect.

A society and religious tradition that gave romantic love the crown would be no society at all, for who would go about the ordinary business set in motion by the lovers? As a reminder that social order is not everything, that there is also a Flight of the Alone to the Alone, it may persist within a largely marital community. The romantic lover, one might say, embodies in the language of personal relationships what that other sort of renouncer, the *sannyasin*, does: a road away from established order in search of the God who is not bound by our expectations. It is necessary to add what ought to be an obvious remark: romantic love, despite its idealizing of the female, is no more a feminist creed than the romanticized notion of motherhood (on which more below). The lady is expected to be passive, mysterious, and unconcerned with children and housekeeping: if her biology betrays her, her lover may be off to follow the true object of his worship, the ever-virgin Lady who only housed herself in the mortal companion. Monogamous society may seem cynical in its depreciation of romantic passion, and has certainly been oppressive in its patriarchalist jealousy, but it embodies moral insights and practical concerns that romanticists forget. Where they agree is in their view that feminity is passive, whether they conclude that all of us are 'female' relatively to God (as Christian and Vedantin teachers have both said), or that God is the Eternal Feminine, the inactive goal of all endeavour.

In confused and changing times conservatives can usually see nothing but betrayal, anomy and despair. It is, however, possible to see new forms of decency developing, and to ask what theological doctrines those forms embody. Even Christian churches now allow divorce; even young believers see no harm in living or sleeping together 'without benefit of clergy', without establishing themselves as expressions of God's love for His Church, pledges of continuing fidelity to the social order and the coming generations. The last bastions of patriarchalist dogma are in the churches, where some people can be heard to insist that God is masculine, that women are suited only to obey, that women are so emotional, so enfeebled by their biology that they would be in total control within the year if allowed equal rights, pay and courtesy with men. Where conservatives see chaos, radicals see the collapse of embattled wickedness, and hope for the emergence of a new covenant, in which there shall be neither slave nor master, black nor white, male nor female. What religion is this?

Sometimes, no doubt, conservatives are right to see mere irreligion: a barbarian conviction that nothing counts but one's immediate whim, a sneering disregard for all ties of honour, history and the sacred. But that is not the only possibility. The forms of sexual relationship preferred amongst modern Westerners have not yet been firmly institutionalized (perhaps never will be), but there are forms. The first and simplest is the model of temporary contract, the undertaking by free and equal individuals to share the costs of housekeeping, the duties of child-care, for a while. Usually such partners 'marry' only when they have children, and till then live as 'ummers' (as in 'this is my daughter's . . . um . . . er'). The notion that free and finite contract is the real source of obligation is deeply rooted in liberal tradition, and no-one should be surprised that partnership in bed and board is now widely understood in that light, whether the partnership is heterosexual or homosexual. Once that model is established, only convention and occasional legal inconvenience prevent the emergence of quasi-marital compacts between three or more adults, the transformation of a couple pretending to marriage into something much more like a club. As long as steps are taken to make sure that children know their biological parents, male and female, it is not clear that such 'group marriages' or quasi-marriages should be opposed. Most such family-clubs, one may suspect, will turn out to be a catena of couples, not a sexual free-for-all, but the couples will change (as they do now, by divorce and the disruption of houses).

If such a development became at all common, our housing arrangements would alter, perhaps into something more like the courtyard system of more ancient patriarchies, with shared culinary and bathing facilities. There might even be chains of family-clubs, linked by exchange of guest-rights and shared assumptions about the furnishings, or about household practices, so that one might expect to find one's club, one's larger 'family' across the world. Those entering such a chain would not retain their older surname, but be adopted, effectively, into a clan. There would be advantages to this arrangement, and doubtless many disadvantages as well. Its emergence would say something about the assumptions we make about our place in the universe, might generate explicit rituals and declarations of faith. If it does not emerge from our present confusion, that too says something about our religious beliefs: maybe, after all, we wish to go on saying that the divine is Two, not multiplex.

One further variation of our possible future may make the religious theme, its accompanying theology, more clear. Such clubs, communes and phalansteries (to adopt the utopian philosopher Fourier's term), if they are to be more than conveniences for independent agents without real interest or involvement in each other or the resulting children (in which case they would not survive), must give their members a sense of belonging, a sense of identity, so that each may say (not 'I am married'; but) 'I am phalansteried'. In a patriarchal marriage, the wife is required to see her husband as a representative of God, the unifying will of the marriage. In a decent phalanstery, each member must see the consensus of the group as it emerges from mutual exchange and living, as the divine among us. The patriarchal God orders the cosmos, though she may resist and fall away. The phalanstery God is in the midst of them, the central point of balance where disagreements vanish, and each individual (liberal individualist no longer) wakes to find her real new opinion. Many such groups, we can be sure, will be torn by mutually irresoluble conflict, and the God be manifest only as the decision to dissolve the company. Their ideal will be of a more organic and responsive deity than our tradition has imagined, save in the words of prophets like Blake. The Council of God may be seen as a multitude or 'as One Man all the Universal family; and that One Man they call Jesus the Christ, and they in him and he in them live in perfect harmony, in Eden the land of life (William Blake, *Vala*, Night the first, line 472 ff.). Even Blake, unfortunately, spoke as if male and female together were one *Man*, one *Brotherhood*, but he undoubtedly intended a suitably non-sexist meaning.

If, on the other hand, we emphasize the separateness of one club from another rather than the idealized communion within a club, we can conceive that the Little Lares, the guardian angels of a family, may grow into larger godlings. Each club has its presiding genius. Anti-realists (for whom religious truths, like any others, are constituted simply by the reasons we have for asserting them) may say that the existence of the genius is constituted simply in the club's devotion to it. Realists may suspect that only those clubs will survive and prosper that find a genuine genius to serve.

Even those of us who, rejecting patriarchy and the spurious feminism of romantic love alike, still hold to our marriages as friends and companions may appreciate the sort of theological statement made by more communal institutions and rituals. We may even come to understand our own 'nuclear families' as variations on the communal ideal rather than the atomic particles which go to make up society. Three competing stories about the building blocks of human society generate their own theologies, their own institutions. The first, that society is made up of individual persons, freely contracting to each other, and taking out insurance for child-care and old age. The second, that society is made up of cooperating nuclear families, which occasionally collapse to burden the air with rootless solitaries. The third, that society is the community network within which ancestral families and colleges and clans can sometimes be distinguished, and individual persons are late historical abstractions, not the first of things. Worshipping the One All Alone, we may find in our individual selves the proper image of the worshipful, and reckon all bonds evil that constrain that thing. Worshipping the Twofold, we find once-married couples the real image, and resist all dissipation of monogamy.

Worshipping the Manifold-in-Unity, we approach another ideal: in the Kingdom of Heaven there is no marriage nor giving in marriage, not because the redeemed are become bodiless or uncooperative monads, but because God is in the midst of them, and they are all one flesh.

This last ideal has not been unknown in tradition. What is different, maybe, in modernist enactment of it is that our predecessors were more wary of allowing sexuality a place in their divine phalansteries. Sectarians who went that way were understood to be overthrowing social order, and the descent of property, as well as (and doubtless they often were) subjecting women (as the child-bearers and home-makers) to more ill-use than even monogamists would wish. Similar problems may yet bring us back to more stable couplings, but not to patriarchy.

Mother-Goddess and Father-God

Relations between male and female as lovers cannot be seen apart from their relationship as co-parents, the relationship between either one and children. Patriarchy, the institutional assumption that it is father who must govern his children, and the mothers of his children, determines much of what passes between mating couples. Children's ambivalent feelings about their parents, a mixture of adoration and resentment, may be projected onto adult mates: men see Mother, women Father in their opposites, and alternately desire to please and to defy the other. In patriarchal societies men are encouraged to maintain their independence, to resist their wives, and scorned if they give in to Mother. Women, conversely, are required to agree with their adversary quickly, and obey Father, even if they also believe that their husbands are like children. Since no sane, adult person can seriously commit herself to doing just what is ordered by someone she thinks immature and childish, the stage is set for a relationship of manipulative intrigue and secret disobedience. Established patriarchal families implicitly proclaim the message that God cannot safely be openly defied, that all the subtleties of personal affection and control have no place in the outside world of absolute, impersonal command, that serious adult life involves the control of 'feminine' emotion. Adult males, convinced that it is weakness, unmanliness to admit to doubts, ecstacies, affections of a kind not licenced by 'masculine' reason, need women to look after that part of their lives. A woman, correspondingly, must learn to express her spouse's fears and affections for him, knowing that he will then be able to dismiss them.

The patriarchal use of father-child imagery defines the most significant part of human life as impersonal obedience to 'rational' law, and exalts the divine above the fleshly and domestic. Children, or male children, are to be called out of the domestic to the outer world, where they can no longer count on personal affections but must share the heady burden of male duty. At the same time, Mother is idealized as unfailingly, but mindlessly, 'loving', undisturbed by any rationally perceived failing in her offspring, and requiring nothing in return. The intolerable burden of such an imagined duty, that can earn only affectionate contempt from her social peers, is doubtless one explanation for the high incidence of neurotic symptoms among mothers: no one should be expected to feel, or display, unlimited and uncritical affection. The equally intolerable burden of that love on its recipients, who must understand that it is wholly self-enclosed, and unrelated to their merits, explains why it is only guiltily returned.

In this convoluted system of mutual repression and deception, Father and Mother are opposing symbols. God as Father is the one who calls His people out from domesticity, who expects them to behave decently and who will be outraged if they do not, who speaks in the voice of universal reason and repeatable experiment. To patriarchalists the attempt to speak of God as Mother evokes the impression that such Goddess-worshippers would have us all sink back into an emotional, uncritical morass, forgetful of adult responsibility in the wider world. It may also evoke the hidden resentment likely to be felt against earthly mothers, for not being the unfailingly responsive comforters that they were supposed to be and for refusing to give the sensual affection the children want. Adulthood, for patriarchalists, requires that we grow out of our dependence on our mothers. Our fathers, by contrast, are reincarnated in successive authority figures, and adulthood requires that we continue to obey, to internalize Father's orders, to grow up to be Fathers too. Women, accordingly, can't grow up, and must always be the Father's daughters.

Opposition to women's candidacy for the priesthood, or the rabbinate, or offices of leadership in general, may be rationalized in many ways. The core of the opposition, however, always seems to be the twin theses that (i) women are naturally suited to the domestic sphere, and (ii) letting them stand as symbols of the divine inevitably says of the divine that it is known through emotion, darkness and partiality. Males embody the powers of formal reason, the rules needed for civil peace; females embody the irrational concession, the sensual involvement of the merely domestic scene. Ordaining women, accordingly, is no mere breach of traditional practice, but an heretical theological claim.

Oddly enough, those masculinist theologians sometimes find un-witting allies among feminists. Justifiably incensed by the way that women have been, and still are treated, some feminists have accepted the symbolic meanings attached to 'male' and 'female' and reversed the values. From the (possibly correct) assertion that women have had to be more in touch with their own and their masters' feelings, more adept at merely social intercourse, less wedded to abstract thought and regulation, feminists have moved to the wilder claim that Womanliness is truly incompatible with formal rules, abstract thinking, language and light. Whereas God-worshippers believe, though they cannot prove, that the divine is rational, abstractly benevolent and holy, Goddess-worshippers have been tempted to conclude that the divine is arbitrary, self-sufficient, unconcerned with morals. The old canard that women can never be really *moral* beings, can never decide to do something because they see that everyone similarly placed should do it, is echoed by feminists who denounce morality, reason and language as a patriarchalist invention.

It seems likely, to put it no more strongly, that this strange agreement between misogynist theologians and self-styled witches rests upon an error.

What patriarchalists insist that women are or Woman is, and what some women under patriarchy have been constrained to be, is not good evidence of how a saner society would read the code. It is one thing to agree that women should not want to become what men have often been made (and neither should men), and quite another to insist that it is really worshipful to be over-emotional, partial, repressive and contemptuous of all that transcends the merely domestic sphere. Formal reasoning, impartial law, science and scholarship are not genuinely 'masculine', however much the normal or socially induced astigmatisms of men have sullied the record. What men and women will grow up to be in a millenarian society whose people have adopted less repressive ways, we do not know.

So how may decent religious traditions use the code of 'male and female' to speak of the Divine? What could we properly say of God as Father, Mother, Child? Is there anything at all to be said for the idea that different images might appropriately be used to make different (even if compatible) theological points? Might it perhaps be true that male and female experience will always be so different that men and women must inevitably mean different things as 'Mother' and 'Father'?

A child's 'significant others' are the figures through whom its information about the natural and social world it must inhabit comes. In societies with a high degree of sexual division of labour, girls must relate to their mothers (aunts, grandmothers) and boys to their fathers (uncles, grandfathers). These 'others' embody for the child all that it must learn and incorporate, the divine in flesh. To betray its trust is to blaspheme, to pretend to be Authority in one's own right, instead of acting out the message of Authority in that day and age. The true teacher cannot say his/her words but 'the words of That which sent her', even if that Sending is from a wider society than the little local tribe. If quite different knowledge and character is genuinely needed by boy and girl, it would seem appropriate that women should worship Goddess, and men God. If it is a male function to take part in the tribe's public ceremonials and offices, God takes precedence over Goddess, save on those occasions when women's rites prevail.

In a society that no longer practises such clear sexual differentiation, it may still be true that only girls will menstruate, give birth, lactate (though not all will). It may even be true that mostly boys will spend their adolescence in gangs of the same sex, risk violent injury and like formal games – our evidence so far is so tainted that we cannot be sure. A wholly non-sexist culture, with little differentiation, may still require some 'women's mysteries', some 'men's'. But such evidence (e.g. the !Kung Bushmen) as we have suggests that such societies will worship a relatively undifferentiated divine: the talk will be of Spirit, not of male Creator or female Container, and no complex mythology or ritual observance will structure religious perceptions. Division in social role increases as the First Cause is pushed further back: the First (Atum, or Ymir, or Purusa) is hermaphroditic, and it is Its offspring, ruling or inspiring different areas of the social universe, that have gender. When those different areas are not very distinct, the offspring are undifferentiated ministers of the One; when those ministers become more individual, and the One retreats into the background, the different provinces of human life take on a more organized form. It does not follow that the religious doctrine merely reflects the social observance: on the contrary, social observances rest upon a religious claim. Only when we remember the One who is, beyond the current social scene, is it possible to weaken the ties of customary observance, what St Paul called 'angels'.

Even the most extreme abstraction may retain a slight 'sexual' bias. At least for mammals, the primary character of males is that they reproduce in another, of females that they reproduce in themselves. To say that Deity is Male is therefore to say that it reproduce its image in something not-itself, in chaos and the dark. To say that it is Female is to say that each new being is contained and fed and grows within the Divine. For the former view, there is a definite division between Creator and Creation, and the latter may, as it were, stand opposite to its God, and not all its qualities be blamed on God. For the latter view, there is no such division, no possibility of standing over against Goddess, and whatever is in the creation is in Her. These things are not so (whichever is so) *because* the Deity is male or female: to speak of it as sexed is merely to convey that these things are so, and not to give a causal account of them. Sophisticated believers would carefully correct and dismiss many apparent implications of either theme: God does not really make the creation out of anything, nor can the creature stand over against its God; Goddess is not just the same as Her child, nor does She expect it never to achieve adulthood. Sophisticated believers, in short, may start with one side or the other, but progressively modify either myth until it says just the same as the other. Once this position is reached social and familial division of labour no longer seems important: the Spirit is One, and known in the agreement of the male and female.

Further reading

Douglas (1973); Leeuw (1938); Lutoslawski (1930); Rees & Rees (1961).

Bernstein (1971) is a discussion of the different codes used by members of different social classes, a distinction that Douglas (1973) uses in her wider account of religious and other symbolism.

Slater (1968) describes the stresses imposed on Greeks by their patriarchalism, and the consequences for their mythology.

On feminist theology in the Christian tradition see Maitland (1983). Whitmont (1983) is a survey of 'neo-pagan' Goddess-worship.

On the family in general, see Thorne & Yalom (1982). One of the oddest features of Christian tradition is the extent to which the Family has been idolized (idealized) despite Christ's demand that His followers abandon family life: we really ought not to confuse parental or romantic love with the Love of God. On romantic love, see de Rougemont (1962), D'Arcy (1945), Van de Vate (1981).

11

Death and Immortality

Individuals and the Eternal Earth

One story found throughout Africa is that God despatched a messenger, the chameleon, to tell humankind that they would die and come alive again. The messenger dawdled on the way, and God sent another, the blue-headed lizard, to say that human beings would die and rot. By the time the chameleon arrived they had accepted the other message. And that is why we do not live again (Mbiti (1969) p. 51).

Religion exists in the relationship of first and second message: the conviction that we were not meant to die eternally; the conviction that perhaps we do. Gilgamesh, in our oldest religious drama, sought the herb of immortality and lost it to the snake: so now snakes shed their skins and humans die. Adam and Eve made the wrong decision: eating the fruit of the tree of knowledge, not the tree of life. I know this self precisely as a self that dies, but cannot conceive what it is for me to be dead, to exist no more, never to come back. I can, to be sure, concern myself for those who may survive me, and may have faced, in some degree, the realization that death stands at my left shoulder. But to be dead is unimaginable, impossible, a silly mistake, as contradictory as frozen fire or a round square. What is it that dies? What is it that could survive?

The first answer, maybe the oldest, is that earth endures. My present plans and thoughts and passions will be forgotten, even while I live, and even by me. All things must change, and have their being in that changefulness: how silly it would be to want things to be so for ever, to be writing this one phrase with a cold in the head, a slight smell of ink, at 11 pm for ever. How silly to insist that this flesh should freeze, and not go through its dances till that movement ends and the new movements start. What goes on, through pain and trouble and the dance, is earth, unfolding its possibilities from one age to the next. All that I can do, in this brief moment of my wakefulness, is to set the scene for the next act to come, the game that earth plays for ever. I can die because there will be a time when earth has changed its pattern, absorbed my being to produce another. Even earth, the literal earth, itself may perish, and the cosmos continue through its changes till all change is done. When Chuang Tzu's wife died, he was found singing and beating on a drum. When asked why, he replied, 'There came a change which resulted in substance. This substance changed to assume form. The form changed and became alive. And now it has changed again to reach death. In this it has been like the passing of the seasons. And while she is thus lying asleep in the Great House, for me to go about weeping and wailing would be to show myself ignorant of fate. Therefore I refrain.'

This great religious theme, of earth's endurance, is embodied for us in the landscape to which our ancestors gave names, the (relatively) unchanging creatures with whom we share the land. We know quite well, if we consider it, that the chequer-board of English fields and hedges, and the upland sheep, and even the granite highlands, are a late invention. Even if the land returned to forest its state would not be as it was 'in the beginning'. What matters to us is not that a particular moment of world history should be unchanged, but that the land carry its history, our history, upon its face. A land which did not do so would not allow us to conceive that our works counted too. If everything were swept away and new creatures, new environments continually created, we could not imagine our return in earth. In such a world we could identify ourselves with the unity of all things only by disregarding, discounting, trivalizing all our personal and immediate projects. What would be the point of writing if no-one would read? Of building if the thing would be torn down? Of bearing and begetting children if they were creatures of another kind? If the one constant law were ceaseless and non-recurrent change, a drunkard's walk through possibility, 'the eternal hills' could not even seem eternal, and the returning swallows would not reassure us.

The religious response to such an age of radical insecurity may be to build firm structures against chaos, pledges of our faith and guardians of time. We may set ourselves to build cathedrals that will take generations to complete, rebuilding ancient houses, uncovering our roots, recalling that earth and our ancestors have weathered storms before. Once the changes are past, we may insist, the world will be re-established and after-ages make the legends of our time. My descendant may admire not trees but some yet unimagined plant; my reader may not take these words from paper, but from microfilm or skringe. But earth endures, and humankind with earth.

This response, this faith, is as unfounded as any other, in the sense that we have no physical or historical demonstration that we can count on things being so. Actually, we should concede that merely historical or natural evidence is quite compatible with its opposite: many nations and cultures, probably, have been lost to history; many species have run dry, or changed so fundamentally that no ancestor could know them. Two other responses, which perhaps come round to the same point, deserve attention.

The first, like Chuang Tzu, takes seriously the thought that all things pass, that there may be a time when only the void remains, not even pregnant with another cycle. Humankind will be forgotten, and earth fail, in 'that long Sabbath that goes on and on'. Behind every sound is silence, round every shape is space, round every momentary flame the dark. It is because there is silence, space and darkness that there can be living things, and because there was and yet will be a time when night and silence is complete that we can speak of a universe at all. In such a world every act, every shape is to be admired for what it is, not for what it may achieve. Some, seeing that the void surrounds and infiltrates us all, may despair, and such despair may take many forms. Some may strive to fill their lives with noise to drown out the silence, concealing the futility of their efforts even from themselves. Others may surrender to their image of the indifferent void, and regard all action, save destruction, as absurd: all projects are doomed to failure save the one that says 'Cooperate in beating all things down.' Even that, of course, will have its reverses: what one nihilist blows up, a million deluded lovers will build up again. But entropy is on the nihilist's side. Others again, as angry as the nihilist, may 'rage against the dying of the light'. Hopeless fury may sustain the efforts of those who would help the victims of epidemic, mass starvation, war. A rich, if rhetorical, defiance is the preferred stance of some atheistical philosophers: considered too closely it becomes absurd – why work to prevent a nuclear holocaust if Omnipotent Matter will inevitably crush all human projects, and itself be lost in universal cold? Utilitarian moralists in particular must have a hard time: no act of ours can possibly much alter the total sum of sentient misery and deluded joy. Of what act, even a thousand years ago, can one seriously think that its particular effects are with us still? What act could make an appreciable alteration in the dying of the fire?

To these real problems, the response of those who have accepted the void is this. It is because all things are mortal that they are lovable, because they pass that they exist at all. We should not act for the sake of any future state, arbitrarily ignoring the billions upon billions of years and places yet to come in which our acts lose all significance, and our beings are lost. Instead, let us do what we do 'as worship', as Lord

Krishna said. A poor performer, in the arts of theatre or games, is always groping for the proper gesture, trying to achieve something, she does not quite know what, and losing the present moment in an uneasy search. The great performer simply does it, without groping or wasted effort or unease at the thought of failure: each gesture is exact, and admirable. Such paradoxical action, even when it looks like an attempt to win a battle or complete a dance or have a picture painted, is not directed at anything but itself. So the good man acts 'for the sake of what is noble', and does his actions 'for their own sake'. It does not matter what else is achieved: it is enough to find that beauty in the perfect leap, the flawless bow-shot, the act of generosity. One who is motivated in this way is quite unmoved by the news that she will die and be forgotten, that the void will 'win'. Immortality, of a kind, is achieved in present nobility.

The second main response to earth's long saga takes our *conception* of it seriously. When we contemplate the first three seconds of the universe, or the predictable decay of stellar energies, or our own place in cosmic time and human history, we seem to stand above or outside time. We are creatures who do not merely respond to local stimuli in terms of their own memories and hopes for the unknown future. We can be conscious of ourselves, our motives and assumptions, and conscious of the whole expanse of time and space. The image we have of it is an historical one, formed in the particular circumstances of our age and culture: but we can recognize that too, and conceive that we may correct our vision of things. The ancient argument used by Plato to prove the soul's pre-existence and presumed immortality rests upon the simple puzzle: how can we find out and recognize what's true if we don't know what's true? Unless I already know that the Truth is (e.g.) such as to be revealed in sense-perception, how can I find out the Truth by way of sense-perception? If I am asked to locate Uncle Jim in a crowded room but know literally nothing about Uncle Jim, I cannot possibly locate him (no, not even by asking everyone there: I don't know whether he tells the truth, or whether he is known to anyone else). How can we know what's true unless there is that in us which once was united with the truth? The puzzle is a real one, but my point here is merely phenomenological. When we contemplate the universe it seems to us as if we stand outside it: how else could it be an object for us if we, as subjects, were identical with it? In feeling ourselves separate we can conceive that we, as subjects, are not involved in the world's debacle. In knowing the world's mortality we already transcend it. Our immortality is our transcendence of time. Because I know that this flesh will die, I know that I am beyond death.

The attempt to articulate a systematic argument to this conclusion is one that puzzled Plato. The attempt to answer a half-formulated argument might puzzle anyone. Fortunately, I do not need to propound it as an argument, but only an observation about how things feel. The first and second responses are alike in this: both redirect our attention from the 'end of the road' in time, to something not 'in time', whether it be the beauty of holiness or the transcendent self. In turning in that direction we must re-evaluate our natural and social yearning toward the future. The worshipful is not ahead of us, up there: nothing 'up there' is likely to be what we would worship, nor will it last.

Souls

So far I have uncovered two main themes in the contemplation of time, death and immortality. Some peoples, on the one hand, so identify themselves with the enduring, cyclic earth as to feel no great trouble when an individual's eyes are closed. Some, on the other hand, do their acts as worship, looking beyond time and the not-so-enduring earth. Neither think it right to suppose that our individual lives should go on, and grow, 'for ever'. What is immortal in the one case is enduring earth, and her patterns, and in the other it is timeless contemplation that turns away from the future considered as a realm of novel action. It is a third theme that most Westerners, and most modern philosophers, expect to discuss: the immortality of the individual self. I have already intimated, almost *ad nauseam*, that there are considerable difficulties about our common notion of selfhood. Setting those aside, we can express the usual notion of immortality or 'survival' as the claim that I myself, the very being that experiences my life 'from the inside', will live forever. Unlike those who expect only a recurrence or re-embodiment of the type, or who draw attention to the time-transcendent quality of moral act and cosmic contemplation, 'immortalists' (so to speak) affirm that there is an individual who survives, a real being. Such immortalists, of course, come in many guises. The surviving soul may go to be with God, or live again in earth. The transcendent soul may, once free of the body, know itself to be the singular soul of all things, or may be one of many individuals. What they have in common is the thought that there is a being, labelled 'I', that does not perish eternally.

Popular religiosity often expresses this by the claim that 'human beings have souls, and are not like the beasts that perish', but 'having a soul' seems an odd requirement for individual immortality: the soul I 'have' may be immortal, but what is that to me? Immortalist doctrine is better expressed by insisting that *I am* a soul. I am, that is, a being with a point of view, an outlook on the world and on my own past history and future possibilities. Popular religiosity, again, often conceives this soul as a peculiarly 'airy' or 'non-physical' body, associated with but not identical to the ordinary 'earthly' body, and surviving the latter's dissolution. Spiritists sometimes speak here of the 'astral' body, something that can (allegedly) be perceived by clairvoyants. I shall argue below that this option has been unfairly disregarded by philosophers, and that it points toward a more satisfactory understanding of immortalism than talk of the Cartesian ego (on which see below), or of bodily resurrection. But these must be considered first.

If we are to survive the death and dissolution of our bodies we must be something other than those bodies. Immortalists have offered two sorts of argument for this conclusion, the moral and the logical. The moral argument rests on the claim that we have other interests than the merely bodily: if we were just bodies, the claim goes, we would have no concern with anything but the feeding and care of that body. But we demonstrably have many other interests, and at least attempt to govern our bodily passions in the name of other, more 'spiritual' ends. Those who deny that we are immortal selves distinct from our bodies seem to be saying that nothing does or should concern us but our material needs, and are correspondingly despised. It is easy to reply that even if we are mortal creatures we may have other interests than those of the proverbial dog with one thought for each paw ('food, food, sex and food'). Why shouldn't mortal and bodily creatures even have 'immortal yearnings', and why should those yearnings suggest that they are themselves really immortal, and not mortal bodies at all?

The reply is a just one, if we are looking for valid arguments to the conclusion that we are not necessarily the same things as our bodies. It is still true that these 'immortal yearnings', or interests in something more than our well-being as short-lived animals, play a part in constructing the imaginative edifice of immortalist doctrine. But a better argument for distinguishing between ourselves and our bodies may be found in logic. If the creature I am is a body (notably, the one that is typing these words) then it is impossible even to conceive that I should exist when this body does not. But it seems perfectly possible to conceive of this possibility: I can imagine what it would be like to continue thinking, imagining and even perceiving although there is no trace of this body left. Accordingly, I am not the same thing as this body, and am not necessarily doomed by its death. 'I' names an immaterial ego, the thing that thinks these thoughts. As René Descartes insisted, while I can intelligibly doubt the existence of the university building in which I am working, and even the body that is fingering these keys, I cannot doubt 'my' existence. In the very act of suggesting to myself that perhaps I do not exist I am bound to agree that I do, whereas there is no such logical compulsion to agree that this body exists (perhaps it is a dream-body).

This latter, Cartesian argument may seem unduly rapid: surely the fact that I might 'imaginably' exist without a brain (in the sense that I can doubt the brain's existence, but not my existence) does not prove that I could? Surely, even though I might not have been a brain (it might have turned out that I wasn't), it might still be true that I am? Just so, it might not be realized that the Professor of French is the Dean of Arts, and he might not have been: but still (maybe) he is. He could be conceived not to be, but wrongly. There are, however, good reasons to suspect that Descartes was right. The Professor is the Dean because the man who (as it happens) is the Professor is the man who (as it happens) is the Dean. We can certainly conceive that this man not be either: being the professor is not the same attribute as being the dean, but there is one man who has both these attributes. But we cannot similarly argue that there is one thing that is (as it happens) Me, and is also (as it happens) this body. This body is this body, and I am I, but neither is the other: if 'I' and 'this body' referred to identically the same thing, there would be no possibility even of imagining that this thing could exist when it didn't. If I can conceive of myself as existing when this body does not, then 'I' must refer to something other than this body. That ego may possibly survive this body.

This argument has drawn renewed force from the logical enquiries of Saul Kripke and requires careful attention. It is certainly not the sort of argument that closes a debate, and although it is probably agreed amongst professional philosophers that Kripke's argument rules out some versions of materialism, there would be no general agreement that it established any form of spiritualism. Those materialists who have wanted to say that we, our minds, have turned out to be the very same things as our bodies or our brains (although there are possible worlds where this is not so), have been proved mistaken. That our minds and our brains are identical cannot be that sort of simple, contingent truth. At the very least, our mental attributes (our thinking and feeling) are not the same attributes as our ordinarily physical, publicly observable ones, and any connection between them must be just that – a connection. Minds and brains, mental states and physical states *may* be causally related (somehow) but they are not identical. Accordingly we have to admit the possibility that our minds, egos or mental states should continue even though our bodies or bodily states did not. Even stern materialists may admit as much, moved to the admission by the thought that 'we' might be re-embodied in computers in some distant technological future.

But what might a bodiless immortality be like, even if we concede that it is not wholly out of the question? God may see all of us 'from the inside', but I only see *me* from the inside, and no other. My conviction that there are other souls rests not upon experience, nor reason, but on natural faith that has not been refuted. If I inhabited an entirely bodiless world, I would 'know of' other souls only by characteristic alterations in whatever sights, sounds, smells or tangible sensations were presented to me, and the conclusion that this was another soul would be as strictly indemonstrable as it is now. I might, we may suppose, be reasonably convinced that the soul I know as G wished conversation by the scent of violets and toasted cheese, the sparkle of purple dust across my view. This might be confirmed by subsequent events: the appearance to me of characteristic phraseology embodying remarks I had not willed to think myself, reminders of past experience and the like. I might, misleadingly, think of this as G's 'approaching' me, but no spatial proximity or distance is implied. Everyone bodiless is at the same place, and could not be closer.

This imagined world does not seem impossible to me. I have assumed that immaterial souls still have sense-experiences. If they do not, but exist in absolute sensory deprivation, without even the images of fancy to enliven them, this is not obviously preferable to, or distinct from, extinction. If there are such experiences, though not such as to give the experiencers reason to think themselves bodily located in a consistent spatial structure, they might still be convinced that they genuinely communicated, and might be right. But who are they? What is to identify S with the soul I now am, or G with Gillian's soul? S 'remembers' being me, and finds shared 'memories' in G, but the fact (?) that S *is* me cannot be the same fact as that S *remembers* me: there would then be no room for error. When S thought to itself 'I am Stephen', this could mean no more than 'I remember Stephen', or even 'I imagine Stephen'. And is S the same S from one second to the next? At any moment nothing is meant by the claim 'I am S' but that, at that moment, a soul 'remembers' S. Maybe 'many' souls do: there is then nothing that one of them is right about (being S, being Stephen) and the others wrong. All that can be said is that the experiences of this bodily being might be 'remembered', but the discarnate souls are not significantly identical with the self I am.

Finally, there is reason to suspect that the apparent clarity and certainty of the Cartesian ego are spurious. The normal use of the first person is to lay claim upon an act or possession within a community of readily identifiable beings who could in principle be tracked through space-time. When I attempt to follow Descartes and think away the world of bodies and ordinary identities it may be that I am left without any understanding of what the word 'I' could refer to. There is a thought but is it 'I' that thinks it? What is added by saying that 'I think it'? Could God Himself say 'I' in absolute solitude or know He was the 'same' God as before?

These reasonings have strongly suggested to philosophers at least since Wittgenstein that there are grave difficulties about the notion of bodiless immortality for human souls, or for God. Talking about things, even 'spiritual' things, seems to require that we have some way of re-identifying them over time, and this seems to require that we be able to locate them, and provide some content for the claim they make to *be* such and such a person, and not merely to have delusive memories of that person. If we think space away can we have selves at all, let alone the 'same' selves as we now are? I am not myself convinced that these arguments are final. It does seem to me that we can grasp the sort of gradual extension of our present concepts that could cope with bodiless, non-spatial identities, even though such existence would be very unlike what we imagine ours to be. It is at least very puzzling that some Christian writers should have been so ready to espouse the argument against bodiless persons (usually adding that ordinary immortalism was a 'Greek' idea alien to the true biblical temperament) without recognizing that it presents an identical difficulty for the supreme bodiless person, God.

Bodily Resurrection

A different immortalist model has been praised by Christian theologians as decently 'Hebraic', by contrast with the perversely 'Hellenic' conception of an immortal soul. Hellenists have some difficulty with the charge that it is 'typically Greek' to distinguish soul and body, and 'typically Hebraic' to think rather of the 'whole person'. It is clearly false to suggest that Greeks generally made a radical division, and probably misleading to suggest that believers in an immortal soul are not concerned for the whole person. Once again, it is extremely odd that some Christians see it as their business to deny that there are souls, or to suggest that the distinction between body and subjective being is the same as a distinction between 'materialist' and 'merely spiritual' concerns (though some weight is given to this view by those who use the 'moral' argument for distinguishing between ourselves and our bodies). It may be right to insist that religion is concerned with matter: it is hardly right to imply that religion has an interest in denying that we are beings with a point of view.

Nonetheless, there has been a degree of agreement that the resurrection of the body is worth investigating. On the one hand, this seems to fit better with biblical conceptions than the notion of an intrinsically immortal, 'bodiless' soul. On the other hand, it seems to avoid the puzzles about the identification of surviving persons that I have described. If I am to survive, it must be a bodily person, within a network of other such persons. But this cannot be the whole story. If S (the resurrected immortal) is to be the same person as Stephen it is not because S's body is the same body as Stephen's. Literally, it will not be, once 'this' body is decayed, burnt, torn to pieces, eaten up. One can certainly imagine that a duplicate, or many duplicates, could be created, but those bodies would not be this body: except by courtesy, because there was other evidence that S was the same person as Stephen (i.e. ought to be treated as the moral equivalent of Stephen, with his responsibilities and rights). S's identity in the resurrection world as S may be easier to manage if S is a bodily person, but the gap between S and Stephen is still there. S might reasonably conclude that he was created as a doppelganger of Stephen, or might decide to build upon his 'memories' to live as if he *were* myself. Who is to say he would be wrong?

The presence or absence of sheer continuity is not itself the issue. Two apparent bodies are continuous if there is a body at every place and moment in between (so that one might trace a continuous path through space-time between 'one' body and the 'other'), but they may not be the same body: I am not the same body as my mother even though my fleshly being is literally continuous with hers, and even if it had happened that my mother died in giving birth to me. Sheer continuity does not guarantee identity. Sheer discontinuity does not guarantee non-identity. It might well turn out to be the case that all bodies are discontinuous at a microphysical level. There might be worlds, or future ages, when 'medium-sized bodies', like the human, were regularly teleported. If it happened often enough, we would have no difficulty about re-identifying persons even though they turned up miles away from where they had last been. It may seem, accordingly, that there is no difficulty in principle in imagining a cosmos where apparently dead persons really reappeared in other areas, leaving behind a simulacrum that decayed. If the community of discourse recognized the resurrectees as 'the same' as old acquaintances, they would be the same.

This idealist approach to the problem – idealist in the sense that what *is* the case is determined solely by what is *thought* to be the case – has some merit. What is lacking is any account of what it would be reasonable to think, and what it is that is thought. If S's being Stephen simply is S's being assumed to be Stephen, what is it that is assumed? Even if we insist that identifying S as Stephen is not a matter of realistic truth, but simply a moral programme, a policy of treating S in a certain way (punishing or praising him for what was done by Stephen), what is to count as a reasonable choice of Stephen-substitute? In Haiti the *gros-bon-ange* of a dead ancestor is recalled from the waters of death to be housed in a jar, which is thereafter the earthly vessel of the one that died. Within the framework of Haitian Voodoo such and such a jar 'is' the place of such-and-such an ancestor. Insofar as the system holds together, what more can be said? Unbelieving realists may simply say that it isn't, that there are better and truer explanations of the phenomena than that. Unbelieving idealists can only, feebly, say that they are not themselves Haitians, that 'their' canons of identification do not allow them to treat a suitably prayed-over jar as grandfather. Idealism, which is born in a healthy respect for social relativity, too often issues in a doctrinaire lack of imagination when confronted by puzzle cases.

The realistic picture requires that identity of person is not simply a 'descriptive' or 'evaluative' notion, but an explanatory one: that is, when we say that S is the same person as Stephen we are not describing surface features of the case, similarities of bodily appearance or memory, nor are we merely urging a particular moral programme. Instead we are attempting to *explain* why S looks or behaves like Stephen or ought to be treated like Stephen. The identity is the cause of the memory, rather than being constituted by the memory; it is the justification for the socially bestowed title, not constituted by that title. What the theory of resurrection lacks, as it is expressed by Christian immortalists like John Hick (1966), is any account of what sort of beings there must be to explain the permanence of memory and character. Ordinary physicalists, who do not expect to survive their bodies' death, purport to explain such things by referring to brain-traces, chemical changes in the neural structure that tend to persist. This explanation may be spurious, as we have no coherent theory to explain the conjunction of brain-trace and subjective image, but it is the sort of explanation which grounds the insistence that my *body* must persist if I am to persist. But if that is why a merely non-bodily survival is held to be unthinkable, those who believe in bodily resurrection have a duty to explain why, after all, there is some other explanation of resurrected memory than mere neurological persistence, but not an explanation that allows non-bodily survival. If it is the continued presence of a certain neurological structure that explains why I remember Isfahan, then that is not what explains why S will (since that structure has not persisted, though it has, allegedly, been reproduced). If whatever it is that explains S's memory constitutes S's identity with me, then what constitutes my present identity with a former visitor to Isfahan is presumably the same: and not my brain.

Simply telling stories about a purported 'resurrection world' is not enough. We need to know what sort of things we are, that can be manifest in this world and the next. The message of immortalists is that I am not just this body, and the message is hopelessly confused by attempts to pretend that this body might survive its own destruction simply because enough people decided to call another creature (resurrectee, great-grandchild or Haitian jar) by my name.

Love and the Individual Creature

Josiah Royce argued, in *The Conception of Immortality*, that eternal life was necessary to our grasp of personal love. It is the mark of such love that we are not satisfied to be told that, were the beloved to die or disappear, there is another just as good. If we were told, and believed, that an extraterrestrial being had cunningly removed our beloved during the night, and left an indistinguishable substitute, a changeling, most of us would be perturbed. Doubtless this would partly be because we would fear that the changeling would not always be indistinguishable, that it would someday turn and rend us. But even if we were persuaded that the extraterrestrial had no malicious purpose, and that it would never be possible to tell the difference between our original love and the changeling, that even the changeling itself would never guess that it was bogus, it does not seem likely that we would think our love requited. It was the original individual that we loved, and still require, although we cannot point to any characteristic of that individual which differs from those of the changeling. Similarly, however many creatures there are in the universe that have the characteristics for which I might unthinkingly say I loved those I do love, it is not those creatures that I love but these. Personal love, although it may issue in compliments on the stubborn integrity, or the clear skin, or the wit, or warmth of the beloved, is not simply admiration or desire for those named qualities. If it were, the changeling would do as well, or a twin sister. No finite list of characteristics is enough to exclude the possibility, unreal as it probably is, that there should be another creature with just those characteristics who is not the one we love.

Royce concluded that the demands of personal love could only be satisfied if every individual had an infinite time to distinguish itself from all possible doppelgangers. To give personal love and loyalty to any individual is to see it as infinitely extended, such that however many characteristics we identify and find elsewhere, there will always be something else to mark it off as itself and no other. The argument is a puzzling one, just because it seems so wrong-headed, and yet does touch on something important. To be 'this individual and no other' cannot be a matter of having any particular characteristics, whether the list is infinite or not. So even infinite time will not produce a list of characters which constitute that individual's identity. Its 'quiddity' is not to be caught by description. Yet Royce is right that that is what we love, the unknown god or goddess of our devotion. That is one reason why efforts to expound identity as some sort of psychological or physical continuity always miss the point. Identity is made known in the personal tie of lover and beloved: the lover, *qua* lover, does not want a cloned doppelganger, even one with the beloved's memories (though this is not to say that he might not be glad of some comfort), but the very being that really is the beloved. But though the lover may want this, it does not follow that he is ever going to get it.

The mysterious and unfathomable thisness of every real identity is not, as Royce indeed admitted, a solid ground for supposing that such things are immortal. But it is perhaps one of the elements that go to make up a conviction of immortality. It is not myself that seems most likely to be undying, but that which I reach out to, the unknown object of my love. If knowledge is a matter of having an adequate grasp of what something is, what properties it essentially has (so that to know uranium is know what it is to be uranium, to be able to characterize the stuff and show how it misses being plutonium or lead), then I cannot *know* the person who is, accidentally, my wife. I cannot tell what properties are essential and unique to her (in that she could not lose them without ceasing to be herself, and anything that has them must be she). Insofar as I do claim to 'know' that person it must be by some other mode. The demand of love is simply that the beloved *be*, even if (agonizingly) she cannot be with the lover. To love is therefore to want the beloved to be eternal, not as being the sort of creature that she now seems to be, not as the bearer of properties that should be eternally instantiated, but simply her unknown self.

If personal love, as devotion to an individual who *ought* to be immortal, who cannot be supposed to be the sort of thing that might dissolve if one or other characteristic got lost (if she grew old, or mad, or wicked), is taken seriously as a mode of knowledge, even ignorant knowledge, learned ignorance, then we can at least see why such love has so often been at the core of religious life. Personal love is a sort of revelation, in that it is borne in on us without our choice and seems to carry with it a demand that something should be which we have no other reason to expect. If there is no eternal life, then the demands of personal love are utterly mistaken, and the sense of 'knowing' something that we cannot adequately describe is an illusion. It may of course be so, but those who are prompt to say so do not always see what the consequences are for our ordinary life. If there is nothing that *has* the properties my wife has and is not identical with those properties, then in loving 'her' I only love her characteristics, and should be satisfied by them wherever they may be. If there is no such 'unknowable quiddity', then my love is only impersonal admiration, desire and benevolence, and not only will but should die if the beloved changes: 'Love is not love that alters when it alteration finds', but such unlove is all that we have left if there is no immortal being in the beloved.

Reincarnation

Some of the problems faced by resurrectionists also confront those who believe in reincarnation. Many traditions expect the dead to reappear in their descendants, in the sense that character traits and facial appearance crop up continually. When a child reaches for her great-grandmother's bonnet rather than her great-aunt's purse that may confirm the diagnosis. Literal, individual identity is not being considered here: only the sort of species immortality that we detect in the endless generations of antelope or bee (not wholly accurately). When a Hindu child purports to remember a life in some other village, and a sudden death, her family may be perturbed, and very insistent that the claim not be taken seriously – not because the claim is incomprehensible, or certainly false, but because the child's loyalties will be divided. Old lives should be forgotten, but it is not doubted that there may be a real identity between deceased merchant and young girl. Buddhists deny (at least at a more theoretical level) that there is a strict identity of self in such cases (or any other): there is only a psychic chain of circumstance, which links the dying thoughts of one creature, the early volitions of another. Causality does not lie at the level of outward, material event, but in the chain of mental acts – a thought to which I shall return.

Standard philosophical discussions of reincarnation are distressingly simple-minded, and usually centre around a claim to 'be' or 'have been' Napoleon. It is clearly imaginable that someone should begin to 'recall' various scenes that fit our historical knowledge of Napoleon's life, and even to provide checkable information that turns out, later, to be accurate. Equally clearly, this cannot of itself constitute the claimant's identity with Napoleon, for there might be several such persons endowed with an equal, unusual knowledge, as if from the inside, of past events. If one were Napoleon simply in virtue of the 'memory', all would be. If all were identical with Napoleon, they would be identical with each other. They are not. Therefore none is identical with Napoleon simply by virtue of 'remembering' his life.

The argument seems formally correct. Where it is ridiculous is in failing to acknowledge the explanatory function of the claim. The 'memory' claim is evidence of the identity, not its essence. That the speaker was Napoleon is an explanation of her 'memories', and not the only imaginable one. Its plausibility depends, in part, on the availability of an ontology which explains how both Bonaparte and the speaker can manifest one and the same individual. It also depends on the relative implausibility of such pseudo-explanations as 'clairvoyance', a term which is merely descriptive, not explanatory.

Western spiritism, whether inspired by Celtic reminiscence, or Vedantin or Buddhist missionaries, has not followed the Buddhist tradition in denying one substantial being to a continuing self. Instead it proposes that each of us is one life, one personality of an immortal selfhood which grows and struggles and sometimes matures till it can take its seat among the gods. Sometimes it is supposed that spiritual families move through time together, embodying themselves in different roles and relations. A woman who seems to recall life as a Cathar does not necessaily claim to be that Cathar, or to be bound now by the obligations of that former life. The claim is rather that there is an immortal self which bears the Cathar and the modern woman as flowers on a vine. We recall 'past lives', if we do, by tapping our immortal Other, who is (in this life) known to us only as a more mature, more experienced figure in our dreams.

The distinctive feature of such spiritism is that the figure under which we know the gods, the image of the divine or our 'higher self', is our real self, the thing in virtue of which we are individuals, and yet not something to be wholly admired or copied. Though my life is only one of indefinitely many lives in the ongoing experience of my Angel, it is the life my Angel needs to grow. This life may disappear without apparent trace, or else may be the growing tip of the angelic life for aeons yet to come, or may be disowned and fiercely repressed until the Angel has grown strong enough to bear it. Such angelic individuals, in their turn, may be the blossoms of a larger tree, and each present life, in the end, contribute something, through the angel, to the divine community itself, the single Manifold-in-Unity that is our eternal mother. 'Proof' that all this is so is hard to come by. If it strikes many people as not wholly implausible, or as a thing that they would like to think is true, that may be a function of our present unrest. Deprived of much reason to think that the world of our present experience is stable, or progressive, we imagine a realm in which we find real families, real growth and gladness, and try to see our present selves as shadows of that promise.

Waking Up

How are we to think of the relationship between our present life and the immortal Self or Soul? One model that has not been much discussed was offered, amongst others, by the great Neo-Platonist Plotinus: the real waking up is from the body, all others being merely staggering from one couch to the next (*Enneads* III 6.6). Our present life is dream-like, in that we have no acquaintance in it with real causes, any more than an ordinary dreamer does. When I dream that by drawing a cat on the wall I cause a door to appear, I may imagine that the drawing 'causes' the door. Once 'awake' I realize that the drawing only preceded the door, and would never have been a 'real' cause, even if my dream were consistent and regular enough to ensure that I could only 'open the door' by drawing cats. We can easily conceive – it is indeed a current staple of philosophy of knowledge – that we are all brains in a vat, being stimulated by mad scientists in such a way as to experience the cloud-capped towers of our vision. Epistemologists have worried that, insofar as we do not know this story to be false, we can really know nothing at all, and tended to reply either that the story cannot really be understood (which is plainly false, if anything is) or that it is at any rate no living option, that no-one could take it seriously. But though vat brains and mad scientists are part of our current mythology, and may have no serious attraction for us, the thesis that this present world is a sort of communal dream, in which 'real causes' (as we conceive them) are not found, and in which weird antinomies of intellect are rife, is not so implausible. On this view, our seeming deaths are simply dream-events. At death we wake up, and have the chance to realize who we are. The one that wakes experiences its life in us as an episode, perhaps instructive or absurd, and remembers or forgets accordingly. Our lives, of set purpose and design, include the material for understanding this possibility, and reasons to expect it.

Social idealists, for whom life and death, sleeping and waking, simply 'are' what 'our community' calls them, may insist that it makes no sense to say that the dead have woken to their immortal lives, their real bodies. Religious realists can disagree. Chuang Tzu dreamed he was a butterfly, and seeming to wake said that he did not know whether he was a man who had dreamt of being a butterfly, or a butterfly dreaming he was a man. The butterfly he was, and is, if such immortalists are right, may be a stranger creature than we think: an immortal, growing beauty with its own life to live, its dreams to remember.

Acceptance of this model does not require any particular decision on criteria of identity. The real world may be a world of bodies, of a kind maybe that we would mistakenly consider airy, as not following the rules of our dream-world. Alternatively, it may be a world of bodiless intellects, distinguished from each other by style, purpose, memory, but growing towards a celestial unity. Whatever the real world is, it houses the real causes of our experience: things happen here not because of mechanical causality, but because the spiritual world requires, at this moment of its growth, just this concatenation of events. What we experience may, or may not, 'reflect' what is really happening: our own lesser dreams sometimes present analogies to our terrestrial lives, and sometimes seem entirely other. In experiencing the world we do, we may be experiencing shifting memories and fancies of the real world – as Plato thought it necessary to assume to explain our ability to recognize or recollect a truth. If this were so, we should not expect that the true waking requires us entirely to forget the world and our dream-history. They are perhaps trial runs for a larger contest, the battle at the end of time or the final flowering. The story is compatible with many religious notions.

The one that wakes up when my life ends may drowse off again, or stay awake for ever, or deliberately sleep to help persistent dreamers, being able (as some of us are in our lesser dreams) to remember she is dreaming and tell others so. Vat-brains (in the sceptics' parable) might realize or be convinced that they were not what they had imagined: realizing this they might attempt to convince others in the network, but could really only say, 'Look, don't things seem peculiar? Can it really be like this?' Maybe deliberate dreamers might be able to manipulate the dream for good or ill in ways not programmed by the Guardians: they could work miracles, acting out the infantile delusion (or remaining memory?) that things should be amenable to conscious will. If such things seem to happen, very occasionally, in our world, this is at any rate what one might reasonably expect if things are really as the model suggests.

Further reading

Hick (1973); King-Farlow (1978); Lutoslawski (1930); Strawson (1959).

There is a large recent literature on immortalism, and on identity. See especially Penelhum (1970). I have not discussed (because I believe it to be entirely worthless) the so-called 'paradigm-case' argument against immortalism, namely that there can be no life after death because a plane-crash in which all on board are killed leaves no survivors. Other philosophers (notably Flew (1964)) disagree.

General questions about identity must take account of the writings of Derek Parfit, especially Parfit (1984), who has helped to demolish the idea that we have any clear account even of our own this-worldly identity; Madell (1981) has an interesting collection of arguments to the effect that we must nonetheless accept that our identity is, *contra* Parfit, an all-or-nothing affair. McGinn (1982) is a straightforward introduction to the complications created by Saul Kripke's analysis for simple mind-brain identity theories (Kripke (1980)).

On reincarnation see Stevenson (1974), Head & Cranston (1977). I have elaborated the notion that we 'wake up' to life eternal in an essay in *Inquiry*, 26, 1984.

Death be not proud, though some have called thee
mighty and dreadfull, for thou are not soe,
for those, whom thou think'st, thou dost overthrow,
die not, poore death, nor yet canst thou kill me.
From rest and sleepe, which but thy pictures be,
much pleasure, then from thee, much more must flow,
and soonest our best men with thee do goe,
rest of their bones and soules deliverie.
Thou art slave to Fate, Chance, kings, and desperate men,
and dost with poyson, warre and sicknesse dwell,
and poppie, or charmes can make us sleepe as well,
and better than thy stroake; why swell'st thou then?
One short sleep past, wee wake eternally,
and death shall be no more; death, thou shalt die.
(John Donne, *Divine Poems*, Holy Sonnet 10)

12

Religious Experience

Emotional Participation

A religious tradition is a system of rituals, a body of texts, a code of practice passed down the generations. Sometimes it involves specifically religious doctrines, about the world, the people and the individual soul, which members of the community are presumed – at least by missionaries and some anthropologists – to 'believe'. Sometimes, at any rate when it has occurred to them that there are alternative cosmologies, 'belief' and 'unbelief' may be the appropriate categories: often, they are not (see Needham (1970)). It would be very odd to say that the British 'believe' that people have heads (though they would doubtless, rather wonderingly, answer 'yes' or 'why do you ask?' if asked whether people did). It would be beside the point to say that the British believe that Christmas is a religious celebration of family feeling: it doesn't matter whether they have thought to think this or not. It would be quite wrong to say that the British believe in Santa Claus, although they tell children stories about the being which they go to some lengths to dramatize, dress up in red, send each other cards with reindeer on them, occasionally (if pressed) devise allegorical interpretations of the story, and are irritated or annoyed by pompous scepticism.

Religious celebrations and stories, in short, may often simply be what people do and enjoy doing. They may embody assumptions which anthropologists and philosophers can tease out (but who exactly 'assumes' them?). They may be made occasions for cosmological speculation, as well as for high art. To reduce all this to the brutal question, 'do you really think it's true?', with the hidden message that, on the one hand, no-one sensible could think it was, and on the other that no-one who saw its falsity could think it worth a jot, is simply naive. Maya Deren, asked whether having been 'possessed' by the Voodoo *loa* Erzulie she 'believed in' the *loa*, replied that she agreed with the principles embodied in the cult, had participated in the ritual, and 'regardless of what (she) might think or believe, (had) served the *loa*' (Deren (1953), p. 289). A religious tradition that did not in any way affect the ordinary experience of the participants, did not offer them anything for their understanding or the endurance of their daily lives, would be very narrow. The question is not 'do you think it's true?', but 'do you find it touches on your life?'. This is the province broadly labelled 'religious experience'.

Most people's religious experience is simply a matter of their experiencing things 'religiously'. The rituals, dramas, sacred sites and stories give them an apparatus for describing things to themselves. A religious experience is participation in a religious ritual, or a sudden perception that some everyday event is like the ritual. Just occasionally a family meal, or a party, is suffused with the sort of gaiety, unforced affection, sweet sadness, or even worshipful terror, that a great ritual occasion is meant to evoke, to praise, to capture. Many of our rituals, like our works of art, are attempts to rediscover some momentary glory, by doing things 'just so'. The gods, being free, do not always oblige, but the occasions when they do are shared, public acts. We can all agree that the coronation did occur, that the sabbath meal was held, that the funeral or baptism or marriage was very moving. Experiencing public events 'religiously' is sharing a community life with the appropriate emotions.

These emotions are sometimes those of confident expectation, or communal reassertion of high courage against adversity, or grief. The rituals that evoke them – partly by their familiarity – are celebrations of the human spirit, and worship is the evocation of the highest we can dare to expect of ourselves. 'Really religious' persons at least hope, or try, to carry those emotions over into their daily lives, but will earn the vague dislike of their compatriots if they are too obviously happy, too much inclined to uncomplaining courage and affectionate joy. The British, at any rate, do not greatly care for uttering 'great shouts of joy' when asked to by their clergy, and reserve the right to pay due service to the minor deities of malicious gossip, complaint, laziness and lechery once outside the church. If these minor deities, so to speak, were consciously sought and cultivated they would be the pantheon of diabolism. As it is, they hardly constitute a systematic rival to the national religion, but only its border territory. They are the states of mind and practice that we are not quite prepared to abandon, and we rather distrust those devotees who do profess a single-minded concentration on the gods of courage, joy and love.

A cynical outsider, who is all of us, might add that the emotions evoked in much national religion are not as honourable as my reference to courage and affectionate joy suggests. Our rituals, like those of any tribal cult, evoke contempt for less fortunate outsiders, pride in our own identities – emotions that our most misjudged poet, Kipling, recognized and feared. Even the affection which ritual occasionally evokes is often entirely spurious: a maudlin and enjoyably soggy emotion quite unable to inspire an ordinarily decent life, let alone an heroic one. Our rituals do not consolidate heroic joy, immortal love, but the sort of jolly, uncomprehending, transient romanticism that is also found in nurse-meets-doctor fictions, softcore pornography, or military songs. A religious experience is one that brings easy tears to the eyes, makes the victim hot and cold, provides an orgasm without need to fear a consequence. Religious experience, in short, is often something that genuinely pious, God-fearing persons should beware. Those seeking enlightenment and release from the wheel are also suspicious: such 'religious' states of mind lead on to others, and are not a true release. If an 'uplifting' service is immediately followed by displays of ill-temper and ennui, who is deceived? The real work of religion goes on in those long years of 'spiritual dryness', while no tears come to the eyes, nor warmth to the heart, head or loins. True piety is to honour our obligations and keep on till the end, without misleading assistance from the sort of spurious affection, drunken excitement and ignorant pride that is evoked, in some, by ritual.

Emotional participation in the rituals of religion and of 'ordinary life' is confined and structured by established codes. Charismatic revivalism is often as distrusted by ecclesiastics as by atheists, and much of the church's organization is directed towards controlling, not evoking, 'transports of delight'. Revivalists, in their first emotional seizure, tend to think that this proves the nullity of the established church, its failure to keep contact with the Spirit. Ecclesiastics, on the other hand, denounce what they see as vulgarity, lack of staying power, a tendency to confuse personal emotion and opinion with full participation in the Divine Omniscience. Both sides are often quite correct. Analogously, a marriage is not made by rhapsodizing over moments of exquisite lustfulness, and fantasizing of an 'ideal marriage' of total openness and constant ecstacy. The sort of sentimental and offensive rubbish spouted by romantic novelists (and some marriage counsellors), somehow intimating that the celibate are not really 'saved', is an exact image of those evangelical religious who demand that one have experienced a tearful spiritual drunkeness if one is to be 'right' with God. On the other hand, a marriage whose partners 'dryly' did their duty by each other, who were never 'carried away' by affection or desire, would strike most of us as rather odd. Do they really gain and enjoy so little from each other? Why do they bother? In some ages, of course, the answer to that is obvious: they bother because there is no alternative, because they owe obedience to family and state, because each partner is yoked to children. Analogously, some 'dry' religions are maintained because they are a duty to the world, because there is no alternative. Once there is, revivialism is a more attractive option than it was, and also a greater danger, if it is forgotten that religion need not depend upon such emotion.

Solitary Experience

Two features of 'religious experience', commonly so called, that my account so far has ignored are its solitariness and its cognitive claims. It is solitary, even when it involves public ritual or revivalist enthusiasm, since (in the last resort) no mortal but the subject of the experience can assure us that it happened at all, that the appropriate emotions were 'really and truly' aroused. Not all enthusiasts do dances, shout hosannas or wear silly grins. Not all those who do these things are 'real enthusiasts'. The 'subjectivity of experience' (the fact that none of us can feel what others are feeling, from 'within') is the ground for generalized scepticism about our capacity to understand other minds, although it can be partly met by the observation that merely solitary experience is a nullity: if I could never know what others think and feel, I can have no concepts with which to describe what I myself think and feel. A more interesting and immediate puzzle is provided by solitary religious experience as distinguished from public ritual.

The moment when someone seems to herself to have stepped out of all her usual habits, all the usual categories, may have been prepared by lengthy meditation and prayer, or may come entirely unexpectedly. It is a peculiarity of most religious traditions (as against secular mind-cure techniques) that there is no training scheme which can guarantee the moment of religious ecstasy, no statistical correlation even between the contemplative programme and that particular spiritual state. Even when it was fashionable to pretend that mescalin or LSD could exalt the taker to the spiritual peaks, it was admitted that the moral intention of the taker was crucial, and that the spirits could not be commanded. Maybe some who took drugs became convinced that saints and mystics had the 'same experience', but others emphatically did not. 'Drug-induced experience' was sometimes peculiar enough to create a distinctively religious response, an awakening of the religious imagination. It did not guarantee enlightenment.

The question is, what is it to be the 'same experience'? If religious experience is essentially solitary, a movement of the individual soul incommunicable to anyone who does not already feel that motion, how can we say the one motion is the same as another? Ludwig Wittgenstein's notorious fable of a people who each keep what they call 'a beetle' in a box, but never inspect any 'beetle' but their own, seems relevant: in such a language 'beetle' only means 'anything in the box', and it does not matter what that thing may be. Analogously, 'religious or mystical experience' is whatever experience is associated with certain public signs: abnormal breathing, half-closed eyes, babbling speech, slowed or quickened heart-beat, flattened brain-waves, unnatural cheerfulness, later conviction of having realized some incommunicable secret. The 'sameness' of the experience is either just the sameness of those public signs or else an unverifiable hypothesis about the subjective occasion for those public events. Similarly my sight of green is the same as yours either if we discriminate grass from buttercups, verdigris from rust in publicly identical ways or if the subjective phenomenon that occurs in me is what occurs in you – an hypothesis we cannot verify (though God or the underlying Self may do so).

Theists, pantheists and atheists may give some public signs of their experience. They report occasions when everything is seen as the illuminated body of the Buddha, as a nut held in the Saviour's hand. Or else they report a 'union' between themselves and the Immortal Ones, a discovery that they themselves are God, or that they are God's beloved. Unity with the creation, community with the Creator are frequent claims. Faced by a remarkable unanimity of public sign and profession, some commentators have concluded that all mystics really do experience the same thing, but then theorize about it. The usual inference is that 'monistic' or atheistic mysticism is an uninterpreted reflection of the event, that speech about Jesus, Mary, Krishna is a theoretical overlay. The 'truth', as it were, is an undifferentiated light of which the mystic knows herself a part; a theistic, personalistic tradition then interprets the event as an acquaintance with the courts of heaven, or sometimes a natural experience fraught with danger. Blake, on the other hand, contended that

> God appears and God is light
> to those poor souls who dwell in night,
> but does a human form display
> to those who dwell in realms of day.
> (William Blake, 'Auguries of Innocence')

Blake's view seems to me to be preferable, first because it is personalist, and second because he distinguishes the experiences. If experiences can only be judged to be the 'same' or 'different' by public sign and profession, we have to conclude that the monist's experience of undifferentiated light is not the same as the theist's experience of encounter and communion with a personal deity (whatever she calls it). Insisting that they are 'really' the same, and that theism involves an extra layer of theory, is simply ideological.

I should add that the dichotomy between 'monistic' and 'theistic' experience is neither exhaustive nor exact. The experience of Julian of Norwich is not the 'same' as that of John of the Cross, nor Richard Jefferies' the 'same' as Gautama's. There are resemblances and shared implications, but there seems no reason to insist that some reports are 'true' and others not. Judged by their professions and public motions, the class of 'mystics' is so heterogeneous as to cast doubt on any careful taxonomy of such experience. The best one can say is probably that, for those we call 'mystics' the doctrines of a creed come alive: all things are seen as the play of their chosen divinity, and they themselves as part of that play. The excitement and consolation and comfort that this brings may be entirely real, and very familiar, but we should not infer that they really experience the same thing and make up different stories about it. Experiences only are 'the same' in any sense accessible to us if they are embedded in a theory of what is real, and what is to be done.

Finally, what are we to say about the supposed incommunicability of these moments? Those who have found the doctrine 'come alive' can recognize the same event in others, by the public signs of stunned recognition, by their own memory of when it woke in them. Those for whom it has not come alive, repeat and even rely upon the very same claims as the enlivened, but without 'real' conviction. They have 'heard of' but not 'seen' the glory of the Lord. That they have not seen is shown by the difficulty they have in sorting out the doctrine, in following its implications, in safeguarding themselves against sudden spiritual crises when the gods are far away, and the world stale. It may also be shown in their self-consciousness, their failure to be self-forgetfully involved in the act. Consider two Zen stories (Zen being the Japanese variant of Ch'an Buddhism, which is in turn a sect of Mahayana Buddhism). A master, when asked the standard question 'What is the Buddha-nature?' would hold one finger up in silence. One day his young disciple, asked the same thing, decided to do the same, perhaps with a slight smirk. The master at once leaned forward and cut the finger off. As the disciple ran for the door he looked back to see the master sitting with one finger raised, in silence. Again: a novice asked the master what was the Buddha-nature, and was told to bring a lighted candle to a darkened room. Whereat the master blew it out. These stories are more puzzling to non-pedagogues than to those who are professionally involved in waking up the young, and usually (in praise or dispraise) elicit paragraphs about the shocking irrationality of Zen. A few commentators fumblingly, and destructively, add that they are parables about the non-existence of the self. A better account can be given simply by considering the subjective aspects of the event, what it is like for the victim. Both disciples are concentrating momentarily on one thing, which is suddenly removed, thus acting out the standard recipe for one first step upon the spiritual path: first to focus on one thing, and then remove the thing, to leave only the unfocused, objectless attention that can fill the whole body with light. The other route involves instead a sensory overload, an attempt wakefully to take account of everything – a task entirely impossible as long as one sees one thing against a background of half-seen or unseen things. The point is not, as psychologizing interpreters sometimes suggest, simply to create or to remember a state of consciousness quite different from our normal object-bound existence. It is rather that until such a state is reached we cannot recognize that thing to which no name is given, and which stands behind and within all thought, all objects of all thought. Few of us can manage to maintain the visions. None of us can hope to see the stars till we blow out the candle.

Santa Claus and Visionary Evidence

In that last paragraph I touched again upon the cognitive aspect of 'religious experience'. Are there experiences of the absolute, or infinite, or source of all experience? Are there incommunicable experiences which warrant our belief in the reality of their objects (if they have objects)? Can religious belief be founded on such experience?

No-one, not even children, believes in Santa Claus. Children do not, because they are not yet equipped to reason about the universe and what their parents say. When they are, they quickly express disbelief, even if they enjoy pretending that there is a bearded old man who annually invades their bedrooms to leave them presents. Their state of mind is not belief, for they do not respond as they would to a realistic belief in such a happening – do not beg not to be left alone to face invasion. They may leave biscuits for him, but only in the same spirit that they demand biscuits for their dolls, or play at battleships. They leave booby traps only when they suspect that Santa is their father and wish to be sure. Such pretend beliefs, that paint a picture of the universe, but take care not to draw the usual implication and rather frown on efforts to 'check', do bear an uncomfortable resemblance to purported religious beliefs. We can make the resemblance more exact: suppose some children claim to have seen Santa in the appropriate and traditional form, and it is made clear that they did not see just their fathers. Others, indeed, in just the same place and time, saw nothing of the kind. Suppose that the children, pressed to answer, either could not tell what Santa wore, or gave replies recognizably related to the pictures they had individually seen (by Rackham, Tolkien or Raymond Briggs). Suppose that, after a while, only a faint memory of happiness was left, a hope one day to 'see' the saint again, but no visible presents, hoof-marks or articulate description. We should say, no doubt, that these were pleasant dreams, quite without force as evidence that Santa Claus 'really existed'. Some adults, tenderly or sentimentally, would welcome such fantasies from their children. Others, realistically or sadistically, would insist on their 'facing facts'.

The Claus-religionists have no way of appealing to agreed facts that are well explained by the hypothesis of a red-coated godling whom some favoured few have see upon his travels. It is not inconceivable that such a story is true, though the godling would have curious properties (a knowledge of all that *children* do and want, a capacity to be outside every house simultaneously though forced to enter through a chimney or other cranny), but there is no non-dreaming evidence that it is, nor is it really compatible with the known provenance of Christmas presents. One response might be to make the dreams an allegory, or a recognition of a common custom: 'Claus only acts and is in existing beings, or men', to borrow Blake's words about God. To reject his existence is to deny that earthly parents love to give good gifts to their children, to mock the familiar romance of Christmas. Some critics may do so out of indignant love: prating of Father Christmas and our love of children is a little sick when thousands of children are bullied, maimed and murdered every year. Others may do so in vulgar irreligion. These responses are well known from other, more self-conscious religious traditions, which evade the charge that their myths are only dreams by emphasizing the moral message encapsulated in them.

But Claus-religionists might think that this response was not entirely right. They might appeal to anecdotes of the miraculous – presents that appeared by no earthly artifice, or were even of no earthly make. Claus inspires by his example, but may sometimes renew that example: not all presents are literally his, but maybe some are. This will hardly convince the unbeliever, who will suspect that an unknown friend of entirely mortal character is really responsible. Evidence of that kind, like 'evidence' of extraterrestrial visitation, is usually unconfirmed, unexamined and not very inspiring. Why did this child get a present from Claus when millions starve? Claus-religionists might add that childhood visions should be taken as more serious evidence, that they do not need confirmation from the public and material world. They might 'spiritualize', not allegorize the story.

Thus, children report that they have been in a presence at once jovial and perceptive who desired them to be good, and gave good gifts. They vaguely remember redness, but add 'not red like blood or pillar-boxes'. If scarlet is like the sound of a trumpet, maybe one can 'see' the quality in virtue of which it is without quite seeing what one ordinarily sees. The children 'see' triumphant warmth and blessing, so that their earthly presents glow, the gift not simply of their parents or their guardians, allegorically, but an extra gift from one who is the cause of their faint, fluctuating and determined love. Claus is the god of true parental (or grandparental?) love, as future archaeologists will doubless say, and the real cause of such love as parents really feel. Meeting him is not like being next to some other mortal being, it is being in his presence, in his world. There may not be two spatially locatable beings in the room where the child 'sees' Santa: it does not follow that there is no Claus, nor that the child is 'only dreaming'.

I have drawn out the Claus-religion (so to call it) at such length for three reasons. First, as a reminder that many archaeological or anthropological discussions of alien cults may be as contrived. Second (and contrariwise) as a hint that the 'real religion' of the British may be more complex than contemporary theorists allow. Third, as a relatively inoffensive way of isolating the problems about such experience. The children's visions cannot be checked against photographic evidence: if a red-coated gentleman were photographed climbing from the chimney, it would not be Santa. They *can* be checked against the total body of traditional lore. If one child swears that Santa wore blue, it would already be a sign that something was awry, for 'seeing blue' is not the same emotional experience as 'seeing red'. If the child declared that Santa snarled at her, or ripped up the presents (so that, though sound the next morning they were forever spoiled for her), or that it was terribly cold or smelly where he was, we should conclude that this was not 'seeing Santa'. Traditional religion, in short, provides the context in which such visions are checked. Visions may expand or change the lore: it is not long since St. Nicholas acquired reindeer, and he may turn to spaceships soon enough. But they cannot contradict its essence: 'Santa molests child' is blasphemy.

Religious experience is our entry into the world of a religious tradition, our being seized of its inwardness. It is recognizable as 'religious experience' because there is such a body. Westerners are no longer trained to experience drunkenness as a sight of Dionysus' world, and have not worked through the possibilities of Claus-religion. Aphrodite is still a real presence, recognized in the beauty and emotion of a sexual encounter or a suddenly suffused lustfulness. It would be merely irritating to insist that there is no one individual, bodily person identical with Aphrodite. We are warranted in taking such experience seriously and 'religiously' because there is a systematic body of information in terms of which we can be said to share our experiences. We build tradition out of these shifting moods and suddenly opening windows, but we probably cannot claim that there is no other explanation, in the abstract, possible for the events. We can be conscious of the presence of 'triumphant warmth and blessing', in the particular mode of parental gift, and call it 'seeing Santa'. The presence is real, by the same standards as anything else – that it is frequently and communally encountered. What its being may be is another matter: did it precede humankind, and is it a person as well as a principle?

If the story with which I concluded my last chapter is approximately true, it is possible to add that those who 'see visions' may not simply be being made acquainted with an enduring presence or world-look (encapsulated in a sense of having literally seen a human figure). They may possibly have stirred from sleep, just as in our lesser dreams we may occasionally seem to see or hear something which turns out to be a figure in our present 'waking' world. On this account some of the things we think are 'dreams' (unreal events) are drowsy awakenings to real events. The archaic dream-pattern that sends a spirit to stand by the dreamer's bed and tell her news may be truer than we think, though the bed the spirit stands by is the real bed, in the real waking world. The 'chimney' that Santa Claus comes down is the child's confused recollection of the ladder between heaven and earth, the apparatus through which we sink from our immortal being to the dreaming world, the shaman's route up and down from the real. What Santa gives is the half-knowledge (more would spoil the adventure)? that there is a better world.

Experiencing the Infinite

The really difficult problem is posed by claims to have experienced the absolute, or infinite. All experience is difficult to convey, and hence to articulate even to oneself, but experience of one being among many, even one 'world-look' among many, seems easier to reckon possible than claims to have known God or the Buddha-nature just as such. First: to experience anything is to have moved from one condition (the object's apparent absence) to another (its apparent presence). Whatever there is which is never noticeably absent is not something I experience. I cannot tell the difference between its absence and its presence, and so cannot say, from experience, what it is. Aphrodite and Santa Claus I do experience, because they are sometimes not experienced: there are subjective realms they do not enter, and places to which I can flee from them. 'But whither shall I flee then from Thy Presence? If I climb up into heaven, Thou art there; if I go down to hell, thou art there also' (Psalm 139:6 f). What is infinite and unconfined is never absent, and to experience it as being infinite is to experience it as never absent – and so not to experience it at all.

Secondly, to experience anything is to be aware of it against a background, as a finite shape or presence. Even if we could experience something that was always there it would be as one thing among many. So nothing can be experienced as infinite.

Thirdly, nothing that we experience, being finite, can require an infinite cause. Crudely, however much power would be needed to hold back the Red Sea or stop the sun, it will always be a finite quantity. So no experience warrants any claim to have experienced the presence of an infinite power.

Fourthly, all experience is conceptually loaded. The very reasons that make it impossible to say that theist and monist have 'the same' experience (that sameness of experience is a function of the public theory and situation), also makes it impossible to experience something not as structured by our limited conceptions.

In all these ways, accordingly, it seems difficult to see how any 'religious experience' could ground a claim to have met God or known the Buddha-nature. Nothing one could meet is God, even if it is Santa Claus. One obvious retort is that if God and the Buddha-nature are indeed incomprehensible it is impossible to say what they can or cannot do to manifest themselves. But abandoning rational comprehension too soon is not sound practice. Consider instead whether these arguments are sound. The claim that we can only experience something that we do not always experience is ambiguous: must the object of our experience sometimes be absent, or merely unnoticed? Our own experience is indeed intermittent, but we can still conceive that something is always present even if we do not always notice it. We may indeed experience it precisely as something that will continue to be even when we close our eyes. To think that God has turned away from the evil is like saying that the sun does not shine upon the blind. It is not unimaginable that at last we have our eyes opened forever.

What of the second and third problems? How can anything we experience be infinite or warrant an infinite explanation? We cannot grasp infinity without being infinite, and the mode and our experience requires the existence of an undifferentiated background against which the object stands out. Visionary reports of Mary or Krishna meet this requirement, but what licenses the visionary to think Krishna, experienced as one figure among many, is the infinite? The story is that his mother saw the cosmos in his open mouth, and that every one of the girls he danced with was simultaneously in his arms. But nothing his mother could have seen could have been literally infinite, nor were there infinitely many girls. Nevertheless visionaries hope

> To see a world in a grain of sand
> and a heaven in a wild flower,
> hold infinity in the palm of (their) hand
> and eternity in an hour.
> (William Blake, 'Auguries of Innocence')

Two routes seem worth exploring. First, consider how aesthetic and religious awakening must differ. All of us find it easier to admire a maple tree in blossom than the stump of a corroded pylon, to love an amiable youngster than a drunken and disagreeable pauper. Aesthetes are content with finite objects for their devotion, and see their gods in comfortable, pleasurable spots. The thrust of the great religions is toward the claim that their God is everywhere, that everything is to become a sign of His presence. We may begin with maple trees and other 'natural' beauties, but must in the end expect the glory even in the lowliest and most contemptible of things. When the religious visionary sees Krishna it is no revelation unless everything becomes Krishna's body. To see a figure as the outward and visible sign of an infinite presence (whether that figure exists in consensus reality or not) is to find all things suffused with the glory which gathers in that form, the glory 'as of the only begotten of the Father'.

Second, consider what the subject of this encounter must be. Only God can see God, and the sight of something as divine is the work of a divine eye opening in us.

> Were not the eye itself a sun,
> no sun for it could ever shine:
> by nothing godlike could the heart be won,
> were not the heart itself divine.
> (Goethe: cited by Leeuw (1938) p. 494)

The mystical claim is often made that the self is identical with God: even Muslims, who have emphasised the altogether Otherness and Dominion of God, have sometimes felt constrained to say that 'I and the Father are one'. This usually alarms the mystic's fellow believers, but it does not always mean 'So worship Me!'. Sometimes it expresses humility, not pride: no-one but God could be the subject of the experience of 'seeing God', which the mystic momentarily shares.

This opening 'of the eyes of man inward into the worlds of thought'

(William Blake, *Jerusalem* 5.18) may also be the answer to the fourth problem, posed by the intrinsic relativity of all our perceptions. For most of us, any theophany can only be of God as He is for us, our highest vision. But if God is at all, and is the true life of all, we cannot quite rule out the possibility that a particular individual's vision may be so swallowed in the eternal vision, that no gap can be found between 'how things are for her' and 'how they are for God'. For most of us, religious experience of this kind can only be to live for a moment in the world of some godling, believed but not experienced to be the angel of the One. Equivalently, we perhaps 'see God' as He is for us, the image planted in our hearts. But maybe some 'see God' by being wholly filled with His Spirit. If this is possible, we could add that whereas ordinary perceptions could be experienced even though their apparent object did not really exist (I could seem to myself to be seeing this computer keyboard, although it wasn't 'really' there), one who 'experiences God' has a perception that could not be false. If the perception is itself one that only an infinite and eternal being could have, then there is an infinite and eternal being. Such a perception of God ('God' here names the object of the perception) would be self-validating in a way that no other perception could be, as being necessarily a perception of God's own ('God' here names the subject of the perception).

The Way of Negation

The account I have given so far fits some kinds of personal religion better than others. To meet with something that is taken to be the One God, or the sign and angel of His presence, is to see the universe as the body of this one, centred upon it, and to feel oneself caught up to communion with that One. Infinite depths are realized in what is at the same time known to be a segment of the phenomenal world. Infinite Selfhood seems to emerge behind and within the ordinary ego: 'not I, but Christ lives in me' (Paul, though he probably did not intend to describe an experience here). But there are other traditional themes, among them the way of negation. If it is agreed that *finitum non capax infiniti* (the finite cannot take in the infinite), might we not conclude, instead of supposing that there is an infinite selfhood within or behind the ordinary ego, that indeed we cannot have any knowledge of the Infinite?

According to the way of affirmation, we may say that this very thing here, a piece of crumpled orange tissue, may be recognized as a unique expression of the Infinite. There is certainly no natural beauty in it, but by careful attention, thanking God for it, we may begin to see the

Buddha-nature even here. This also is Thou, and, recognizing it as such, all other phenomenal and physical realities are filled with light. Only the greatest saints can carry this project through (or only the One God), but any of us may catch a glimpse of it, though we are more likely to settle for the finite joys revealed in great music (not in noise and riot), in Botticelli (not in paint splashed at random), in maple trees (not in rusty wire). Such a project is itself a sort of negative way: the saint who says 'The Buddha is in excrement' (and so practises the way of affirmation) in effect rejects the little gods of cleanliness and order. Gandhi, in striving to remove the taint of impurity from excrement was, as I have remarked before, hoping also to remove it from the Untouchables, the excrement removers. By seeing it, and the act of cleansing, as holy, the poles of Hindu culture, Brahmins and Untouchables, were to be joined in a new service of the One beyond the petty categories of ritual life. The way of affirmation is also a way of negation.

The main way of negation, however, is a different route: 'neither is this Thou'. Nothing that we can imagine or encounter is the One God. Even to imagine that we could ever be united in a beatific vision with the Incomprehensible Lord is, for some religions, blasphemy. Our task must not be to seek God, but simply to obey His word, as revealed in the bible-reading community. We cannot even be said to love God, but must walk without consoling image in mere faith. This extreme Protestant piety is obviously only an inch away from secular agnosticism: a God that we cannot dare to conceive and must not pretend to love is as superfluous a deity as one can well imagine. All that is left of piety is a certain style in one's spiritual and social life. The alternative form of apophatic theology shares the belief that the One God is wholly outside our categories, not to be grasped in intellect. It rejects the conclusion that there is therefore no way of approaching – or being approached by – the One. When Lao Tzu instructed his disciple, 'Do not try to hold on to Tao – just hope that Tao will keep hold of you!' (Chuang Tzu 23: Merton (1965), p. 133) it was with the unspoken thought that those who consented to be led by Tao, to be a child of Tao, would at last be shown what exceeds intellectual comprehension.

Certainly even the highest image that we have, an image that in a sense we ought to have (as being likely to rouse in us the necessary emotion of adoring obedience) is strictly false (for reasons mentioned earlier, in chapter 4). Certainly the disciplined mystic will regard special emotional states, beatific visions and raptures, as merely providential aids, no more 'like' God than are the occasions of despair and dereliction when 'God seems far away'. Anyone who would approach God must do so via a progressive shedding of all images, a constant rehearsal of the arguments that show the impossibility of speaking truly about God, a deliberate asceticism of the intellect. 'God' is a term that functions solely as a dummy, a place-holder: it does not name anything that we can conceive or identify. 'Coming-to-God', on the other hand, names a certain sort of spirituality, characterized by a radical sense of one's own finitude and unworthiness. In taking that sense seriously the follower of the negative way places herself at the disposal of the Unknown.

If such a project is considered in the abstract we are likely to get the wrong impression. Protestants who wish to maintain the altogether otherness of deity, our complete inability to measure deity by human standards, end, paradoxically, by sounding just like secular moralists, since there is nothing we can do but deal with our fellow creatures in accordance with traditional morality. Those who insist that there is after all a mystical way, though one that involves the stripping off of all images and all enjoyable affections, may end by simply advocating that particular style of spirituality, without any suggestion that it involves an approach to a metaphysical reality. Similarly, many Westernized accounts of Zen Buddhism made it sound like a merely antinomian cult of self-expression. Only when one realizes that Zen is indeed a Buddhist sect, that its adepts are disciplined, well-read and religious as well as deliberaturely oblique in all their responses, can one catch a glimpse of what it really is to be a Zen adept. Only when one understands that mystics like John of the Cross, for all their talk of Nothingness and the complete absence of any object for true piety, were engaged in normal sacramental and ceremonial duties, and regularly and sincerely professed their belief in the established creed, can one see the negative way in context. The claim that there is no way of understanding God or reaching Him by any effort of ours, that our religious duty is to live by faith, not sight, is not a bland agnosticism of a kind that any modern might accept, but an expression of humility before and within a presence 'known' as being unknown, and as requiring our whole devotion.

The Sense of Being Loved

The experiences and projects of personal religion that I have been describing are largely the province of spiritual athletes. Most believers are probably more familiar with the rituals of their tradition. An age that has forgotten its polytheistic past is also not well trained to see the angel or godling in moments of awe or excitement. In one respect, however, the late Abrahamic tradition seems to have uncovered a novel and popular mode of divine contact. Whereas 'the god of the philosophers', admired by sophisticated Hellenes, loved only the wise and virtuous, and the Olympians simply had favourites, the God of the Jews and Christians purports to love each one of us, and to have endured in Jesus or His people all that we may.

The experience of knowing oneself to be the object of an infinite love, knowing that God Himself is a co-worker, a co-sufferer with us, seems to have no clear precedent in other traditions. Even the Bodhisattvas, who have vowed to be available to all sentient creation, from compassion for their distress, do not actively and enthusiastically value each particular being. Krishna's love for Radha, Eros' love for Psyche, are allegories of God's desire for the soul or the soul's pursuit of God, but they do not appear to issue in a regular, almost comfortable perception of a love at once erotic and parental that will not let the 'least' of its beloveds fall, however hard the path. 'Almost comfortable': popular reports may even verge on the cosy, but there is usually a thread of alarm in the experience. Loving someone is often, weirdly but not quite unreasonably, felt to be something of an impertinence, an implied claim, a threat. There is a voice in all of us, maybe, which wishes to be ignored, not loved, as there is also one that requires only to be given justice, not mercy (foolishly enough). The pervasive theme of Christian tradition is that we are loved, personally and at infinite cost, by someone who has experienced all our ills, up to and including a sense of absolute dereliction. Whatever happens 'He' has been there, and whoever else abandons us 'He' will not, even if we rather wish He would.

It is on regular experience of this conviction that a continued belief in the Incarnation is founded. Merely biblical evidence, and the testimony of the early church, cannot demonstrate even that the early Christians thought that 'Jesus was God'. He was inspired, anointed of God, the word to the ages: none of this requires that he was identical with God (whatever identity strictly is). Not even the claim that he, as known to us through history, is our best image of the divine quite catches what is generated in the felt presence of a being at once God and Human, the lover that was from everlasting, who knows us from inside. The doctrines that have swarmed around this experience are not, in the abstract, very clear nor yet demonstrable. It is understandable, however, that ordinary believers tend to resent theological criticism. It may, in the abstract, be very difficult to make sense of the Chalcedonian definitions (formulated to exclude alternative accounts that were considered heretical). It may, historically, be clear that early believers did not have and would not have appreciated the claim that Jesus was God-made-flesh. But all modern attempts to rationalize the creed regularly conflict with the ordinary believer's insistence that she is loved as a person by God, and that God must have shared our troubles, must have come (as it were) an infinite distance to meet us. God 'ought to have been', He 'must have been' incarnate, not merely (as spiritists allow) because God, the highest spirit, has travelled up the same road as us all, through wire-worm and whale to godhead, but because the very ground of Being, the First Cause, was born and suffered and died.

That paradox is what prevents the Christian tradition from simply vanishing within the reformed Abrahamic religion, since Islam and Judaism alike suspect Christians of exalting a creature to godhood, and Judaism in particular would insist that God has no need of special incarnations to know us from within (but does that knowledge involve His suffering with us?). Other traditions may insist that the wish to be loved is 'immature', that really adult believers do not care whether God knows of them at all, being content to admire God's glory. High-minded persons add that even those believers who avoid the vulgarity of supposing that those the gods love prosper in this life merely postpone the privileges they expect until the next. There is something to be said for these complaints, but most of us, not being high-minded, find it difficult to maintain any sense of our own worth in a universe where no-one else values us. It is perhaps because we have a sense of being infinitely valued that we are assured of being selves at all, not merely moments in a shifting sea. It is no accident that atheistical philosophers and psychologists are busily dismantling the last bastion of secular intelligence, the indomitable ego. There is, on some views, nothing special about the relation between the present state of mind of that person who calls himself 'Stephen Clark' and the state of mind of that person who called himself that ten years ago: that person was not identically *me*, but merely shares a large number of psychological and physical characteristics with 'me' (as will 'my' son in thirty years' time, and an indefinite number of strangers in the millenia to come). There is no single self underlying my changes of belief and character, and nothing especially rational about prudence, as against 'self-sacrificing altruism'. It is only if we are convinced that 'we' are loved despite our characters (as we love our true loves: see above, in chapter 11) that we have reason to deny this secular No-Self doctrine. The Christian priest reported to have said 'I know I exist, because I know God loves me' expressed the theistic answer to Descartes' erroneous claim to know that he existed because he indubitably thought.

Further reading

Clark (1984); Cupitt (1971); Deren (1953); James (1960); Merton (1965); Needham (1972).

Zaehner (1957) is a riposte to the exaggerated claims of 'drug-mysticism'. Staal (1975) is unduly critical of Zaehner, but contains much of interest on the different modes of supposedly 'mystical' experience. Kenny (1973) is an excellent introduction to Wittgensteinian attacks on 'private language'.

Hay (1982) is a sympathetic study of the 'religious experience' of ordinary people, believers and unbelievers.

As kingfishers catch fire, dragonflies draw flame;
as tumbled over rim in roundy wells
stones ring; like each tucked string tells, each hung bell's
bow swung finds tongue to fling out broad its name;
each mortal thing does one thing and the same:
deals out that being indoors each one dwells;
selves – goes itself; myself it speaks and spells,
crying What I do is me: for that I came.

I say more: the just man justices;
keeps grace: that keeps all his goings graces;
acts in God's eye what in God's eye he is –
Christ. For Christ plays in ten thousand places,
lovely in limbs, and lovely in eyes not his
to the Father through the features of men's faces.
(Gerard Manley Hopkins, 'As kingfishers catch fire')

13

The Future of Religion

Prayer and Obedience

As I intimated in an earlier chapter, one response (that of the *Book of Job*) to the problem of evil is to realize that, whereas we would like to see a single project (ours) driven through against all odds, the Lord allows His creatures, all His creatures, liberty to be themselves. The Oneness of a domesticated universe, eternally at 'peace', is not the Life He offers. The One wills multiplicity. Complaint is not exactly pointless:

> Thou dost see fit
> that their words take wing,
> thou dost inspire their questioning,
> thou dost see fit
> that from all of them arises a great
> lamentation.
> (Clastres (1977), p. 140, from Guarani chant)

But if I did start shouting at the sky,

> The sky would only wait
> till all my breath was gone
> and then reiterate
> as if I wasn't there
> that singular command
> I do not understand.
> Bless what there is for being,
> which has to be obeyed, for
> what else am I made for,
> agreeing or disagreeing?
> (W.H. Auden, 'Precious Five')

This 'religious response' is a half-ironic resignation to the Will, a resignation that does not issue in lethargy, but in being what we are set to be, calling on the One to aid us, 'crying, What I do is me: for that I came'. One crucial element in this response, making the difference between non-idolatrous religion and humane agnosticism, is prayer, the formal recognition of our mortality and of the Unborn and Indestructible.

Prayer has a bad name amongst both atheists and irreligious. Is it not an 'immature' confession of helplessness and heteronomy, an attempt to seize an unfair advantage by offering emotional blackmail to the Lord? 'Man come of age' must put aside such childish things. The notion that 'man' has come of age presumably means that 'he' is no longer dependent on others for 'his' life and health, nor duty-bound to serve 'his' creator. My own view is that this doctrine has only to be stated for it to be obvious that the first half is false, and the second unproven. We are wholly dependent on others, and cannot complete a sentence without the aid of the whole universe. Certainly, if the Beginning (an ancient label for the Father) is blind, deaf and lazy, we cannot look to it for Law, nor for assistance. We are then imprisoned in a futile world which we have no rational hope of understanding or controlling. If the Beginning is not blind, or deaf, or lazy, it is simply rhetorical nonsense to speak of defying it. The idea that 'coming of age', or maturing, requires us to entertain delusions of remaking the universe to 'our' requirements, or ignoring all standing obligations, is richly comic. Do we usually think that people like that are very grown-up?

Mutual insult and recrimination apart, there is good logical reason to resist Oedipal impulses to 'defy' God: if the Beginning is not to be trusted, nothing that follows from it can be trusted either. To say or think that God's authority should be disregarded is as self-contradictory as to say that one's own brain-processes are diseased (assuming that these processes are the ground of one's own thought), or that everything one says is false. God, as the sole origin and sustainer of all our life and thought, can only be 'defied' in imagination, and at the cost of total incoherence. At the same time, it must be admitted that much of what God ordains or allows would be unendurable without God's grace, and even that God does not always (pious rhetoric notwithstanding) 'temper the wind to the shorn lamb'. There are at least five responses to the existential crisis imposed on us, that we can do no other than accept and worship, but cannot quite do that either.

The first is the simply or decently atheistical: we must make the best of things while we can, and try to act so as to get the best consequences for those we care about, while never quite forgetting that we have no rational hope of more than momentary happiness. It ill becomes any of us to sneer at this response, or to undermine it. Believers may even reckon it God's grace to the unbelieving, that they are allowed to live for the moment and in unreasonable hope.

The second response is diabolistic. Disappointment breeds a despairing hatred of 'bourgeois' complacency and the established order. Some of these diabolists ('accusers') will drift into open revolution, purporting to be anarchists or Fifth Monarchy men, but without any real intention of establishing justice upon earth: 'justice' is only a name given to the judge's self-interest, and no-one deserves better. Other diabolists infest the literary and socio-political magazines, applauding all books that preach despair and disillusion, sneering at all that seem to offer any more convivial hope, thinking the very worst of all human motives (save their own), and using all the usual tricks of rhetoric to suggest that more ancient ways have been refuted.

The third response may veer towards diabolism or towards piety. It can be, and has been, claimed that there is in us, in our awakened humanity, a power to mould the world. Faced by a universe in which no allowance is made for good intentions, we devise a system of law that exculpates those who know not their right hand from their left, who did not intend nor culpably allow an evil. Instead of the selfishness embodied in all natural individuals (whereby every one pursues its own good), we can look to a higher unity in which we serve the common good (not as defined by some self-selected clique, but by the 'common sense' of all humankind). This power is held to be a 'natural' power, one accidentally arranged by mechanically operating systems, but one which can (as it happens) master its own origin. The supposed evidence for this claim is all about us, here in the developed West. What such progressive humanists do not always admit is that our relatively secure existence has not been built merely on technological innovation and humane legislation, but on the raw materials and labour forced from less fortunate peoples, and species. It is not self-evident that this method of hoisting the few upon the backs of the many can be continued indefinitely, nor extended to the larger populace.

The fourth response is more fashionable than once it was. If desires always multiply as soon as they are satisfied, and if there are natural limitations on energy and materials, we must draw a line somewhere. For a long time, the rich could expect that the less rich and the impoverished would accept their station, because they could expect their own situation to improve. But if we have reached a limit, we can no longer hope to improve the lot of the less-well-off without causing the better-off to lose a little, or a lot, of what they have. Where there is always more cake, everyone can have a little more: if the cake is no longer growing, or if it grows more slowly than the number eating it, we cannot all have more. In this situation (and it is no part of my present brief to decide how far this is a realistic account of the problem) we may, some of us, be a little readier to agree with Hellenic moralists that *pleonexia*, the desire to have more, is the root of evil. Better that we be content with less – a doctrine preached more often to the poor than to the rich. The preachers of a new poverty (which need not be impoverished or pauperized) also often urge that 'we' (family, town or nation) try to be self-sufficient, and even seem to hope that at the last humankind will become once more one species among many, forgetting our grandiloquent pretensions, and being no great loss when once evolutionary forces have restored earth's climax community. Why should it matter much if there are people left to talk and strive to understand the world? What matters more is the Whole Earth's future. In seeking our own aggrandisement we not only hurt our fellow humans, but tilt the 'balance of nature', which will one day swing back again.

The fifth response is piety, directed not toward the natural powers of humankind, nor toward the supposed 'balance of nature', but to the One. To pray for aid and comfort may sometimes involve us in religious error (vain repetition, idolatry or neglect of obvious duty), but failure to do so is certainly irreligious. Religion is the way of prayer. Guides to the prayer life regularly insist that all images and expectations must progressively be abandoned, though without ever losing hold of a necessary, open-ended faith.

Where this piety differs from the versions of religion that recent philosophers have usually discussed is that it is not tied to any particular belief about the future. Naive believers may suppose that, if religion is 'true', no righteous person ever suffers, or that all suffering is simply justified by its spiritual consequences. Better informed believers understand that their faith is not the simple-minded assertion that bullets do not harm the righteous, those favoured by the Lord. Their faith is rather the open-ended one, that whatever happens they will be right to trust the Lord. No-one but an innocent could think this easy, or deny the possibility that even our fidelity may be taken from us. Piety, or prayerfulness, in this context is simply the recognition that we are at the One's disposal, and should not expect to build the divine kingdom here on earth. What can be built or has to be built is not the divine, which can only be revealed, and only to those whom it has chosen to inhabit.

This-Worldly Visions

What can be expected in the future? Atheistical fancy varies. Some suppose that, if we survive at all, things will go on very much as before. We shall learn, and forget; we shall make new arrangements and misunderstand old ones. We may achieve occasional, fleeting happiness, but all things fail and are forgotten. Other fantasists (making the third of the responses I described above) prefer to believe that 'we' or our successors will rise to seize the thunderbolt, and sit ourselves upon the throne of God. A few such atheists imagine that the Ultimate Intelligence will roll back time, retrieve us all from ruin, or at least remember us. In an infinite universe must not all possibilities be realized?

Other, less dogmatic secularists have suspected that secular modernism is an aberration, that 'religion' will return in power: the need to recognize our cosmic place, to acknowledge the powers that make the worlds, to realize ourselves as something more than transitory states of matter, or bundles of perceptions. New, sectarian philosophies spring up among the deracinated young; an old awareness of the living world as something more than material for technocratic control is widespread, whether it is expressed in ecomysticism or Goddess-worship or a simple love of television documentaries. At the same time the developed West can hardly escape an intense guilt about what our peoples have done by way of slaughtering, oppressing and exploiting our human and non-human kindred (even if other peoples would have done as ill). It would almost help if we could feel that we were being punished, or likely to be punished: how else can we look our fellows in the face, how else start square?

The need to make amends, the need to believe that we will not forever be excluded from the great congregation, may be dissipated in futile (even harmful) pieces of do-goodery or emotionalism. They may, alternatively, be the occasion for a resurgence of decent humility, trust in the Divine, a prayerful service of the World-to-come, which is also the World that 'really' is. Prayer, contrition, renewal are recurrent moments in humankind's religious history. It seems to be a universal experience that old rituals are devalued, new ones swiftly established. The stories we tell ourselves are deeply involved in ritualist and counter-ritualist movements: the Divine is Spirit, and not to be confined by any ritual of ours (whether it be a careful recital of the sacred words, or the more 'personalistic' insistence that God is known in the experience of human sociality), but we must think of the Divine according to our best ideals of beauty, decorum, justice and amiability.

One possible response is to take, as our best image of the Divine, the network of living nature itself. The days of sentimental humanism are numbered: the ill-formulated guilt which all informed and prosperous human beings must feel at what we have done to our world and neighbours, the sense that 'human beings' are as ill-drawn a category as 'Westerners' or 'whites', the admiration we must feel for the orderly and beautiful economy of nature, all issue in a religious movement which has not yet achieved its climactic form. The living Earth, set against the lunar sky, awakens in us a reverent tenderness. The stellar universe, on a longer view, is 'the blast of the thundered Word' extolled by St Hildegard (an eleventh-century nun and naturalist). All of us are co-operating in uttering that Word, all of us together are 'the voice of God'.

Ecomysticism may take many forms, some of them merely senti-mental. At its best it involves a realistic respect for 'Earth's Household', an understanding that we human creatures are not all-important, a readiness to worship by living up to the demands of unity-in-multiplicity. We do not yet know (if we ever shall) whether the living earth is unique, and all stars shine for her, or if the stellar creation is itself alive and conscious of itself, in other lives than ours. It may turn out that there are finite intelligences elsewhere in the universe, that some day before the end of time a network of exchange will have grown up. It may turn out, on the other hand, that we are 'alone' in this creation, or effectively so. Neither result would do any necessary damage to the cause of religion; either would affect its future course. Suppose that the living earth is unique: other powers stalk the stellar heights, themselves unconcerned with the painful delights of flesh and blood, but all constrained to serve the continuing being of earth and her members. This vision of things matches ancient myths, of Marduk's fight with Tiamat, of the little life that crawls out of the great, dead giant to serve the gods of justice, love and knowledge. Our love and worship may be aroused by the very vulnerability and finitude of Earth. Suppose, on the other hand, that our world is one of uncounted millions, that life and conscious being is as powerful a force as gravity or electro-magnetism, that the ufologists (however mistaken in detail) are essentially correct. When we look outward to 'the fire-folk sitting in the sky' we do indeed see the anatomy of a living universe (as our medieval predecessors thought). This vision too has precedents: the fire-folk and their self-conscious members may be angels or demons or merely fellow-citizens of the cosmic city.

If conscious life looks up to heaven on a million worlds, what can we say of our world's special claims? The Christian tradition must face this problem particularly: other traditions of piety do not claim, and may expressly deny, that they, their prophet or their sacred text are the unique expression of the Divine. Christian thinkers have often claimed that Jesus alone is the Word, not merely that the Divine speaks and acts through him (as it may through many), but that this very historical creature is the one true centre and point of existence. What can Christians say to hydrocarbon arachnoids from Betelgeuse 17? Could they be expected to believe that a primitive hominid was the beginning and end of all creation? They might agree that the story was, in the abstract, an intelligible one, that the One might indeed have begotten

Jesus 'before' all worlds. But would it be reasonable to believe the story? Would not strict Christocentrism seem as parochial as anthropocentrism, or simple egotism?

One reply regularly found in popular Christian song is the universalist: the Divine has begotten Itself a myriad times, and wears as many bodily forms as there are worlds. The unique centre of creation is manifested, even 'crucified' many times. Jesus is the incarnate Word, and so are (so to speak) Corixil of Betelgeuse 17 and innumerable others. This story fits well with a Spirit-christology (that Jesus was inspired by God), or an ordinarily neo-Platonic one (that he, like Moses, perfectly embodied God's idea of Humanity), but less well with mainstream Christian doctrine. Would not Jesus then be the same entity as Corixil, since 'both' are identically the Word? And, since Jesus and Corixil are separate and local beings, how can they be identical? If they are not the same, they cannot be identical with one and the same thing. As so often, the argument is inconclusive: perhaps, when correctly viewed. Jesus and Corixil are the same entity (as multiple pieces of communion wafer all are the veritable Body of our Lord): we only see one facet of the transdimensional being.

But other theologians may prefer either to express a pious ignorance, that we do not know what other course the Divine has take to involve itself in sentient creation, or to insist that, after all, we are right, that arachnoids and crystalline intelligences and self-conscious stars must all look to the Babe lying in the manger, and recognize in Him their prophecies and intimations. If there is to be a centre for all conscious life, if all of us are to be moulded into one body through recognition of our common derivation, our common goal, that centre might as well be here, out in the boondocks, or the cosmic slums, as anywhere. These fantasies may sometimes help us to face believers of other cults and traditions with more equanimity. Whatever the right answer, we could not afford to ignore our alien friends, and would most probably conclude that the Divine is a mountain, and we are deployed about its foothills. It may be that there are easier and harder routes up hill, but we should not spend too much time trying to walk round the mountain. Where we are, there should we start to climb: in climbing we shall meet our neighbours, and learn new tricks from them. As we draw 'closer' to the infinitely distant peak we shall meet stranger company. We do not need to go to alien worlds for that.

The End of the World

Another, and less hopeful, future does not rest on any renewed appreciation of the Spirit that moves in Earth's Household or the

Universe. The spectres of totalitarian rule, or catastrophic violence, or ecological decay sometimes seem very powerful. If we suffer the unimaginable effects of nuclear spasm or ecocatastrophe, or the all-too-familiar effects of tyranny or mob rule, the direction of our religious attention will be towards the Other World, not our glorification of the Name in this world. Prayer will not be an opening of the door between the worlds to let the Good God in, but an opening to let us out. The distinction may not be clear, nor universal. The victims of tyranny and disaster do characteristically turn to religious forms that tend to strike liberals as relatively 'magical' or 'mystical'. Where earthly instruments fail, the heavenly must serve. But those same magical and mystical forms may be the ones that are needed to sustain those victims as they build new social forms, repair the world and look to their earthly future. In looking to the eternal, they do not necessarily expect to abandon time. But, despite these qualifications, there is a real difference between the two prognoses. On the one hand, we are to continue working out 'God's purpose' in the world; on the other, we are to recognize that here we have no continuing city.

It is this latter doctrine that usually seems most offensive to atheistical intelligence. Religious 'activists', so to call them, are often allied to atheistical reformers who desire the happiness and liberation of their chosen clientele (the oppressed masses, humankind or the natural world). Religious 'ritualists' are often (accurately or not) perceived as conscious or unconscious allies of the great oppressors: if the business of religion lies elsewhere, the business of this world is left to earthly rulers. From this point of view it hardly matters whether those who would withdraw from the world think that the rulers are agents of the Divine sent to govern the unruly, or representatives of the 'God of this world', who is the very devil. In either case true piety demands that we ignore them, 'give Caesar what is Caesar's' – not in the bland and unchallenging sense beloved of preachers, but in the original and radical conviction that money, power and position can be no concern of the true believer. All this world shall go down in flames, and the New World (which is also very old) receive its citizens out of the wreck. Expecting, even longing for, the wreck may take further alarming forms. Nuclear spasm is not to be feared, as it is only the working out of divine providence, God's judgement on the nations; and the elect will, in any case, be 'caught to meet Him in the air'. Ecological catastrophe is no concern of ours, because the Second Coming is at hand, when the Land shall be changed. The fierce hope of vindication by the immortal Judge, who will destroy the shoddy commonplaces of this world's dream, is not only an emotion of the obviously oppressed. Even people who are to outward appearance both prosperous and influential may feel themselves despised by cultural elites with whom they cannot compete: witness the fervour of midwest America. The hope of vindication may also be joined by an almost hopeful dread of judgement: consciousness of acute and humanly irremediable sin may create its own fantasy of punishment which it will be almost a relief actually to endure. The Aztec empire, one may suspect, was toppled so easily because its ruling peoples could no longer endure the headless corpse that wandered their hallucinatory forest, the hideous wound in its chest opening and shutting with the sound of a woodman's axe. The arrival of Quetzalcoatl, sometime opponent of the dreadful Tezcatlipoca, was a welcome relief, even in the unpromising guise of Cortes and his men. The penance that had been sought in self-scourging and self-immolation as well as in the slaughter of captured warriors and slaves now took the shape of world's end and the conquistadors.

That world's end, of course, was not absolute: the new world of the Spanish occupation was not noticeably millenarian, nor the end of time. We can understand how the oppressed might fantasize about the retribution to come, and how even the confused oppressors may come to fear a fall, but outsiders with any historical sense do not expect such endings to be final. Survivors will take up their lives again, and continue the long story of earth's revenge. It will not have been World's End, but only one moment of the eternal wheel. The religious question is: can there be a true World's End, 'an end of time', and what would it be?

Liberals are usually not inclined to think of such an end. Just as religious Amerindians have turned away from the eschatological hopes of the Ghost Dancers to the experience of God-within and the Peyote cult, so liberals prefer to dwell upon the image of life indestructible, fireweed growing in the ruins of London, the regular games of children beneath the guns. Life goes on, and in its going makes the faulty choices, forges the chains and endures the consequences of this world's ways. There is no way out that is not also a way in to a new, temporary world of alliances and accidents. What has been done before will be done again, and piety must lie in our endurance. The endurance itself may bring a secret joy, an intimation of the eternal, the light beyond the sky. But liberal piety, while requiring a devoted loyalty to reformism, social justice, does not expect the eternal ever to make a final end of time. Heaven lies outside the circles of this world, or else (in piety's final decay) is sentimentally identified with human love and sociability. The coming of God's kingdom is simply to be our unending approximation to the ideals of liberal humanism. But neither sentimental humanism nor the rationalist conviction that the eternal never competes with time is quite true to the Abrahamic tradition.

Hellenists who turn to Christian theologians are regularly exasperated by the assertion that 'the Greeks' had no true historical sense, or that 'they' had a cyclic view of history, whereas 'the Hebrews' preached a strictly linear history, with a beginning, middle and end. Attempts at psycho-history rarely do anything but enrage knowledgeable historians. But though the contrast between Hellenist and Hebrew is overdrawn and inexact, there is some truth in the suspicion that natural, pagan humanity does expect life to continue, new things to age imperceptibly but ineluctably, the flood of causation, *karma*, to wash away all seemingly permanent structures. Stability lies outside the stream, or else in the very patterns of the stream. The prophetic, millenarian expectation manifested among the followers of Zarathustra (the real one, not Nietzsche's), and the Hebrews, and the Tupi-Guarani, is of a final stability that 'no pettiness alters', that time will not wash away, not simply another condition or state of the world and consciousness, but the Real Thing. World's End is the final reckoning.

Although we have images of such an end, and of the dawn of eternity, we cannot take them literally. Any serious attempt to imagine what might happen in a world suddenly transformed can hardly avoid turning into novelistic fantasy: either life goes on (and life is inconceivable to us unless it involves change, decay and accident), or it is a sterile, unchanging, boring pseudo-perfection, an everlasting Sunday afternoon. The absence of adequate image can be endured: what is more worrying is the uncertainty about what 'the end of time' could be.

The most abstract interpretation is that time, the before-and-after, will have an end. There will be a last moment, and nothing happen after that because there will be no moment after that. Our ordinary understanding of time seems to require that there can have been no first moment, and no last, any more than there can be a highest number or an end of space. But this infinite time may be quite unreal. Cosmologists are now familiar with the thought that cosmic history cannot be traced back before a certain moment: that is when time began (though some cosmologists hope, without empirical evidence, that our beginning will prove to have been a moment in the eternal breathing in and out of Brahman). Similarly, there may be a literally last moment: not merely that nothing happens afterwards, but that there is no afterwards. This story seems intelligible. Maybe our universe of space and time is strictly finite, even if the Real World is not. When we awaken from our sleep, our immortal selves stand outside the temporal flow and can conceive the whole of our world's history as a completed story. When we die, in terms of the dating systems of our communal dream, makes no difference: all of us awaken as 'contemporaries' in whatever Real Time our world's time has copied. But the story does not quite catch the prophetic hope of transformation: it simply leaves the world of time (our time) behind, in favour of an unimaginable Real whose before-and-after has quite other properties.

Can the end of time be understood not as the literally 'last moment', but only as the last moment of distinguishable change? Much religious and philosophical thought seems directed to this possibility: the Divine is absolutely unchanging, and the coming kingdom will not lose its way, not change. This doctrine, taken in abstraction from the whole religious field, results in paradoxical conclusions: a god who does not know anything of its creatures' experiences, and is never affected by them. Such a being is so far beyond or below anything we can conceive to be personal that it seems odd that so much ink, and blood, has been spilt in the dispute between atheism and religion. On such terms God's worshipfulness simply is the unchanging n-dimensional matrix that is the real world, immune to change because it already contains all change. Even this doctrine is not without religious merit, but it is as well to remember that the timelessness and changelessness of the Divine are religious notions, to be understood within the context of prayer and worship. Changelessness is a matter of absolute fidelity and reliability rather than simply never being different, in any respect, from one moment to another. 'Timelessness' rather connotes the irrelevance of period, age or date to God: He has no special time any more than He has any special place. In this context 'the end of time', correspondingly, need not involve the end of literally all distinguishable change: it may simply be the hope that, some day, there will never again be any falling away, even in seeming, from the Divine life. The prophetic message does not seem to be that all life will at last become unchanging splendour, the beauty of statues, or Keats's lover. If the wolf lies down with the lamb (Isaiah 11.6), it is not because they are frozen solid, but because (by whatever unimaginable contrivance) all powers and oppositions of the world are reconciled, and never again imagine that they are antagonistic individuals.

One very ancient conception of our situation is indeed that Time and the World are formed within the Abyss, 'the infinity, the nothingness, the nowhere and the dark' (as some Egyptian texts have it). Atum made His/Her own space and time, and will at last be reabsorbed in the Abyss. More horribly, the Fifth Sun whom the Aztecs fed with maniacal persistence, will perish and the endless dark begin. Fire and Frost, that met in the Abyss to generate gods and insensate matter, will roar inwards to bring all things low, at Ragnarok. Sometimes there may be some hope of a new beginning, a new differentiation within the endless sea: new halls appear, new gods play upon the renewed meadows: new people step from the wood of dreams. Or else Brahan, after aeons, may breathe out again, and the worlds reform. Modern cosmologists waver, as I mentioned, between the thought that this universe is a one-off affair, that entropy will reach its maximum and nothing distinguishable happen afterwards, and the groundless hope that, in infinite time, the worlds may re-emerge. The underlying reality, the 'natural' state of things, in either case is the undifferentiated Abyss, where no direction is any different from any other, no moment distinguishable. If that is how things are, humane intelligence can indeed do little more than admire the momentary brilliance of this island universe.

The prophetic message, on the other hand, assures us, not merely that we can break out from the cosmic egg and realize our identity with the 'timeless realities' of which this changing, atomized universe is a copy or nightmare distortion, but that the Real World will break in, and so transform the copies that they are new 'real things'. There will be, simultaneously, a casting away or burning up, and a transformation into a new mode of life.

> In a flash, at a trumpet crash
> I am all at once what Christ is,
>   since He was what I am, and
> this Jack, joke, poor potsherd, patch,
>   matchwood, immortal diamond,
> is immortal diamond.
> (Gerard Manley Hopkins, 'That Nature is a Heraclitean Fire and of
> the Comfort of the Resurrection')

The connotation of 'diamond' for Hopkins was probably its undiminishing fire, not its adamantine unchangeability. For the prophetic mind it is not stasis that is the 'real', 'natural' condition of things, but unwearying activity. 'The end of time' is the end of weariness and boredom, the end of that process by which what we do becomes 'past', over and done with, inaccessible and stale. But the adamantine quality of diamond may also express a truth (or a supposed truth): maybe there will be an end of fatal decision, so that all serious decisions will have been taken, and 'where the tree falls, there let it lie'. This is not altogether comforting, but we cannot quite leave it out of consideration without falsifying our tradition. Buddhistic thought allows an infinity of further chances: even if our life-stream goes down to hell, that will only be a stage upon the way back up to humankind, which is the only exit from the wheel. Abrahamic thought has taken much more seriously the idea that fatal decisions can only be taken here and now, that in the world to come the decision will have been made, and our eternal selves will prove to be inhabitants of heaven, or hell. No finite sin could deserve an infinite punishment, any more than any finite well-doing could deserve infinite reward, but that is perhaps not the point. The end of time will simply show us what we eternally are: diamonds, perhaps, or rubbish. The analogy I have mentioned in earlier chapters perhaps represents the truth: my eternal self is, as it were, the shape raised upon the line of my mortal existence, and even the slightest movement of repentance and obedient love will be foundation enough for God's action. As a square is to a line, or a cube to a square, so is my angel to this linear existence, and the world will one day be opened up to the higher dimension.

If this is what the end of time is to be, those who expect it may not be quite so much at odds with those who simply hope to make the best of our present world. They believe, to be sure, that there is a radical break coming, that on some singular morning something unknown since the beginning will occur: a happening described in whatever convenient terms, as 'the sky's opening', or 'the Son of Man's coming on the clouds of heaven'. On That day we shall see that we have only ever seen the 'backside' of things: the commonest of things will 'turn around and look at us'. Such an event may perhaps come as the final, or the first, moment of a nuclear spasm, but it is not identical with that expectable disaster (even if that disaster is also the gods' judgement on iniquity). There is indeed an easy equivalence between what has been feared or hoped for in That Day and the frightfulness of nuclear spasm:

> *Dies irae, dies illa,*
> *solvet saeclum in favilla,*
> *teste David cum Sibylla.*
> (Thomas of Celano, *fl.* 1255)

But what David and the Sibyl saw was a religious judgement, a breaking in of God's ways upon the unruly with irresistible power, not the expected result of distrustful fear, bellicose stupidity. 'The time is coming when you will hear the noise of battle near at hand and the news of battle far away; see that you are not alarmed. Such things are bound to happen; but the End is still to come' (Matthew 24.6). God does not need nuclear bombs.

Further reading

Brundage (1979); Clastres (1977); Lewis (1943); Miskotte (1967); Rundle Clark (1959); Zimmer (1967).

Tense-logics for 'the end of time' are offered by Prior (1967). The theological debate between supporters of the more traditional 'timeless' deity and one who shares time and change with us is sometimes misrepresented as a contrast between Hellenic and Hebraic conceptions. The dispute is hardly likely to be resolved while theologians retain such stereotypes (on which see Clark (1975)), if ever. Process theology, so-called, is sometimes associated with a more holistic approach to the natural world (as by Cobb & Birch (1981)). The religious need for deity to be at once timeless (infinite, eternal, transcendent) and 'in time' (finite, responsive, immanent) has been used by O'Hear (1984) as a reason for thinking religion incoherent. My own view is that the doctrine that Nirguna manifests itself as Saguna (see also Cole & Sambhi (1978)), Atum as Life and Order, the Father in the Son, has to be counted as a mystery or paradox, not a refutation (see Stace 1952). Those who can swallow modern physics should not blench at religious metaphysics!

Puccetti (1969) is the only philosopher known to me to have considered the logical difficulties of multiple incarnations of the One Word.

14

Reasons and Conclusions

Reasons for Believing

In earlier chapters I have offered some arguments for believing that certain religious doctrines and practices were not unreasonable. I have even urged the merits of one particular metaphysical system as a way of making sense not only of religious but of secular practice, namely Neo-Platonism. But my chief aim has simply been to describe the landscape for my fellow-travellers. There are plenty of books which argue for or against particular religious doctrines on the basis of what are taken to be agreed premises. Very few of them ever quite convince the opposition, because the supposedly agreed premises are usually not agreed at all. Theists and atheists regularly talk past each other, as do Buddhists, Christians and Hindus. I have no assurance that I have succeeded in doing differently.

What I have argued, and what I do, broadly, believe, is that the whole phenomenal universe is the actualization in time of an ideal image or project that is best grasped, by us, as a community united in love. We cannot seriously claim to be the sort of creatures that might ever understand the universe, unless that universe, and ourselves with it, is founded on rational principle. The universe is made by the ordering intellect, the Logos, and filled with the Life that proceeds from the unimaginable One through the Logos. Without that Trinitarian faith it does not seem reasonable to put any trust in the little capacities of human curiosity. Moreover, unless it is at least conceivable that human character and actions should be just what the Logos is, we have no chance of fully grasping anything – the Logos would remain wholly inaccessible to us. Consistent neo-Platonists may therefore be ready to admit of some genuinely human person, born within the cycles of this world, that he or she is the very word and intellect of God. They may also accept that it is at least possible that the life flowing from the One should be renewed in us through our association with the company of the Divine Man's disciples. We live, as it were, on two levels – the 'ordinary' level of competitive individualism and material interest, and the 'original' level of divine conciliarity, *sobornost* (in the language of Russian Orthodoxy: Bulgakov (1935) p. 74 ff). That original level is also the life of the world to come.

I think that there are good reasons for holding to some such system, and also that one of the reasons for the 'decline' of religious faith among the half-educated masses and the more self-opinionated intelligentsia is the failure of churchmen to understand and unfold the riches of their metaphysical heritage. Once religion is reduced to the level of sentimental moralism on the one hand, and equally sentimental ritualism on the other, it is hardly surprising that a lot of people lose interest. When it is understood that there is something to be said for a hard metaphysical theism we can at least get a sensible discussion going.

That discussion will not get far, however, without some consideration of the rules of evidence. There are at least two views of evidence which lead people astray. The first, that we should never believe anything 'without evidence', and should proportion the strength of our belief to the weight of the evidence. The second, that everything depends upon a 'leap of faith', which it would be sinful to query. This second thesis, historically dependent on particular versions of Protestantism, has a merely social twin – the conviction that it is somehow impolite to comment on anyone else's 'religion'. The two theses together amount to the assertion of a radical division between reason and religion – a division which it has been my chief endeavour to deny.

What is wrong with the two theses? Crudely, that they each make both reason and religion quite absurd.

The first thesis, like many another dictum which eventually proves unacceptable, at first seems entirely sensible. We ought not to believe things without any reason: to say otherwise seems to leave the way open to any sort of arbitrary or self-contradictory belief. 'Arbitrary' belief just is unreasonable belief, believing at one's own private whim. But what is it to have a reason? I have a reason for believing p if I can produce some other proposition, q, which 'implies' the truth of p. But what is implication? And what is the status of that other proposition? Obviously, if I have no reason to believe q then the fact the q implies p gives me no reason to believe p. And if 'implication' is to be understood as 'logical implication' then we will, at best, only be entitled to believe those propositions that could not logically be false if q were true. At worst, we shall have to ask ourselves what reason (i.e. what proposition r) we have to believe that q implies p.

In other words, when we set ourselves to defend our belief in p (say, that Amerindians have as many teeth as Europeans) by referring to some other of our beliefs, we find that we now have to defend our belief in those other beliefs, as well as in the rules of logic (and of probability, if we feel constrained to agree that 'implication' can mean more than merely logical implication). Every attempt to prove a proposition merely increases the number of propositions we have to prove. It is no exaggeration to say that the very point of a 'proof' is not to establish a conclusion, but to suggest how that 'conclusion' might be subverted. On these terms no belief at all is reasonable, for every belief needs to be justified by an infinite number of prior justifications.

One response has been to insist that there are some privileged beliefs that require and can receive no prior justification. They are self-evident, and constitute the foundations for a reasonable system of knowledge. Candidates for this honourable post have included the axioms of logic and mathematics, as well as the 'immediate' pronouncements of sense-experience. On these terms, reasonable belief is founded on logic and personal sense-experience. Unfortunately, all attempts to reconstruct what we would ordinarily regard as knowledge on this basis have failed. Firstly, there is no general agreement on what is to be regarded as self-evident – a term that certainly does not mean 'evident to all'. Secondly, there seems no non-arbitrary reason not to extend the list of 'self-evident' claims. Perhaps I find it as difficult to deny the existence of God as other people (they say) find it to deny that they see red, or that $2 + 2 = 4$. Thirdly, how exactly could we move from statements of immediate sense-experience and the rules of logic to assertions which we would ordinarily think well-grounded about, say, the number of dead in the Falklands campaign? At the very least, this will involve us in claims about the trustworthiness of testimony, as well as metaphysical theories about the relation of sense and fact.

Faced by these difficulties, most modern philosophers have preferred to found knowledge not on any privileged set of self-evident propositions but on the 'normal' consensus reality of suffering humanity. That people have heads is not a recondite deduction from formal logic and reports on sense-data (twinges, floating patches of colour, high-pitched whistling sounds), and it needs no defence, though it is supported by a mass of other beliefs, about hats and eyes and the like. Every bit of ordinary knowledge is supported by a mass of other bits, but the whole floats on emptiness. It is mildly amusing that philosophers who whole-heartedly reject the church's claim to infallibility, and sneer at those who rest themselves on faith, should themselves be entirely credulous of what they are told in newspapers and everyday conversation. It is quite clear that our ordinary 'information' about the world rests on our willingness to trust the testimony of our neighbours and our text-books.

We carry on believing until there is positive reason to withhold belief.

The rationalist's rule, that we should only believe what is 'self-evident' or what can be inferred from what is self-evident (by rule of logic, or of probability), must in practice give way to a more generous rule, that we should accept common discourse until we have reason to dismiss it. We cannot get outside our whole system of belief in order to check it against reality, or find an unquestionable starting point from which we could rationally reconstruct that system. What then can we do when faced by apparently irreconcilable systems? One response, the most complacent, is simply to deny that there is or could be any other system than 'ours' – which usually, in this age, means the vaguely naturalistic system that educated Westerners imagine has been 'proved' by 'science'. Our rationalist predecessors could at least claim that they had thought through the steps which led from incontrovertible axioms of logic or sense-experience to belief in ordinary material bodies, locatable in space-time, which operated according to mechanical laws. They recognized that there were alternative explanations, and other ways of looking at the world, and hoped to show that only their way was rational. Once it became clear that their system could not be deduced from incontrovertible axiom, their successors quietly dropped the rationalist demand, except when dealing with the 'religious', who were required to meet standards of proof that the naturalists themselves could not possibly manage. There is no adequate proof, in rationalist terms, that bodies exist, or that our memories are broadly accurate, or that the future will resemble the past. All that can be said is that this is what 'we' assume in carrying out our chosen projects.

A less parochial response than myopic denial that there is any alternative to naturalism, and acceptance of testimony only when it is that of 'normal' or 'qualified' people (but not when it is the testimony of mystics or of vulgar people who speak in tongues), is that of social relativism. It is claimed that 'our' reality (which is to say, the body of information agreed by respectable people) includes reference to bodies, mechanical laws, and spatio-temporal locations, but not to spirits, Platonic forms and a real, waking world beyond the illusions of time and chance. Other societies' realities (that is, their bodies of information) may be otherwise, but we cannot question 'our' world. This very strange doctrine somehow combines a naturalistic reality with an idealist meta-reality: claims about bodies, or spirits, are 'true' in being central theses of agreed bodies of doctrine, not in being accurate reflections of the one and only world. Though less parochial, this doctrine is, in effect, as complacent as the first: alternatives are not taken seriously as what they profess to be, namely pictures of reality.

If rationalism is a clearly unviable project, are we reduced to arbitrary faith, whether in the consensus reality of modern naturalism or the religious metaphysic in one of its various forms? A good many Protestant theologians have held as much, insisting that 'human reason' cannot cope with these immensities, and must give way to a leap of faith. What we cannot prove we must assume, and we can offer no distinct reason for what it is we assume. In drawing this conclusion they have themselves accepted the notion that rational demonstration and arbitrary act of will are exhaustive alternatives: what cannot be demonstrated must be arbitrarily selected as the soul's starting point. There can then be no rational quarrel between those who arbitrarily select different beginnings. Each person must choose her own Book of Law, which derives its authority over her solely from her own act of will – so that Koran, and Bible, and the Guru Granth Sahib may all be available as a personal fetish in a court of law or a Freemason's initiation.

But how can a genuinely, traditionally religious person suppose that the authority of her God derives merely from her 'own' authority over her acts and judgements? Such a god, such a sacred text, is not God, nor sacred: 'to believe in God' is to acknowledge a higher authority than oneself; to swear 'on the Book' is to put oneself at risk. In religion and in realistic science alike we consent to be led, to submit our imaginations and judgement to the Truth, not simply to social pressure or wish-fulfilment fantasy. God's authority does not derive from the consent of the individual believer, and the truth is not simply what 'we' all agree on. Rational demonstration and arbitrary judgement are not the only possibilities: demonstration must take its beginnings from indemonstrable premises, but these need not be the choice of the individual will. If they are, that individual is being irrational. What we must take as our premises is what is borne in on us when we approach the universe and ourselves in the proper spirit, of pious obedience. Anything else will lead in the end to intolerable confusion. 'Faith' and 'intellectual intuition' (or '*nous*') amount to the same thing, that initial recognition and welcoming of That-which-is, which is independent of our wills and preferences.

If we are to get anywhere we must assume that our best and most honest efforts will, in general, be rewarded, and therefore that this is the sort of universe where that hope is not merely ridiculous. This does not constitute a 'proof' that this is so, as if we had prior assurance that what we have to assume must in fact be true. But neither is it wholly arbitrary. It is the essence of the only bearable or humanly livable life. We have to think of the universe as rational – though not necessarily as readily comprehensible – even though we know that we have no independent proof that it is. The beginning of wisdom is the 'fear' (that is, respectful obedience) of the Lord, of That-which-is.

Only those who have a 'high' doctrine of reason, who think that we may encounter and recognize the truth, have any right to demand rational argument from the believer. Those who have only a 'low' doctrine, that reason is only the name we give to certain practices which have served well enough to maintain social order and agreement, have no business to complain if others seek a different 'reality'. Those with a high doctrine may be justly reminded that this makes real sense only in a religious context. Particular religious doctrines may rationally be doubted and discussed: the fundamental premise of religion, that That-which-is has absolute authority over us, is also the fundamental premise of reason.

The Case against Heresy

The case for heresy, for private judgement (and so for the happy notion that a sacred text has no real authority over us, beyond that which the believer freely gives it), is relatively easy to state. On the one hand, no-one is as wise or well-informed as to be, of her own nature, accurate in all her judgements. For that very reason, no-one ought to be allowed to forbid her fellows to follow the argument exactly where it leads them. On the other, religious belief is pre-eminently a movement of the personal will, and cannot be dictated by others. If I 'believe' p merely because I am forbidden on pain of torture or excommunication to believe differently, it is not clear that I really believe at all. Just so, if I only do something out of fear or personal interest, and not because I conceive it to be right, I do not act morally – so that the law cannot compel people to be really moral, even if they are forced to be law-abiding. It is surely best to allow the maximum liberty of conscience and profession compatible with an equal liberty for all. Attempts to control belief merely undermine the real piety even of those who outwardly conform, and probably result in massive error (for want of adequate discussion and experiment). What academic could disagree? Even the most rigid of sectarians will concede that there is a field of debatable opinion, where it is permissible to argue for and against theories that have not yet been settled.

The common view that it is typical of science to be willing to question all theories without exception, of religion to adopt an unquestioning credulity, is clearly exaggerated. Most specialists are in fact very unwilling to take radical criticism seriously, or to spend any time in worrying about the ruling axioms of their particular disciplines. Those who do begin to have doubts, or to play at sceptical enquiry, may find that they do not easily obtain employment, publication, grants or tenure. There will, of course, be debate on some issues, but these will be fringe concerns, matters of applying accepted theories and techniques to novel areas. They will not involve radical, Cartesian questioning of the sort that doubts everything that can logically be doubted. It is also clear that however often scientists claim to trust nothing but their senses and experiments, science of any kind would be quite impossible without a general acceptance of testimony. If every investigator had to question and recheck every piece of 'received opinion' no-one would ever get any new work done. Indeed, if it is wrong to accept the received opinion, it would also be wrong to rely on one's own memory and records. Every experimental result would have to be 're-confirmed' each day.

In other words, not only do scientists, in fact, display a considerable reluctance to re-open questions that their community considers settled, but there is also good reason to suggest that this conservatism is appropriate. It may sometimes be excessive, and it is certainly very irritating for original or hyper-critical thinkers, but we have to concede that science or scholarship could not be run on Cartesian principles. Conversely, religious traditions have devised ways of checking their results, translating them into contemporary idiom, or dismissing earlier orthodoxies, without entirely subverting their view of things or making out that their predecessors were entirely wrong. Even the most rigid of sectarians do not suppose that the founders of their sect said and believed exactly and literally what they themselves believe. Maybe they would have agreed that the new way of putting things was strictly implied by what they did say, but maybe they wouldn't. Tradition and innovation work together in any human enterprise.

Heretics, who prefer their own judgement or that of their immediate circle to the accumulated testimony and orthodox theory of the sect or discipline whose judgement they wish to sway, are likely to have a hard time. Usually they will not even be answered (or will be answered patronizingly in a variety of mutually contradictory ways); they will be typed as cranks, and their arguments as obvious sophisms. Occasionally these sophisms will turn out to be truisms. This is hard on the heretic; but she has no absolute right to complain. She wishes, after all, that her 'truth' may one day be the relatively unquestioned context of debate. Whatever people say in praise of the 'open society', where no theories are sacred and novices are encouraged to question everything, they rarely intend their own theories to be on permanent trial. But if heretics want there to be an orthodoxy (namely, their own theory), they cannot justly complain if present opinion thinks them heretical, and therefore of less moment and authority than the established creed. Gnosticism, to borrow a term from religious history, is the conviction that my friends and I have access to the truth, and that no-one else is qualified to judge what we do and say. It is not wholly impossible that there are such a privileged few, but they cannot expect to convince the rest of us.

Honest and humble enquirers, accordingly, unavoidably conduct their investigations within the context of received opinion, and submit not only to the Truth, but to the judgement of their fellows. 'Questioning everything' is an impossible project; insistence that one's own judgement is bound to be superior to one's superiors' is merely egoistical. None of this, to state what should be obvious, in any way supports the cruel and conceited measures that have been taken against innovators in the past. If intellectuals have a duty to submit in the end to common judgement, the judges have a duty not to close their ears entirely, and not to kill, torture, insult or ostracise the questioners.

The Nature of Authority

The parallel I have drawn between science and religion is intended to subvert a current orthodoxy. A reasonable reply might be that although the two sorts of institution are alike in their conservatism, even their proper conservatism, they are very unlike in their criteria for proper authority. Whereas scientists and scholars gain authority by displaying intellectual excellence that has some connection with the acquisition of truth, religious authority is wielded by religious officials or charismatic personalities. Professors are believed because it is judged that they have special knowledge and expertise; priests because they preach the church's creed and wield its magic implements: prophets because they work miracles or look and sound impressive.

The distinction is perhaps not as clear as rationalists suppose. Professors are as vulnerable as priests to the conviction that what they say must be so, whether or not they 'really' have any special knowledge of the field. Priests are usually only accorded that status after training in the arcana of their tradition. Prophets do claim an authority of a different kind, 'supernatural' rather than 'natural', owing little to any human training or information. In no case is it unreasonable for others to believe what the authority says, merely because she says it. Rationalists tend to suggest that believing on authority is intellectual sin, though it is one that we clearly cannot avoid. It is regularly contrasted with 'believing on the evidence', but wrongly so: if an authority says that p is true, that is itself evidence that p is true, because an authority would not have said it was true if it wasn't. This principle itself may require justification if we are to believe it, but it is not one that we can dismiss out of hand – as if there were a rule of evidence that said that nothing anyone else says is ever good enough reason to believe. On the contrary, if we trace any piece of evidence far enough we shall find that it rests on the authority of someone.

Authority may be widespread and diversified. Each of us is an authority of sorts on our own life and person: it is conceivable that we are often mistaken, forgetful or self-deceived, but if we honestly say that we remember some past episode we have some right to be aggrieved it no-one will believe us. Any of us may also be a channel for information that depends for its authority on the veracity, skill or luck of others. We cannot claim to be authorities on that information unless we have some grasp of how it was acquired, how it might be checked and expanded. Who is an authority on God?

Personal experience of enlightenment or the divine presence may convince us that we have a slight right to be aggrieved if no-one will believe us (though only if there is some change in our lives that others might reasonably notice). But such personal experience cannot be the final ground of our belief, for reasons discussed in chapter 12. Only if we already have reason to believe that there might be a divine presence, that it might make itself known to selected persons, can we claim authority for our convictions. In short, we need an established tradition within which mystical utterance can take its place. How may we reasonably conceive that such a tradition be organized?

One religious response has been to allow the maximum diversification. Like-minded persons may form their own conventicles, dismissing all others (according to temperament) as 'relatively right' (which has been Buddhist practice) or 'relatively wrong' (which has been Christian). Alternatively, we may prefer what is, technically, the 'catholic' response ('catholic', because *kath'olou* – for the whole world), refusing to concede that particular groups within the living tradition might be entitled to ignore their fellow-believers. Catholicity sometimes lays claim to a rule of evidence known as the Vincentian canon (ironically, after an early Christian schismatic) that we should believe what has been believed everywhere, at all times and by everyone. It is clear that this canon is vacuous, particularly as it is only invoked to ground the speaker's rejection of a doctrine which she dislikes but which is in fact believed by others. Once a doctrine is in dispute it is pointless to appeal to the canon, since neither side can claim universal assent. The intention behind the canon may be more reasonable: maybe there is a common body of belief that enables the community to continue 'in communion'. Schism and heresy are constituted by the refusal to accept the common judgement of believers; crass complacency by a refusal even to listen to dissentient voices.

As in political affairs, so in religious, there are in essence three forms of authority for such a catholic community: the democratic, the oligarchic and the monarchical. On a democratic view, all members of the community have a part to play in defining doctrine, and the creed which gives the context for personal innovation and debate is settled by consensus, over time. On an oligarchic it is the qualified few, the bishops or theologians, who must meet in council to decide. On the monarchic, it is the single leader of the church, 'the vicar of Christ' or the like, who has the final word. A purely democratic view must, in practice, go along with considerable diversity of opinion, since there are few doctrines on which there is a view shared by 'all who profess and call themselves Christians', still less all God-fearers or pious persons. The duty of pious obedience remains, but there is little dogmatic content to that duty. Oligarchic rule tends toward the scholastic, the maddeningly exact discrimination of positions and rejection of potential heresies. It may also result in very peculiar doctrine, as committees struggle to accommodate the obsessions of their members, or deal with one error without falling into another. Monarchists may have an easier time, though they run the risk of imposing on later ages the particular foibles of one individual.

In each case it is only reasonable to believe these authorities if there is reason to believe that the world is such as to make them more likely to be accurate than not. In each case what the world is believed to be depends on what our authorities say it is. At best, this will be circular; at worst, it will be self-contradictory. If the world, for example, is what modern naturalists say, we should have no reason to believe that common consent, rational thought or scientific observation bore any systematic relation to the truth: we should have to regard all our best theories as merely pragmatically useful, not as saying how things really are. If the world is what, say, Abrahamists declare, we have some reason to expect that what is approved by Abrahamists, over the long run and under God, will not be entirely mistaken. This does not prove Abraham correct, since we have no prior assurance that what is consistent is veridical, nor that what is pragmatically self-refuting is false. It does give Abraham the edge.

Is it reasonable to go further, and insist not merely that believers should submit to general, long-term judgement as that is embodied in the received opinion of the body of believers (it being unreasonable to think that God would leave His people entirely without aid), but that we should also defer to the *ex cathedra* utterances of a church official, or the majority vote of an ecumenical council? Do papal or conciliar pronouncements, in other words, get their authority from the eventual consent of the church, or do they carry authority in themselves, and effectively define who is to count as a real church-member?

The authority of a scientific theory is, in practical terms, a function of its helpfulness to a range of practitioners and the support given to it by a few highly esteemed scientists. In the scientific and scholarly world no-one remains at the top forever: however expert one has been, it is accepted that one will eventually be regarded as a has-been, remembered (possibly) with affection and respect, but without any claim to protect old theories from assault or approve new ones. This (politics apart) is doubtless because it is generally recognized that age may reduce intellectual capacity and imagination, and new theories require the acquisition of new techniques and concepts. In the religious world this gradual surrender of authority is less marked. We do not expect our great religious leaders to admit to decay, and rather honour the aged than cheerfully despise them.

One way to understand this contrast (which is, of course, a very inexact one) is to see religion as a matter of tradition, science as essentially innovative. To be 'religious' is often to be traditionalist, and the old are often more alive to what things were like than they are to contemporary happenings. To honour the old, and revere their sayings, is to hold on to something, the nugget of irreplaceable truth, that scientific innovation must not wholly destroy.

Another explanation is that it usually takes a lifetime for anyone to become a saint, and that process can continue indefinitely, even if intellect and memory and self-control decay. Habits of devotion and kindliness, at least when founded in a real and prayerful intention, are relatively well-protected against destruction, though not absolutely so. An old man has a better chance of being a saint than a great scientist or scholar, and the elderly deserve a higher status in religion than in science for that reason. Again, it may be true (and many traditions have thought it true) that the soul's eye becomes clearer as the body nears its end. Some of the elderly see or remember the celestial city with more clarity, even if they can no longer be trusted to remember phone numbers or the names of their grandchildren. The heavenly sun shines brighter as the earthly lamps decay. If this is so, then the religious do well to look to the elderly and dying for their authorities, guardians not merely of tradition, but possible examples of saintliness and witnesses to the undying light.

It is clear in any case that religious authority does not rest simply on intellectual gifts, and it is not the class of educated theologians and philosophers that have the last word. Churches, unlike scientific disciplines, cannot be governed solely by the scholarly. Human wisdom may be required of us, but it is not the criterion of religious truth. For that we must look to the believing masses, the ones who prayerfully intend to be saints, those old in the faith. There is therefore more reason in religion to believe nothing radically inconsistent with the eventual judgement of elderly and saintly persons, than there is in science or scholarship.

But religious authority rests at last with God or the Buddha-nature. Insofar as 'being God' is being worshipful, being such as to be followed and obeyed as an ultimate end of thought and action, and 'being the Buddha-nature' is being enlightenment, that much is a tautology. Those who take 'science' as their final authority (so that science alone is to be believed in considering what the world may be, and science alone served in considering what we may do) are, in effect, worshipping that form of life which we may call Apollo (on which see chapter 5). Science as such, as the effort to make sense and humane use of the world in which we find ourselves, may be an exercise of piety, or else a rival religion ('scientism'). Those who are commonly thought to be 'religious' are those who think that there is something more important than science, and other ways to truth. They are surely right to think so, but it is easy to equate that Truth with the ordinary lives of reasonably decent citizens, so that 'being religious' becomes a synonym for convention. From that perspective science and scholarship may serve as sound reminders that 'God is greater than our hearts, and knoweth all things'. Neither the conventions of everyday society, nor the theories of science, can easily be equated with the One above all other, the source alike of science and of society. Pious citizens and scientists alike let themselves be guided by 'something not themselves that makes for righteousness'.

Those who refuse all such guidings, who deny absolute authority to anything but the momentary will of the individual, have achieved an extraordinary success in our day. Our predecessors would recognize such persons as having a criminal mentality, the kind that say 'I must have this because I am Me' (with no acknowledgment that every other ego could say as much). Recent moral philosophers have proclaimed that it is only these criminals who are truly 'moral', preferring their own 'autonomy' to any divine command or purpose. To deny divinity (which is to say absolute authority) to anything but the momentary will makes it impossible even to bind oneself to one's own present purpose: why should a past Me have authority over the present, any more than a present friend or neighbour? Real autonomy, which includes the capacity to plan one's life in company with the whole congregation of earth and heaven, rests upon obedience to the laws of 'God and the Buddha-nature' (see Merlan (1963) p. 114 ff).

True piety must stand above the worship of science, society or the momentary self. All these lesser things have value only insofar as they serve the Father (who is the Beginning), through the Son (who is the

Word and Wisdom of God), by grace of the Spirit (who is that which spoke through the prophets). By the same token, Enlightenment shows up the lesser gods as 'thieves and rebels, destroyers' if they are separated from 'the vine of eternity' (Blake (1966) p. 571). Apollo has his place in religion, as do Athena and Aphrodite, but they are not the Lord, and neither (obviously) am I.

Pascal's Wager

Philosophers, at best, are map-makers. I hope that these maps of the realms of piety may be of service to travellers. Even in the Heavenly City there may be those who enjoy looking at quaint maps of far-off countries. But the map is not the territory, and philosophy no substitute for pious endeavour. Those who have understood these maps will tuck them away and follow the approved signposts up the mountain. What, after all, have we go to lose? As Blaise Pascal pointed out, when life is uncertain we must calculate our possible gains and losses. Forced to lay our bet on Piety or irreligion, we may allow at least some possibility that Piety is the accurate response. We stand to win an infinite prize if this is so, or lose as much. If it is not, then the gains of irreligion will be finite and fragile joys. Rational gamblers calculate their moves by reckoning up the product of the probability and the expectable gain. An infinite gain, even one relatively improbable (which piety's is not) has more weight than any finite gain. Which error would be worse: to practise piety although there really was no worthy object of our devotion, no Unborn and Indestructible, no Presence whose adoptive children we might be, or to look only to earthly satisfactions when in fact there was? The pious, even though they may be diverted into diabolic parodies of true religion, are preparing for the next stage of a journey. The atheistical, all the more so if they are humane and civil atheists, must bind themselves to satisfaction of finite and ultimately futile projects. If atheists and materialists are right, we have no rational hope of understanding or settled prosperity, nor reason to think that these things much matter. So there is little reason to think that the pious, insofar as they are asked to surrender certain earthly satisfactions (the pleasures of malice and self-aggrandisement, for example) and un-reasonable hopes, are losing anything of value even if they are 'factually' mistaken. Those who do not learn in time to reach out to eternity, on the other hand, may lose an infinite reward. So mistaken disbelief is a worse failure than mistaken faith. Let us, accordingly, practise piety.

This argument clearly offends some people, who suspect that an indecent image of the deity, rewarding self-interested make-belief at the expense of honest doubt, is involved. Others remark that there are more than two alternatives, that it is not wholly inconceivable that the Aztecs were right after all, and the survival of this world's sun, and our felicity, depend on mutual slaughter: are we to bet that they were right because it would be a worse outcome if they were right and we did not back their judgement? Any number of deaths-in-agony, after all, must be a finite cost. Both these responses miss the point. Pascal's wager is a choice between Piety and Irreligion just as such: what form of piety, what precise metaphysic should be regarded as the best bet is another question that might be settled by more normal means. Nor is it necessary to think that it is Nobodaddy who dispenses infinite rewards for a pretended piety. The point is that if religion is correct, then the lives and character we build must be the basis or the earthly manifestation of our celestial life, however great the help that may be available. If it were not so, if there were no real connection between earthly and celestial lives, how could the latter be our lives at all? But if there is a real connection, so that the celestial could be regarded as the mathematical solid raised upon the plane of our earthly existence, then our policies and acts here-now are of an infinitely greater weight than we had supposed. On what we do and feel here-now depends the shape of our celestial life, whether for good or ill. Maybe the divine is able and willing to mend any botch we make, but that would be a risky bet to make. If that life depends at all on us then we had better seek what help we can now, while we are confident that we can. If nothing beyond this life rests with us (because there is no life of ours beyond this life) yet the life of piety is not all that disagreeable, the irreligious life not all that happy. Better to assume that what we do may have infinite reper-cussions: if it does, we shall have done our best; if it does not, we have lost, in comparison, nothing.

Further reading

Bulgakov (1935); Clark (1984); Merlan (1963); Ware (1963).

Contemporary epistemology, the study of criteria for knowledge, has moved away from 'foundationalism' (the requirement that there be self-evident foundations for knowledge) to the assumption that all claims to knowledge must be justified within our 'ordinary' form of life. Epistem-ologists have not always been too scrupulous in picking out such an ordinary life: see Chisholm (1982), Dancy (1985), Price (1969). On the philosophy of science in particular see Barnes (1974), Lakatos (1976). On Pascal's wager, and related topics, see Levi (1967).

Give me my Scallop shell of quiet,
My staffe of Faith to walke upon,
My Scrip of Ioy, Immortall diet,
My bottle of salvation:
My Gowne of Glory, hopes true gage,
And thus Ile take my pilgrimage.

Blood must be my bodies balmer,
No other balme will there be given
Whilst my soule like a white Palmer
Travels to the land of heaven,
Over the silver mountaines,
Where spring the Nectar fountaines:
And there Ile kisse
The Bowle of blisse,
And drink my eternall fill
On every milken hill.
My soule will be a drie before,
But after it, will nere thirst more.

And by the happie blisfull way
More peacefull Pilgrims I shall see,
That have shooke off their gownes of clay,
And goe appareld fresh like mee.
Ile bring them first
To slake their thirst,
And then to tast those Nectar suckets
At the cleare wells
Where sweetness dwells
Drawne up by Saints in Christall buckets.

And when our bottles and all we,
Are fild with immortalitie:
Then the holy paths weele travell
Strewde with Rubies thicke as gravell,
Seelings of Diamonds, Saphire floores,
High walles of Corall and Pearle Bowres.

And this is my eternall plea,
To him that made Heaven, Earth and Sea,
Seeing my flesh must die so soone,
And want a head to dine next noone,
Just at the stroke when my vaines start and spred
Set on my soule an everlasting head.
Then am I readie like a palmer fit,
To tread those blest paths which before I writ.
(Walter Ralegh, 'The passionate mans Pilgrimage', 1–34, 51–9,
supposed to be written by one at the point of death)

Bibliography

Philosophy of religion is a field so wide that a comprehensive bibliography would be a large volume in its own right. What follows can be no more than a list of those books to which I have referred in composing my present discourse. I am sure that I have been influenced by more authors than I cite. Contemporary journals dealing with these matters include *Downside Review, Modern Churchman, Modern Theology, Religion,* and *Religious Studies.*

Aho, J. P. (1981), *Religious Mythology and the Art of War* (Aldwych Press: London).
Atkins, P. W. (1981), *The Creation* (Freeman: London).
Auden, W. H. (1966), *Collected Shorter Poems* (Faber: London).
Banton, M. (ed.) (1966), *Anthropological Approaches to the Study of Religion* (Tavistock: London).
Barfield, O. (1965), *Saving the Appearances* (Harcourt, Brace & World: New York).
Barnes, B. (1974), *Scientific Knowledge and Sociological Theory* (Routledge & Kegan Paul: London).
Berger, P. L. (1969), *The Social Reality of Religion* (Faber & Faber: London).
Berger, P. L. (1970), *A Rumour of Angels* (Allen Lane: London).
Berger, P. L. and Luckmann, T. (1967), *The Social Construction of Reality* (Allen Lane: London).
Berkeley, G. (1948), *Alciphron: Collected Works*, Vol. 3, p. 21 ff (Thomas Nelson & Son: Edinburgh).
Bernstein, B. (1971), *Class, Codes and Control*, Vol. 1 (Routledge & Kegan Paul: London).
Berryman, J. (1971), *Love and Fame* (Faber: London).
Blackburn, S. (1984), *Spreading the Word* (Clarendon Press: Oxford).
Blake, W. (1966), *Collected Works* (ed. G. Keynes) (Oxford University Press: Oxford).
Bloom, A. (1980), *Living Prayer* (Darton, Longman & Todd: London).
Bolton, J. D. P. (1973), *Glory, Jest and Riddle* (Barnes & Noble: New York).

Bowes, P. (1977), *The Hindu Religious Tradition* (Routledge & Kegan Paul: London).

Bowker, J. (1973), *The Sense of God* (Clarendon Press: Oxford).

Brundage, B. C. (1979), *The Fifth Sun* (University of Texas Press: Austin).

Bulgakov, S. (1935), *The Orthodox Church* (tr. E. S. Cram, ed. D. A. Lowrie) (Centenary Press: London).

Cardenal, E. (1974), *Love* (tr. D. Livingstone) (Search Press Ltd: London).

Chang, G. C. (1972), *The Buddhist Teaching of Totality* (Allen & Unwin: London).

Chesterton, G. K. (1933), *Collected Poems* (Methuen: London).

Chisholm, R. M. (1982), *The Foundations of Knowing* (Harvester: Brighton).

Clark, S. R. L. (1975), *Aristotle's Man* (pbk 1983) (Clarendon Press: Oxford).

Clark, S. R. L. (1977), *The Moral Status of Animals* (pbk 1984) (Clarendon Press: Oxford).

Clark, S. R. L. (1982), *The Nature of the Beast* (pbk 1984) (Oxford University Press: Oxford).

Clark, S. R. L. (1984), *From Athens to Jerusalem* (Clarendon Press: Oxford).

Clastres, P. (1977), *Society against the State* (tr. R. Hurley, A. Stein) (Blackwell: Oxford).

Cobb, J. and Birch, C. (1981), *The Liberation of Life* (Cambridge University Press: Cambridge).

Cohn, N. (1970), *The Pursuit of the Millenium* (Paladin: London).

Cole, W. D. and Sambhi, P. S. (1978), *The Sikhs* (Routledge & Kegan Paul: London).

Cupitt, D. (1971), *Christ and the Hiddenness of God* (Lutterworth Press: London).

Cupitt, D. (1980), *Taking Leave of God* (SCM: London).

Cupitt, D. (1982), *The World to Come* (SCM: London).

Dancy, J. (1985), *Contemporary Epistemology* (Blackwell: Oxford).

D'Arcy, M. (1945), *The Mind and Heart of Love* (Faber & Faber: London.

Davies, B. (1980), *Philosophy of Religion* (Oxford University Press: Oxford).

Davies, P. (1983), *God and the New Physics* (Dent: London).

Deren, M. (1975), *The Voodoo Gods* (Paladin: London); first published as *The Divine Horsemen of Haiti* (Thames & Hudson 1953: London).

Derrett, J. D. M. (1973), *Jesus' Audience* (Darton, Longman & Todd: London).

Dodds, E. R. (1951), *The Greeks and the Irrational* (University of California Press: Berkeley).

Donne, J. (1929), *Complete Verse & Selected Prose* (ed. J. Hayward) (Nonesuch Press: London).

Douglas, M. (1966), *Purity and Danger* (Routledge & Kegan Paul: London).

Douglas, M. (1973), *Natural Symbols* (2nd edn) (Barrie & Jenkins: London).
Drury, M. O'C. (1973), *The Danger of Words* (Routledge & Kegan Paul: London).
Dumont, L. (1972), *Homo Hierarchicus* (Paladin: London).
Durkheim, E. and Mauss, M. (1963), *Primitive Classification* (tr. R. Needham) (Cohen & West: London).
Eliade, M. (1959), *Cosmos and History* (tr. W. R. Trask) (Harper & Row: New York).
Eliot, T. S. (1957), *Four Quartets* (Faber: London).
Empson, W. (1955), *Collected Poems* (Chatto & Windus: London).
Evans-Pritchard, E. E. (1965), *Theories of Primitive Religion* (Oxford University Press: Oxford).
Falkner, J. M. (1935), *Poems* (Westminster Press: London).
Fawcett, D. (1921), *Divine Imagining* (Macmillan: London).
Flew, A. (ed.) (1964), *Body, Mind and Death* (Macmillan: New York).
Frankfort, H. (ed.) (1949), *Before Philosophy* (Pelican: Harmondsworth).
Fraser, J. T. (ed.) (1968), *The Voices of Time* (Allen Lane: London).
Gale, R. (ed.) (1978), *The Philosophy of Time* (Harvester Press: Brighton).
Geach, P. (1977a), *Providence and Evil* (Cambridge University Press: Cambridge).
Geach, P. (1977b), *The Virtues* (Cambridge University Press: Cambridge).
Glatzer, N. N. (ed.) (1969), *The Dimensions of Job* (Schocken Books: New York).
Gordon, R. L. (ed.) (1981), *Myth, Religion and Society* (Cambridge University Press: Cambridge).
Gudmunsen, C. (1977), *Wittgenstein and Buddhism* (Macmillan: London).
Gunstone, J, (1982), *Pentecostal Anglicans* (Hodder & Stoughton: London).
Gustafson, J. M. (1982), *Theology and Morality* (Blackwell: Oxford).
Hay, D. (1982), *Exploring Inner Space* (Pelican: Harmondsworth).
Head, J. and Cranston, S. L. (eds) (1977), *Reincarnation: the Phoenix Fire Mystery* (Julian Press: New York).
Helm, P. (ed.) (1981), *Divine Commands and Morality* (Clarendon Press: Oxford).
Hick, J. (1966), *Evil and the God of Love* (Macmillan: London).
Hick, J. (1973), *Philosophy of Religion* (Prentice-Hall: New Jersey).
Hooykass, R. (1972), *Religion and the Rise of Science* (Scottish Academic Press: Edinburgh).
Hopkins, G. M. (1967), *Collected Poems* (ed. W. H. Gardner & N. M. Mackenzie) (Clarendon Press: Oxford).
Hudson, L. (1968), *Frames of Mind* (Methuen: London).
Hume, D. (1976), *Natural History & Dialogues* (ed. A. W. Colver & J. W. Price) (Clarendon Press: Oxford).
Hussey, E. (1972), *The Presocratics* (Duckworth: London).
Jaki, S. (1974), *Science and Creation* (Scottish Academic Press: Edinburgh).
James, W. (1960), *The Varieties of Religious Experience* (Fontana: London).

Jaynes, J. (1976), *The Origin of Consciousness in the Breakdown of the Bicameral Mind* (Houghton Mifflin: New York).

Johnson, S. (1924), *Journey to the Western Islands*, with J. Boswell's *Journal of a Tour to the Hebrides* (ed. R. W. Chapman) (Oxford University Press: Oxford).

Kelsey, M. T. (1973), *Tongue Speaking* (Hodder & Stoughton: London).

Kelsey, M. T. (1974), *Encounter with God* (Hodder & Stoughton: London).

Kenny, A. (1973), *Wittgenstein* (Allen Lane: London).

King-Farlow, J. (1978), *Self-Knowledge and Social Relations* (Science-History Publications: New York).

Kipling, R. (1927), *Collected Verse 1885–1926* (Hodder & Stoughton: London).

Kolakowski, L. (1982), *Religion* (Fontana: London).

Kripke, S. (1980), *Naming and Necessity* (Blackwell: Oxford).

Laing, R. D. (1960), *The Divided Self* (Tavistock: London).

Lakatos, I. (1976), *Proofs and Refutations* (ed. J. Worral & T. Zohor) (Cambridge University Press: Cambridge).

Larner, C. (1982), *The Thinking Peasant* (Pressgang: Glasgow).

Leeuw, G. van der (1938), *Religion in Essence and Manifestation* (tr. J. E. Turner) (Allen & Unwin: London).

Levi, I. (1967), *Gambling with Truth* (Knopf: Boston).

Lewis, C. S. (1943), *The Abolition of Man* (Bles: London).

Lifton, R. J. (1970), *Boundaries* (Vintage Books: New York).

Lutoslawski, W. (1930), *The Knowledge of Reality* (Cambridge University Press: Cambridge).

MacCormac, E. R. (1976), *Metaphor & Myth in Science & Religion* (Duke University Press: Durham, North Carolina).

McGinn, C. (1982), *The Character of Mind* (Oxford University Press: Oxford).

Machan, T. R. (1975), *Human Rights and Human Liberties* (Nelson-Hall: Chicago).

Macintyre, A. (1981), *After Virtue* (Duckworth: London).

Mackie, J. L. (1982), *The Miracle of Theism* (Clarendon Press: Oxford).

Macpherson, T. (1972), *The Argument from Design* (Macmillan: London).

Macquarrie, J. (1981), *Twentieth Century Religious Thought* (SCM: London).

Macquarrie, J. (1984), *In Search of Deity* (SCM: London).

Madell, G. (1981), *The Identity of the Self* (2nd edn) (Edinburgh University Press: Edinburgh).

Maitland, S. (1983), *A Map of the New Country: Women & Christianity* (Routledge & Kegan Paul: London).

Mbiti, J. S. (1969), *African Religions and Philosophy* (Heinemann: London).

Mehta, V. (1977), *Mahatma Gandhi and his Apostles* (Penguin: Harmondsworth).

Merlan, P. (1963), *Monopsychism, Mysticism and Monoconsciousness* (Nijhoff: The Hague).

Merton, T. (1965), *The Way of Chuang Tzu* (New Directions: New York).

Miskotte, K. H. (1967), *When the Gods are Silent* (tr. J. W. Doberstein) (Harper & Row: New York).

Mitchell, B. (1980), *Morality: Religious and Secular* (Oxford University Press: Oxford).

Morenz, S. (1973), *Egyptian Religion* (tr. A. E. Keep) (Methuen: London).

Mosley, N. (1976), *Julian Grenfell* (Weidenfeld & Nicholson: London).

Muir, E. (1960), *Collected Poems* (Faber: London).

Nagel, T. (1979), *Mortal Questions* (Blackwell: Oxford).

Needham, R. (1972), *Belief, Language and Experience* (Blackwell: Oxford).

Nielsen, K. (1982), *Introduction to the Philosophy of Religion* (Macmillan: London).

Ogilvy, J. O. (1977), *Many-Dimensional Man* (Oxford University Press: New York).

O'Hear, A. (1984), *Experience, Exploration and Faith* (Routledge & Kegan Paul: London).

Ong, W. S. (1982), *Orality and Literacy* (Methuen: London).

Otto, W. F. (1954), *The Homeric Gods* (tr. M. Hadas) (Thames & Hudson: London).

Palmer, H. (1973), *Analogy* (Macmillan: London).

Parfit, D. (1984), *Reasons and Persons* (Clarendon Press: Oxford).

Penelhum, T. R. (1970), *Survival and Disembodied Existence* (Routledge & Kegan Paul: London).

Philips, D. Z. (1965), *The Concept of Prayer* (Routledge & Kegan Paul: London).

Plantinga, A. (1975), *God, Freedom and Evil* (Allen & Unwin: London).

Popper, K. (1957), *The Poverty of Historicism* (Routledge & Kegan Paul: London).

Price, H. H. (1969), *Belief* (Allen & Unwin: London).

Prior, A. (1967), *Past, Present and Future* (Clarendon Press: Oxford).

Puccetti, R. (1969), *Persons* (Herder: New York).

Rahula, W. (1967), *What the Buddha Taught* (Gordon Fraser: Bedford).

Ralegh, W. (1951), *The Poems* (ed. A. M. C. Latham) (Routledge & Kegan Paul: London).

Rees, A. & B (1961), *The Celtic Heritage* (Thames & Hudson: London).

De Rougemont, D. (1962), *Passion and Society* (tr. M. Belgion) (Faber & Faber: London).

Royce, J. (1906), *The Conception of Immortality* (Constable & Co: London).

Rundle Clark, R. T. (1959), *Myth and Symbol in Ancient Egypt* (Thames & Hudson: London).

Schon, D. A. (1967), *Invention and the Evolution of Ideas* (Associated Book Publishers: London).

Schutz, M. (1971), *Collected Papers: The Problem of Social Reality* (Nijhoff: The Hague).

Skorupski, J. (1975), *Symbol and Theory* (Cambridge University Press: Cambridge).

Slater, P. E. (1968), *The Glory of Hera* (Beacon Press: Boston).

Smart, N. (1972), *The Concept of Worship* (Macmillan: London)

Smart, N. and Hecht, R. D. (eds) (1982), *Sacred Texts of the World* (Macmillan: London).

Smith, W. Cantwell (1978), *The Meaning and End of Religion* (SPCK: London).

Smith, W. Cantwell (1981), *Towards a World Theology* (Macmillan: London).

Snell, B. (1953), *The Discovery of the Mind* (tr. T. G. Rosenmeyer) (Dover: New York).

Soskice, J. M. (1985), *Metaphor and Religious Language* (Clarendon Press: Oxford).

Staal, F. (1975), *Exploring Mysticism* (Pelican: Harmondsworth).

Stace, W. T. (1952), *Time and Eternity* (Princeton University Press: New Jersey).

Stevenson, I. (1974), *Twenty Cases Suggestive of Reincarnation* (University Press of Virginia: Charlottesville).

Strawson, P. (1959), *Individuals* (Methuen: London).

Swinburne, R. (1980), *The Existence of God* (Clarendon Press: Oxford).

Te Velde, H. (1967), *Seth, God of Confusion* (tr. G. E. van Baaren-Pape) Brill: Leiden).

Thorne, B. and Yalom, M. (eds) (1982), *Rethinking the Family* (Longmans: London).

Toynbee, A. J. (1956), *A Historian's View of Religion* (Oxford University Press: London).

Turner, V. W. (1967), *The Forest of Symbols* (Cornell University Press: Ithaca).

Turville-Petre, E. O. G. (1964), *Myth and Religion of the North* (Weidenfeld & Nicolson: London).

Van de Vate, D. (1981), *Romantic Love* (Pennsylvania State University Press: University Park & London).

Vivekananda, Swami (1959), *Bhakti-Yoga* (Advaita Ashrama: Calcutta).

Wallas, G. (1926), *The Art of Thought* (Cape: London).

Ware, K. (1963), *The Orthodox Church* (Penguin: Harmondsworth).

Whitmont, E. C. (1983), *Return of the Goddess* (Routledge & Kegan Paul: London).

Wilhelm, R. and Baynes, C. F. (1951), *The Book of Changes* (Routledge & Kegan Paul: London).

Wilhelm, H. (1960), *Change*   (tr. C. F. Baynes) (Harper & Row: New York).

Williams, C. (1938), *Taliessin through Logres* (Oxford University Press: London).

Williams, C. (1950), *He Came Down from Heaven* (Faber & Faber: London).

Wilson, B. (ed.) (1970), *Rationality* (Blackwell: Oxford).

Wisdom, J. (1953), *Philosophy and Psychoanalysis* (Blackwell: Oxford.)

Wolfson, H. A. (1947), *Religious Philosophy* (Harvard University Press: Cambridge, Mass.).

Wordsworth, W. (1977), *Poems* (Penguin: Harmondsworth).

Yates, F. (1966), *The Art of Memory* (Routledge & Kegan Paul: London).

Zaehner, R. C. (1957), *Mysticism: Sacred and Profane* (Oxford University Press: Oxford).

Zaehner, R. C. (1974), *Our Savage God* (Collins: London).

Zimmer, H. (1967), *Philosophies of India* (ed. J. Campbell) (Routledge & Kegan Paul: London).

Index

34   12